Chinese WMD Proliferation in Asia: US Response

Chinese WMD Proliferation in Asia: US Response

Dr Monika Chansoria

Foreword by

Brigadier **Gurmeet Kanwal** (Retd)
Director
Centre for Land Warfare Studies

KNOWLEDGE WORLD
KW Publishers Pvt Ltd
New Delhi

in association with

Centre for Land Warfare Studies
New Delhi

KNOWLEDGE WORLD

KW Publishers Pvt Ltd

NEW DELHI: 4676/21, First Floor, Ansari Road, Daryaganj, New Delhi 110002
Email: mail@kwpub.in/knowledgeworld@vsnl.net Tel.: +91.11.23263498 / 43528107
MUMBAI: 15 Jay Kay Industrial Estate, Linking Road Extn., Santacruz (W), Mumbai 400054
email: mumbai@kwpub.in Tel.: +91.22.26614110 / 26613505

www.kwpub.in

ISBN 978-81-907431-9-8

Published by Kalpana Shukla, KW Publishers Pvt Ltd
4676/21, First Floor, Ansari Road, Daryaganj, New Delhi 110002

Printed at Rajkamal Electric Press, New Delhi

Contents

Foreword

China began its quest for nuclear weapons with help from Soviet Russia in the mid-1950s. Russian assistance included nuclear advisers, "an experimental nuclear reactor, facilities for processing uranium, a cyclotron, and some equipment for a gaseous diffusion plant." Subsequently, China's relations with the Soviet Union soured and China had no option but to master the final intricacies of the nuclear warhead and delivery systems on its own. On October 16, 1964, China conducted its first nuclear test at Lop Nor with a uranium-235 warhead that yielded 25 kilotons. The first nuclear-tipped missile was fired on October 25, 1966, and the first hydrogen bomb was exploded on June 16, 1967. With these developments, China acquired nuclear deterrence capability and broke the superpowers' monopoly over nuclear weapons. Today, China has 400 nuclear warheads and possesses 12 to 15 intercontinental ballistic missiles (ICBMs) and is a major stakeholder in promoting nuclear weapons and ballistic missiles as a currency of power.

From acquiring the status of a nuclear weapon state (NWS) to exploiting it as an instrument of state policy was but a short step for a dictatorial Communist regime that had not yet grasped the key advantages of integrating itself with the rest of the world. Under the pretext of providing technical information for peaceful purposes, China is alleged to have provided direct assistance to Pakistan's nuclear weapons programme in the 1980s, including handing over warhead designs and "enough HEU (highly enriched uranium) for at least two nuclear bombs." China is also said to have provided assistance and transferred dual-use materials that have application in the development of nuclear weapons. China transferred M-9 and M-11 nuclear capable ballistic missiles to Pakistan in fully assembled mode as well as missile technology, and looked the other way when its protégé North Korea transferred Nodong and Taepo Dong ballistic missiles to Pakistan.

The nuclear weapons assistance provided by the Chinese to Pakistan was passed on by rogue Pakistani scientists to countries such as Iran, Libya and perhaps some others. It has been long suspected that nuclear weapons know-how may even have been passed on by the Pakistanis to the senior leadership of the Al Qaeda. Pakistan is still unable to justify or explain the proliferation activities of Dr AQ Khan to the international community given the fact that Pakistan's nuclear and missile development programmes are completely state controlled. While the government of President Pervez Musharraf had continued to deny for several years that Khan's proliferation activities had taken place with the explicit knowledge and acquiescence of the state, it was too blatant a lie for the world to have taken it seriously.

In keeping with its traditional practice of double-speak, China advocates lofty principles of non-proliferation while having been the world's greatest proliferator. In a speech entitled "Reinforcing Efforts to Prevent Proliferation: China's Perspective", Ambassador Sha Zukang said at Wilton Park, UK, on December 17, 2002, "China has always stood for the complete prohibition and thorough destruction of all kinds of weapons of mass destruction and is firmly opposed to the proliferation of weapons of mass destruction and their delivery systems. China has steadfastly pursued a policy of not advocating, encouraging or assisting any other country in developing weapons of mass destruction. China's policy and practice in nuclear nonproliferation give eloquent proof of its unswerving position." Nothing could have been further from the truth. Despite grand policy pronouncements, it will be a long time before China becomes a consistently reliable partner in the global battle against nuclear and missile proliferation.

Non-proliferation Ayatollahs in the United States had loudly lamented former President George W Bush's "concessions" to India after the US-India Civilian Nuclear Cooperation Agreement was signed on July 18, 2005, despite India's impeccable record on proliferation. However, most of them had maintained incomprehensible silence about Chinese nuclear proliferation activities, some of which are probably continuing even today. Even at the height of its unabashed nuclear proliferation, China had no difficulty in importing nuclear reactors from France and Russia and exporting such reactors to Pakistan primarily due to the silence of the Western Alliance. The US government chose to ignore China's proliferation as Pakistan had become a frontline state in the fight against the Soviet occupation of Afghanistan and it was considered more important to ensure continued Pakistani support for the anti-Soviet *jihad*. Pakistan is now a nuclear-armed state whose very existence is increasingly being threatened by "Taliqaeda" radical extremists. The Af-Pak region is rapidly becoming the world's most unstable region and the spectre of Pakistan's nuclear weapons falling into *jihadi* hands has been giving nightmares to national security planners the world over.

India bore the brunt of Chinese nuclear and missile proliferation over the decades. According to K Subrahmanyam, "The NPT regime was damaged beyond repair when the China-Pakistan combine carried out proliferation and the European countries failed to check the black market linkages between their companies and Pakistan and China... no other country was placed in the situation India faced of a proliferating China on the one side and a proliferating Pakistan on the other, both in an alliance with each other." By transferring nuclear warhead and ballistic missile technology to Pakistan and blessing North Korea's ballistic missile transfers to Pakistan, China has permanently and irrevocably altered the geo-strategic equation in Southern Asia. There appears to have been a sinister purpose behind this carefully calibrated move and, in any case, despite what China may continue to claim, there could not have been a more unfriendly act.

Dr. Monika Chansoria, Research Fellow, Centre for Land Warfare Studies (CLAWS), New Delhi, has taken careful stock of China's nuclear and missile proliferation, the response of the international community, in general, and that of the US, in particular, in her book *Chinese WMD Proliferation In Asia: US Response*. She has analysed the key issues that drove Chinese proliferation activities and has arrived at balanced and well argued deductions. This book is a major case study on how a serious international challenge like nuclear proliferation should not to be dealt with by the international community. The ambivalence of the US and its promotion of its own short-term interests at the cost of major long-term damage to strategic stability and the non-proliferation regime have been well documented.

Dr. Chansoria's book should be compulsory reading for diplomats and other government officials and scientists engaged in nuclear disarmament negotiations as well as for academics and scholars pursuing non-proliferation and disarmament studies. It is also recommended for officers of the army, the navy and the air force who must understand the background developments that led to India facing nuclear adversaries on two sides of its borders.

April 2009
New Delhi.

Brigadier **Gurmeet Kanwal** (Retd)
Director
Centre for Land Warfare Studies,
(CLAWS)

Preface

Through the Cold War years, US nuclear strategy and arms control experts demonstrated diminutive concerns over the Chinese nuclear capability, as it did not figure as a major factor in the US nuclear calculus that remained centred on Soviet nuclear arsenals. At that time, the context of an international system was highlighted by the cut-throat competition between the two superpowers, the US and erstwhile USSR, vying for global hegemony. Since the end of the Cold War, China managed to increase its regional influence beyond its immediate region. Based on rising Chinese economic and military power and expanding Chinese diplomatic and political interchange abroad, the overall power and importance of the People's Republic of China (PRC) rose and is expected to persist in a similar direction in the coming future.

During this time period, the Sino-American relationship could best be described as a complex interplay of conditions. While the United States and China had enormous interests at stake in their bilateral relationship, neither was particularly deft in dealing with the other. Significantly, this included the issue of nuclear and missile technology transfer by China that took shape as one of the most prominent stumbling blocks, leading to a divergence of Chinese and American security interests.

From Washington's perspective, Beijing showed a darker side in its dealings in the realms of proliferation and technology transfer. Of greatest concern to Washington was the documented Chinese behaviour contributing to the spread of technology relating to the weapons of mass destruction (WMD) along with their means of delivery to states located in regions that were a cause of concern to the United States. China's transfers of sensitive nuclear, chemical, biological technology along with their means of delivery became the focus of considerable international attention since the 1980s, when Beijing emerged as the foremost supplier of WMD technology to nations within Asia and beyond. Supplies from China have aggravated trends that result in ambiguous technical aid, more indigenous capabilities, longer-range missiles and secondary (re-transferred) proliferation. In June 1997, the Director of Central Intelligence (DCI) testified to Congress that "China was the most significant supplier of nuclear, biological, chemical (NBC)-related goods and technologies to foreign countries."[1]

During the early 1990s, in concentrated efforts to reduce its isolation owing to the 1989 Tiananmen Square massacre, China appeared coming into the fold of non-proliferation and its regimes, riding on a campaign to garner a greater international image and exhibit itself as a responsible player on the international podium. This period witnessed increased Chinese participation in international regimes, including those directed at controlling the proliferation of NBC weapons. However, this participation was marked by lacunae on many accounts of Beijing's violations of the terms and conditions of the non-proliferation arrangements. Since 1991, Beijing has taken steps to address US and other countries' concerns by increasing its partial participation in international non-proliferation regimes and issuing export control regulations, but questions have remained. The issues relating to proliferation and China were highly charged on Capitol Hill. China's missile and chemical exports raised threats to the existing regimes on nuclear non-proliferation and the US viewed China as an increasingly assertive power in Asia that was expanding its military reach. Even though Chinese sales have fallen in recent years, much more progress will be needed to curtail China's behaviour.

China's transfers of ballistic missiles and nuclear weapons technology, as well as equipment and materials that could be used in the manufacture of chemical and biological weapons caught the attention of the United States, and this study documents China's principal arms-transfer relationships within Asia (Pakistan, North Korea and Iran), analyses the motivations of supplier and recipients, evaluates the clauses of each transfer, and classifies the likely constraints on Chinese WMD proliferation. Thereafter, the study assesses the threat posed by

1. As quoted in Shirley A. Kan, *China's Compliance with International Arms Control Agreements*, CRS Report for Congress, January 16, 1998, Washington DC, p. 1.

these transfers running through Pakistan, North Korea and Iran along with the examining China's strategic and commercial motivations for arms transfers. The study has been structured into six chapters, beginning with the first chapter that entails the emergence of a nuclear China, the Sino-US nuclear agreement, the debates on the resultant convergence and divergence in the Sino-US strategic paradigm in addition to the US response towards the 'China threat' and the nuclear espionage activities that were highlighted by the findings of the Cox Committee. The second chapter analyses US non-proliferation policy in the post-Cold War era, China's involvement in the multilateral export control regimes, particularly dual-use technology controls and its compliance with international arms control agreements. Thereafter in the third chapter, the study undertakes a detailed look into the nature and extent of China's nuclear and missile collaboration with Pakistan and further the Chinese-Iranian WMD axis. The fourth chapter gives an indepth analysis of the North Korean nuclear issue and the direct and indirect assistance provided by the PRC to the Northeast Asian nation's nuclear and missile capabilities.

The fifth chapter deals with the issue of the deployment of US missile defence systems that were touted and to a certain extent, justified as a counter-measure to the ever-increasing threat emanating from nations that posed a threat to the US homeland and its allies. This chapter provides an insight into the infrastructure of the national as well as theatre missile defence systems that aim to develop and deploy a defensive screen for the whole of the US, and further its allies, with an ability to track and destroy incoming ballistic missiles. Washington is working towards amalgamating radar and communication systems with satellites in space so as to provide early warning of an attack. The incoming missiles would then be destroyed by sophisticated interceptors based in the US and territories of its allies. However, the larger the area to be defended, the greater the technical challenge ahead coupled with the negative responses from both China and Russia—the most vocal critics of this programme. As for the United States, there were resolute reiterations in the US policy formulation, especially under the Republican George W Bush Administration that crucial to any engagement policy is the maintenance of a robust defence and deterrence capability. This strategy appeared to be a combination for combating WMD capabilities, with a robust, layered missile defence and other counter-proliferation capabilities that could threaten to neutralise 'rogue' WMD capabilities, reduce the strategic utility, and, thus, attractiveness, of these weapons to would-be aggressors. Accordingly, the Bush Administration adopted the deployment of the missile defence systems to bolster the US deterrent military posture. The concluding chapter provides my analysis of the study in the backdrop of the changing trends in the American and Chinese conceptions of security in the post-Cold War age.

February 2009
New Delhi

Dr Monika Chansoria

Acknowledgements

We do not walk in solitude while on foot during the journey of life, thus leading me to ask myself—where do I start to thank those who joined me, as well as steered me on to the right path all along this voyage. Over the years, those that I have met and worked with have endlessly inspired me in their own distinct manner. Hence, even though I might express gratitude time and again in the following pages, one fact remains—every single recognition emanates from the core of my heart.

First and foremost, I wish to earnestly thank Almighty God for always having showered his blessings upon me, manifested in the form of a wonderful and privileged life that I deeply cherish.

Heartfelt appreciation goes out to Brigadier Gurmeet Kanwal, Director of the Centre for Land Warfare Studies, for being an immense source of support and optimism. Brigadier Kanwal's sustained encouragement over the years has motivated me immeasurably in my research career. It is an absolute pleasure and learning experience to work under his benevolent guidance as he has spearheaded an intellectually driven milieu requisite for credible research and analyses.

The American Studies Division at the School of International Studies, Jawaharlal Nehru University, will always remain a special place since it has played an instrumental role in the shaping up of my career. I owe immense gratitude to my mentor, Professor Chintamani Mahapatra for his unwavering support and encouragement throughout the course of this study and for making me gain deeper and finer insights into several facets of American foreign policy. In large part, he has been my driving force and I owe my initial interest in American studies to him.

Wholesome support was forthcoming from Professor Christopher S Raj, Professor Abdul Nafey and Dr KP Vijayalakshmi at the Centre for Canadian, US and Latin American Studies, whilst they provided constant direction and valuable advice through the course of my research and beyond.

Many institutes and libraries helped to bring this book to fruition. Among these, I would like to acknowledge the assistance provided by the American Information Resource Centre (New Delhi), British Council Division (New Delhi), American Library (Paris), Sciences Po Bibliotheque (Paris), Indian Council of World Affairs (Sapru House, New Delhi), Institute for Defence Studies and Analyses (New Delhi) and the JNU Library. Moreover, I would like to take this opportunity to acknowledge a heartening work atmosphere at the Centre for Land Warfare Studies, for which I thank Deputy Director, Colonel Ravi Tuteja and all my colleagues.

Appreciation in abundance goes out to Air Commodore Jasjit Singh, Air Vice Marshal Kapil Kak, Dr Manpreet Sethi, Group Captain Atul K Singh, Wing Commander AK Singh, Wing Commander Ramakrishnan, Dr Nirmal Jindal, Professor Manoranjan Mohanty, Professor Neera Chandhoke, Professor Rajeev Bhargava, Professor MP Singh and Professor Shanta Nedungadi Varma for contributions that remain indispensable.

I have the good fortune of having friends who have always been there for me, wished me well all the way through for which I would like to profusely thank Naveen Raheja, Neil Mackerel, John Scott Brady, Anusha Sareen, Kalyani Behl, Arada Saengsakorn, Kallol Bhattacherjee, Richa Bhasin and Dolkar Tsering.

Warm affection goes out to all my friends at Cité de Paris and elsewhere in France for being exceptionally caring and supportive in so many distinct ways. I sincerely thank Raed Bader, Devié Vallée, Max Jean, Didier Celestine, Dr Bano Singh, Thierry Vallée, Lenita Perrier, Carmen Diop and Dr Pramod Rao for all the pleasant times coupled with special moments.

A special mention for my closest pal, Sara Rmich, for being a fantastic friend who has constantly supported me through the years, for which I remain grateful. *Coco, tu rends les souvenirs de Paris encore plus spéciaux et je chéris tous les moments qu'on a passés ensemble. Merci pour tous ces instants merveilleux.*

Thanks are due to my publishers at Knowledge World, including Kalpana Shukla, Rehana Mishra and Jose Mathew. Rehana made meticulous efforts during the entire process of copy-editing the manuscript, which I truly appreciate. Besides, Jose has particularly been forthcoming with fine suggestions during publishing of the book.

Finally, above all, I wish to express eternal gratitude to my mother, Sheela K Chansoria, and my father, Keshav Kumar Chansoria, for being evermore supportive and encouraging in all my endeavours. I am indebted to them yet again for being my guiding force and pillars of emotional strength. Moreover, it is their resolute patience matched by great efficiency, compassion and unflagging enthusiasm that saw me through the numerous impediments that I encountered in the various segments of this journey. In all certainty, I would not have been able to accomplish my goals had it not been for them.

New Delhi **Dr Monika Chansoria**

1

China's Nuclear Emergence

A 'Nuclear' China Surfaces

Since its inception, the People's Republic of China (PRC) has made robust efforts within its economic and technical capabilities to develop a nuclear force and appropriately related delivery systems in order to help deter superpower or regional aggression and intimidation by any nuclear power. The aim was to secure a strategic retaliatory capability in case of a nuclear war and, most significantly, gain strategic leverage regionally as well as on the global platform.

China's strategic nuclear weapons programme dates back to the mid-1950s. The significance of possessing a nuclear weapon was depicted by the position that Mao Zedong took in 1946 when he stated that the atomic bomb was a "paper tiger, which the United States (US) reactionaries use to scare people."[1] It could well be that Mao's talk of paper tigers arose more from the need to shore up the courage of his own people than from an underestimation of the role that nuclear weapons could play in warfare or political conflict when one side had them and the other did not. Significantly, the Chinese decision to go nuclear was influenced by growing US involvement in Indochina coupled with past US nuclear threats to China during the Korean War and the again in the crisis over the islands of Quemoy and Matsu in 1954-55, as did the growing prominence of nuclear weapons in US military strategy more generally, with the adoption of the "massive retaliation" policy.[2] Understandably, Mao read both these crises as blatant American nuclear blackmail. The Chinese also realised that Chiang Kai-shek, on Taiwan, was still intent on a return to the mainland, and they paid more attention to noisy American sympathy with Chiang than to the less noisy but more important recognition in the White House that such an adventure was out of the question.[3] Following the Chinese bombing of the Taiwanese-held islands, namely, Quemoy and Matsu, the US and Taiwan went ahead and signed a crucial security pact in December 1954.[4] President Eisenhower was apprehensive that the Chinese might try to invade Taiwan or the islands surrounding it. Subsequently, Beijing, under the leadership of Chairman Mao, decided that the time had arrived for China to obtain its own nuclear arsenal to counter the US nuclear arsenal. Notably, the formal Chinese decision to start a nuclear weapons programme was made in the middle of the Quemoy crisis, on January 15, 1955.[5] In a revealing Politburo address to Party leaders in 1956, Mao explained, "If we are not to be bullied in the present-day world, we cannot do without the bomb."[6] The timing of this statement, just a year after President Eisenhower's public warning over Quemoy, visibly suggested as to who was being referred to as the "bully" by Mao. From the American standpoint, it appeared paradoxical that the first confrontation over Quemoy and Matsu was considered the precipitating factor of Mao's decision to go nuclear courtesy his continued perception of the Americans as nuclear bullies.

In the opening years of their nuclear effort in the 1950s, while receiving extensive aid from the Soviet Union, the Chinese were able to establish a workable basis for future development of nuclear weapons. Soviet aid included not only technical support in the construction of a facility for the enrichment of uranium but also an undertaking to deliver "a sample of an atomic bomb."[7] Crucially, between 1955 and 1958, China and the Soviet Union signed no less than six agreements on nuclear cooperation during which the Soviet Union provided Beijing with a cyclotron, a nuclear reactor and fissile material for research. Moscow also agreed to undertake joint surveys in China for uranium and to provide assistance with nuclear physics.[8] This included the foundation of the Chinese nuclear weapons programme that was laid out in the 1957 Sino-Soviet Agreement on New Technology for National

Defence. Under this, the Soviet Union agreed to supply China with a prototype of an atomic weapon and related technical data. Moscow, also agreed to assist in the construction, training and operation of a gaseous diffusion separation plant in Lanzhou, northwest China, to produce weapons-grade enriched uranium-235. In addition, both Mao and Khrushchev were optimistic about prospects for the continued rise of socialism. Mao particularly was hopeful that the Soviet Union would be effective in neutralising any nuclear threat from the US.[9]

However, the Sino-Soviet split during the late 1950s, owing primarily to the mounting differences between Khrushchev and Mao, abruptly ended cooperation between the two countries. Thereafter, the Soviet Union refused to part with any more technical information concerning nuclear weapons. By August 1960, Moscow withdrew all of its technical experts from the Chinese bomb programme. According to the August 1963 Chinese account, the Soviets "tore up the agreement" and refused to provide the sample bomb after the open split between the two Communist nations.[10] The withdrawal of the Soviet technical expertise and financial assistance severely hampered the rapid development of the Chinese programme. Once the Soviets pulled out, the PRC was left to manage on its own projects that were earlier conceived and executed under wide-ranging Soviet guidance. China was left with no choice but to keep on engineering the available data and the process ended up taking many years.[11] Adequate uranium supplies were not a problem, because China had extensive unquantified uranium deposits. In the meantime, China also completed two plutonium production reactors near Baotou, Inner Mongolia, and freed itself from overdependence on uranium.[12]

Carrying on from this modest beginning, the Chinese leadership continued to give the nuclear weapons programme a high priority and successfully managed to insulate it from the uncertainties generated by internal power struggles in China since the late 1950s. China was aware of its limited economic and technical resources and the fact that the strategic environment in Asia was heavily influenced by the US and the erstwhile Soviet Union. Thus, it worked meticulously so as to deploy a small but varied nuclear force that could survive a superpower attack, penetrate existing enemy defences and hit significant targets of potential aggressors. This remained China's persistent view until it actually went nuclear. In fact, it would be apt to state that the Chinese faith in nuclear weapons has never wavered since. China is believed to have developed nuclear weapons due to its destructive capacity, political significance and also to break the nuclear monopoly of the Western nuclear powers.

Interestingly, in order to prevent the possibility of an inadvertent nuclear war, the Soviet Union and the US signed the Hot Line Agreement in June 1963 and established direct radio and telegraph communications between the countries' leaders with the aim of preventing future crises. President Kennedy also announced that the Soviet Union, Great Britain and US would meet in Moscow to continue discussions toward a nuclear test ban. Expectedly, in August 1963, elongated negotiations eventually led to the Limited Test Ban (LTB) Treaty. The treaty allowed only underground nuclear tests by the three nations. The impact of these negotiations on China was inescapably negative—a country not yet ready to test naturally saw support for a test ban as an unfriendly gesture. Understandably, the nuclear weapon that was first sought by Mao in order to not feel bullied by Washington was, in fact, deployed in what could be interpreted as a measure to discourage bullying by Moscow.

Amidst this backdrop, Communist China on October 16, 1964, exploded its first nuclear fission (atomic) device with a 22-kiloton yield over the Lop Nor test site.[13] The Chinese considered this a major achievement in their efforts to increase defence capability and simultaneously oppose, what they considered, the US' "imperialist policy of nuclear blackmail and nuclear threats."[14] Soon after testing a nuclear device, a Chinese government statement said: "To defend oneself is the inalienable right of every sovereign state. China cannot remain idle and do nothing in the face of the ever-increasing nuclear threat posed by the United States. China is forced to conduct nuclear tests and develop nuclear weapons."[15] The Chinese government pointed out long ago, "The treaty on the partial halting of nuclear tests signed by the United States, Britain and the Soviet Union in Moscow, in July

1963, namely the Limited Test Ban Treaty, was a big fraud to fool the people of the world. It tried to consolidate the nuclear monopoly held by the three nuclear powers and increased the nuclear threat of US imperialism against the people of China and of the whole world."[16] This was considered to be crucial since the US was the sole threat to the Chinese at this point. However, a fortnight after the third Chinese nuclear explosion in May 1966, the US intimated to the Chinese that a "no first use" pledge might, after all, be acceptable if China on its side would become a party to the Moscow test-ban treaty—thus, of course, renouncing the right to conduct further nuclear tests in the atmosphere, in outer space, or under water. The American statement palpably reflected a long-standing US interest in breaching China's self-imposed abstention from international disarmament discussions. Beijing expectedly chose to dismiss it outright by portraying the LTB Treaty as an effort to preserve the nuclear supremacy of the Western nuclear powers, while limiting China's ability to develop and improve its nuclear capability.[17] Interestingly, China not only claimed its right to acquire nuclear weapon capability but also defended the right of every other nation if they chose to do so. Significantly, China rejected the 1968 multilateral nuclear Non-Proliferation Treaty (NPT) on similar grounds where it declared that it would not assist other countries in developing nuclear weapons, but would certainly defend the right of non-nuclear states to acquire such arms.[18]

Moreover, China accused that Washington "had not stopped manufacturing various nuclear weapons on the basis of the nuclear tests which it had already conducted. Furthermore, seeking forever-greater perfection, the United States has during this same period conducted several dozen underground nuclear tests, thereby further perfecting the nuclear weapons it further manufactures. In stationing nuclear submarines in Japan, Washington is posing a direct threat to the Japanese people, the Chinese people and the peoples of all other Asian countries."[19] It further pointed out that the United States had declared, after signing the LTB Treaty, that conclusion of such a treaty did not mean that the US could not conduct underground tests, or would not use, manufacture, stockpile, export or proliferate nuclear weapons.

The Chinese government justified its nuclear tests by solemnly declaring:

> ...China will never at any time and under any circumstances be the first to use nuclear weapons. The mastering of the nuclear weapon by China is a great encouragement to the revolutionary peoples of the world in their struggles and a great contribution to the cause of defending world peace. We, hereby formally propose to the governments of the world that a summit conference of all the countries of the world be convened to discuss the question of the complete prohibition and thorough destruction of nuclear weapons, and that as a first step, the summit conference should reach an agreement to the effect that the nuclear powers and those countries which may soon become nuclear powers undertake not to use nuclear weapons, neither to use them against non-nuclear countries and nuclear free zones, nor against each other.[20]

Beijing's initial deterrence logic was combined with the purpose of breaking the superpower monopoly. Later, China's nuclear strategy was defined as "anti-nuclear blackmail", which primarily meant that no power could threaten or intimidate Beijing with nuclear weapons and not face nuclear retaliation. Since this strategy relied heavily on a small number of weapons to conduct a retaliatory second strike, it came to be known as "minimum deterrence."[21]

In fact, about a month prior to Beijing's nuclear test, US Secretary of State, Dean Rusk acknowledged that it was known since the 1ate 1950s that the Chinese Communists had been working to develop a nuclear explosive device. Therefore, China's refusal to sign the LTB Treaty that was already signed by over a 100 countries was clearly understood by the US policy-makers. Sensing that China was on the verge of testing a nuclear device, Rusk had acknowledged that the detonation of a first device would not mean a stockpile of nuclear weapons and the presence of modern delivery systems. The US had, in fact, fully anticipated the possibility of Beijing's entry into the nuclear weapons field and had taken it into full account in determining its military posture and its own nuclear weapons programme. Rusk stated, "We would deplore atmospheric testing in the face of serious efforts made by almost all other nations to protect the atmosphere from further contamination and to begin to put limitations upon a spiraling arms race."[22]

Furthermore, reacting to the Chinese testing of a nuclear device, US President Lyndon B Johnson affirmed that Communist China's nuclear development programme came as no surprise to the US government. Moreover, he believed that its military significance should not be overestimated since many years and great efforts separate testing of a first nuclear device from having a stockpile of reliable weapons with effective delivery systems. President Johnson reaffirmed the US' defence commitments in Asia. He stated that even if China should eventually acquire an effective nuclear capability, it would have no effect upon the readiness of the US to respond to requests from the Asian nations for help in dealing with "Communist Chinese aggression."[23] He considered the nuclear weapons programme a tragedy for the Chinese people, who were suffering under the totalitarian Communist regime, given that sparse economic resources, which could have been used to improve the well-being of the Chinese people, were instead being used to produce a crude nuclear device that would only increase the sense of insecurity among the masses. President Johnson condemned the Chinese action by stating, "We join all humanity in regretting the contamination of the atmosphere caused by the Chinese Communist test."[24]

By this time, the world community appeared convinced with a widespread view that the reasons for China's going nuclear were two-fold. Firstly, the Chinese policy-makers believed that their alliance with the Soviet Union did not provide adequate security, as reflected by events during the Korean War in 1950-53 and subsequently the Taiwan Straits crisis in 1954-55. The Soviet Union under Khrushchev attempted to promote peaceful coexistence with the Western world and confronted the US only when the Soviet vital interests came under threat. Soviet support for China was muted and belated when it faced US coercion during the Taiwan Strait crisis over the islands of Quemoy and Matsu. The decision to reduce dependence on a potentially irresolute ally saw the birth of the Chinese nuclear weapon.[25] Prominently, China was threatened by the US during both these crises. The US adopted the policy of "massive retaliation" with nuclear forces as the core of its declared national military strategy and enhanced China's sense of insecurity. The second probable reason why the Chinese developed the bomb was a realisation that a strategy of self-reliance was better than seeking an alliance partner.[26]

Interestingly, it was while President Johnson was in Thailand that China conducted its fourth successful nuclear experiment and the second of the year in October 1966. It was a Hiroshima-size nuclear warhead fitted on a guided missile with an estimated range of nearly 400 miles. The test indicated that Washington was unsuccessful in preventing rapid progress in China's quest for nuclear weapons. Reacting to the Chinese test, President Johnson only renewed his promise of America's support for non-nuclear nations confronted with any threat of nuclear blackmail. China's pursuit of a national nuclear capability, the president rather ambiguously added, "invites danger to China itself" in as much as "any nuclear capability they can develop can and—will be—deterred."[27]

About a year later, on June 17, 1967, China successfully tested a fusion (thermonuclear/hydrogen) bomb with a 3.3-megaton yield over the Lop Nor test site. Markedly, it took China only 32 months to move from its first atomic test to a thermonuclear weapon, the shortest period for any nuclear weapon state thus far. This test was accompanied by the usual assurances that China would under no circumstances be the first to use nuclear weapons. However, the explosion caused significant political and psychological fall-out in Japan, and elsewhere and seemed likely to intensify the impending American preparation for defences against Chinese missile attacks. But the US was not unduly perturbed over the emergence of China as a new nuclear power. First of all, compared to the size of its own nuclear arsenal, China's was of very little significance. Secondly, the Sino-Soviet rift had encouraged the US policy-makers to think that the Chinese were ultimately going to turn their guns against the Soviet Union.

Beginning with 1964, Beijing conducted 45 nuclear detonations before it opted to accommodate US-backed international arms control pressures by signing the NPT in 1992, and later terminating the programme in 1996 and signing the Comprehensive Test Ban Treaty (CTBT). Since its first nuclear detonation in 1945, the United States had carried out 1,030 nuclear tests and had built more than 30,000 nuclear weapons by the early 1990s. In contrast, after 1979, China increased its number of average yearly tests marginally from 1.3 to 1.7 until it stopped testing in 1992, whereas the US averaged 13.6 detonations a year. The greatest number of tests in any given year was 18 for the US and two for China.[28]

Table 1.1: Nuclear Tests Conducted by US and China, 1945-1996

	United States	China
Atmospheric	215	23
Underground	815	22
Total	1,030	45

Source: Statistics from United Nations sources quoted in *The New York Times,* September 11, 1996, p. A3.

Although until the late 1960s, China's nuclear programme was directed at Washington, thereafter China focussed on the Soviet threat owing to the bitter Sino-Soviet split and envisioned the US as the central counterweight to Soviet power. China's objective to deter Soviet power and intimidation was partly achieved after deploying a number of missiles capable of delivering nuclear warheads inside Soviet territory. Therefore, the Chinese bomb, first undertaken in conscious partnership with Moscow, primarily became a safeguard for China against the massive nuclear armament of a deeply antagonistic Soviet Union.[29] By putting in place an NPT, the US indirectly legitimised the Chinese nuclear weapons. In a roundabout way, the US allowed China to proliferate vertically. By the time the NPT came into existence in 1970, the US policy-makers were all set to embark upon a détente policy vis-à-vis China. The new nuclear Communist power came to be viewed as a potential strategic partner and a counterweight to the Soviet Union. All this makes one wonder whether the Americans, in fact, had stopped worrying about the Chinese nuclear arsenal.

Crucially, the larger incident of Chinese nuclear apprehension was deftly given shape during the Sino-Soviet Crisis of 1969, when there occurred a confrontation between the nuclear powers that included ground force combat and real nuclear threats, along with striking demonstrations of determination by both sides. More than a million Russian troops were deployed along the 5,000-mile Sino-Soviet border; hundreds of Soviet nuclear missiles were targeted against Chinese cities and border clashes were growing in frequency and intensity.[30] The Chinese were determined to demonstrate to Moscow that they could not be pushed around any more. The border fighting, for instance, on the frozen Ussuri river in northern Manchuria, was sporadic and both Beijing and Moscow were cautiously aware of the latent nuclear danger. The Soviets indeed engaged in atomic diplomacy by spreading rumours of plans to use nuclear weapons—enough to stir alarm in the Nixon White House and enough to produce a typically Maoist retort that any act of atomic aggression would be met by "revolutionary war."[31] The prevailing rhetoric paved the way for moves to defuse the crisis and in October 1969, the Chinese announced that negotiations on the border conflict had been agreed upon and subsequently the conflict drew to a close.

From the Chinese point of view, their bomb was bound to give the Soviets reason enough to avoid an exchange of nuclear warheads and this crisis indeed proved beyond doubt that the Chinese judgement to invest in nuclear deterrence had been wise. It became clear by now that China's need for nuclear weapons was a requirement for providing a specific nuclear deterrent to what were seen as specific nuclear dangers as witnessed in 1969.[32] The reality of the Chinese nuclear policy, at least since 1969, concluded to a considerable extent that in the view of the Chinese government, the Chinese deterrent remained untested precisely for the reason that it existed.[33]

As for Mao and Zhou Enlai, this period was seen as an opportune moment to advocate a new global diplomatic strategy that defined the Soviet Union as the focal adversary, wherein they wanted a tactical accommodation with the US.[34] As it happened, the strategy coincided with American interests and soon witnessed President Richard Nixon's momentous visit to China in 1972. Following his visit, President Nixon came to believe that as a great power, China could check the Soviet expansionist policies and accommodate the Western interests. When President Nixon met Mao Zedong for the first time in February 1972, both agreed that their two countries could gain leverage in dealing with Moscow by providing a closer association between Washington and Beijing. However, Nixon's advisers did not want to openly antagonise the Soviet Union by siding with the Chinese. The objective was to tactically play a balance of power game involving the two largest Communist powers. The normalisation of relations between the United States and the People's Republic of China could well be termed as one of the geo-political paradoxes of the 20th century. While containment of Communism remained the cornerstone of the US foreign policy until the end of the Cold War, and disintegration of the Soviet Union, Washington began to build security ties with China—another Asian Communist country—since the late 1960s. The goal was, of course, to contain the spread of influence of Communist Soviet Union through the help of Communist China.[35]

Thus, Henry Kissinger recorded in his memoirs that the President and he shared "the same fundamental judgement: that if relations could be developed with both the Soviet Union and China, the triangular relationship would give us a great strategic opportunity for peace."[36] For China, the need to gain a degree of deterrence against Soviet pressure along its borders was foremost. As Chairman Mao put it to President Nixon, "The issue of the international situation is an important one. The small issue is Taiwan; the big issue is the world."[37]

By the time the Carter Administration came into being in 1977, it took a broader view of the country's relationship with Beijing than his predecessors, attaching more weight to potential economic collaboration. Nevertheless, like Nixon and Kissinger, Carter too believed in China's "strategic importance" in international affairs.[38] He subscribed to the longer-range objective of engaging China fruitfully in the international system and thereby giving it a stake in the global community compatible with American interests.

On the Chinese front, the existing geo-political realities made the "anti-Soviet rationale" central to Deng Xiaoping's thinking. And at the same time, cooperation with the US to further China's economic and technological modernisation topped his agenda and the economic progress of China became his apex priority. According to Deng, an economically frail China would be futile in opposing "hegemonists", reuniting Taiwan or building a strong national defence. As he said in 1984, "Our political line is to take the four modernisations (agriculture, industry, science and technology, and national defence) as the key point, from beginning to end to not let go of this, unless another world war arises."[39] By the time the two countries signed an agreement on normalisation in late 1978, the respective leadership already had multiple motives in doing so. Gaining leverage in dealings with Moscow was central for both China and the US.[40] For Washington, the constructive involvement of the PRC in the international community was equally pivotal and for Beijing, gaining American cooperation in economic development was paramount. On the basis of these initial objectives, bilateral cooperation in the 1980s was remarkably successful for both countries, culminating in a nuclear cooperation agreement.

US-China Nuclear Agreement

Under the 1954 Atomic Energy Act (AEA), as amended by the 1978 Nuclear Non-Proliferation Act, nuclear cooperation agreements were a prerequisite for US companies to export nuclear materials, technologies and services. Recipient countries were supposed to guarantee that US exports would be used strictly for peaceful purposes, place transferred US equipment and materials under safeguards, and maintain adequate physical security over imports and nuclear materials produced through their use. These countries were to obtain prior US consent to retransfer US-origin technology or materials and to reprocess or enrich US-origin materials or materials produced in US-supplied facilities.

Under the Act, the United States was required to have a bilateral agreement on nuclear cooperation as a clause for nuclear cooperation with any nation. The US and China negotiated such an agreement in 1985, stating the terms under which the United States could supply China with technology, materials, equipment and technical services to build and operate nuclear power plants and other nuclear facilities. It also provided some controls over what China could do with US assistance. The agreement required Beijing to use any such assistance strictly for peaceful purposes, to get prior US approval before reprocessing spent fuel of US origin, and to receive US permission to transfer US-supplied equipment, materials and technology to another country. The agreement also allowed the US to verify through visits and information exchanges that cooperation under the agreement was not misused.[41]

However, in the run up to signing the agreement, China's substantial assistance to Pakistan's nuclear weapons programme since the early 1980s created concerns among US policy-makers and led the Ronald Reagan Administration in 1982 to suspend talks it had initiated with Beijing on an agreement for cooperation in the field of nuclear energy.[42] The ensuing events and their ramifications have been discussed at length in Chapter 3. In mid-1983, Beijing began an apparent shift in its position and indicated that it would join the International Atomic Energy Agency (IAEA). A statement by the Chinese Premier, Zhao Ziyang, claimed, "China does not advocate or encourage proliferation... we do not help other countries develop nuclear weapons."[43] China also notified to the United States that it would begin requiring IAEA safeguards on its nuclear exports to non-nuclear weapon states.[44] In January 1984, China joined the IAEA and subsequently advised the United States that in the future, it would require IAEA safeguards on its nuclear exports to non-nuclear weapon states. In a series of statements beginning that month, top Chinese leaders reiterated China's firm commitment to non-proliferation.

These developments paved the way for Reagan and Zhao to initiate discussions on a draft of the nuclear trade agreement. The nuclear dialogue took place during President Reagan's April 1984 visit to China. The Reagan Administration, however, did not submit the accord for the required review by Congress until July 1985, reportedly because of concerns that Chinese nuclear aid to Pakistan was continuing.[45] After further talks, however, China agreed to implement its non-proliferation policy, according to US officials, "in a manner consistent with basic non-proliferation practices common to the United States and other suppliers," apparently intending to signify that any Chinese assistance to Pakistan had been halted.[46] The final Sino-US agreement of 1985, negotiated by the Reagan Administration between 1981 and 1984, authorised the sale of nuclear reactors, major reactor components and low-enriched uranium (LEU) fuel. It certainly was a milestone in the history of Sino-US relations as the accord was the first US nuclear trade pact with a Communist country and the first bilateral agreement with another nuclear weapon state.

A controversial provision of the Sino-US agreement addressed the issue of safeguards. Article 8, Section 2 of the agreement declared that since both parties were nuclear weapon states, bilateral safeguards on transferred items were not required. The Reagan Administration acknowledged that it had sought to persuade China to accept IAEA safeguards on US exports, but that Beijing refused on the ground that it was a nuclear weapon state and that it should be treated equally with the United States. However, Administration officials testified that information exchanges and visits would be negotiated before any exports were approved.[47] To critics, beyond the specific provisions, loomed the much larger question: how credible were China's non-proliferation commitments? Section 129(2) (B) of the Atomic Energy Act requires termination of US nuclear exports to any country that assists non-nuclear weapon states in developing nuclear weapons. There were many critics of the Sino-US agreement who argued that China did not meet the standards mentioned above. They highlighted a series of Press reports that appeared through the 1980s describing unsafeguarded Chinese nuclear exports to countries seeking to develop nuclear weapons. Apparently, Chinese transfers reported during this period included:

- Sixty tonnes of low-enriched uranium to South Africa in 1981.
- Heavy water and low-enriched uranium to Argentina in the mid-1980s.
- Assistance with uranium enrichment and possibly a tested bomb design to Pakistan.[48]

Nonetheless, the Reagan Administration continued to pursue the nuclear cooperation agreement, which it viewed as an incentive for China to adopt stronger nuclear non-proliferation policies. Along with that, US officials projected major economic benefits from nuclear trade with China. Citing Beijing's plans to install 10,000 megawatts (MW) of electricity from nuclear power plants between 1985 and 2000, they estimated the potential Chinese reactor market at $20 billion, with US companies in a position to win a share worth $3 billion to $7 billion. The Administration also predicted that winning a share of China's nuclear energy business would enhance US companies' chances of participating in China's other energy sectors. However, the Sino-US agreement drew bipartisan criticism on Capitol Hill from liberal Democrats and conservative Republicans, who predicted that the loose provisions of Articles 2, 5 and 8 would not prevent China from retransferring US technology and materials to non-nuclear weapon states. The General Accounting Office found the accord acceptable on balance, but, at the same time, noted that the agreement:

> ...does contain certain vague and unclear language, which could lead to misinterpretations. In several respects the language in this agreement differs from that in other nuclear cooperative agreements, but for the most part, these differences appear to have more symbolic than practical effects. Nevertheless, the changes represent a departure from the long-standing US practice of encouraging more stringent controls on the use of US nuclear exports.[49]

The Sino-US nuclear agreement required the US president to submit a report on the history and current status of China's non-proliferation policies to Congress and allowed 30 days of continuous legislative session to review this information before the agreement could enter into force. Concurrently, the US-Chinese nuclear trade remained in limbo for the next several years due to growing US concern over China's nuclear and missile related exports. Most significantly, Beijing continued to support Pakistan's nuclear weapons programme despite its non-proliferation pledges. In addition, China sold CSS-2 intermediate-range ballistic missiles (IRBMs) to Saudi Arabia and began marketing the M-series missiles to Iran and Syria—issues that are dealt with in detail in the subsequent chapters.

According to a Congressional Research Service Report published in March 1994 for the US Congress, China had sought to develop nuclear weapons also in order to increase its influence in Asian and world affairs. Beijing went far toward demonstrating its global strategic importance in the 1980s when it became only the third world power to test successfully an intercontinental ballistic missile (ICBM). The deployment of a sea-launched missile and continued development of short and intermediate range, solid-fuelled, land-based systems have underlined China's position as a key player in the international security calculus of Russia, the US and others. China's willingness to sell its IRBMs and new solid-fuelled, land-based missiles or related technology to Third World countries reinforced this trend. Chinese accomplishments in nuclear weapons development seemed to appeal to Chinese patriotism and add to the political benefit of leaders associated with the military advances. The following is a tabulated format of existing Chinese nuclear power plants spread across China (Table 1.2).

Table 1.2: China's Nuclear Power Plants in Operation, Under Construction and Planned, December 31, 1996.

Name	Location	Plant Capacity (Megawatts)		Reactor Size and Number
In Operation		Design	Existing	
Daya Bay	Guandong Province	1,800	1,800	900 x 2
Qinshan Phase 1	Zhejiang Province	2,900	300	300 x 1
Under Construction				
Qinshan Phase 2	Zhejiang Province			600 x 2 700 x 2
Ling'ao	Guandong	2,000		1,000 x 2
Planned				
Qinshan Phase 3	Zhejiang Province	1,400		700 x 2
Lianyungang	Jiangsu Province	2,000		1,000 x 2

Source: US-China Commercial Nuclear Commerce: Nonproliferation and Trade Issues, CSIS Report, September 1997.

Sino-US Strategic Paradigm: Convergence vs. Divergence

The end of the Cold War left American foreign policy in a drift that gradually appeared to be ending as the United States paved its way towards a new role in the world. This process included devising a new strategy for its relations with Asia where the core concepts were engagement and leadership— reflecting the belief that the US should be engaged in Asia militarily, economically and politically, and should lead efforts to promote security, interdependence and democracy in the region.[50] However, it should also be stated that in addition to both these concepts, the US aimed to bring about "containment" of China; this, in fact, has been the continuing policy of Washington towards Beijing wherein it envisages an "engaging containment" of China within Asia. Washington recognises the importance of Asia to its vital interests and acknowledges the fact that the world's centre of strategic and economic gravity has shifted from the Atlantic to the Pacific—a process that is unlikely to reverse in the coming years. Undoubtedly, placement of China was essential to Washington's evolving Asian strategy. Based on its size, strategic location and rising economic and military power, China is considered the leading regional power in Asia; and factors of geography and interest continued to make Asia the main international arena where the Chinese government would exert influence.

According to a Congressional Research Service Report published in 1994:

> ...China exerts worldwide economic influence and is the leading military and political power in Asia, but its importance and influence would be much greater if Chinese leaders were inclined to assert Chinese influence in world affairs more forcefully. Post-Mao Zedong leaders generally eschew such a global approach. Preoccupied with a long list of domestic economic, political, and social priorities, China's leaders focus on maintaining the internal stability and economic prosperity essential to the Chinese Communist Party's monopoly of power. In sharp contrast to Mao's messianic vision and provocative behavior, Chinese reformer Deng Xiaoping and succeeding leaders

> have been prepared more to deal with the world as it is, seeking out opportunities that help the massive Chinese task of nation building and over time build greater comprehensive national power.[51]

This observation in a way captured the US view of China in the early years of the post-Cold War era. Former Chinese President Jiang Zemin and his successor, President Hu Jintao had begun to follow a focussed policy in Asia involving enhanced diplomatic, economic and military exchanges; increased Chinese participation in Asian multilateral organisations; and greater Chinese flexibility on territorial disputes that, on the whole, has served Chinese interests well.[52] China remains a crucial peg of the emerging security and political architecture of Asia. In fact, much of Asia's future depended on the way China would shape its policy in the post-Cold War years. The direction of China's evolution as a major power, however, contains many imponderables—namely, the issues of sovereignty over Taiwan and the Spratly Islands in the South China Sea, given that Vietnam, Malaysia, Philippines and Brunei all claimed sovereignty over these islands. In this backdrop, modernisation of China's conventional and nuclear forces as well as its arms control policies could lead to a security dilemma in Asia unless matched by restraint or security cooperation with the US.[53]

The focus for Sino-American security relations in the first post-Cold War decade reflected a number of developments. With the USSR's decline and eventual fall in 1991, the Soviet threat that had unified the US and China vanished. Thus, bilateral issues that had been subordinated for years rose on the agendas of both nations. China's economic, diplomatic, and military growth throughout the 1980s and 1990s meant that Chinese and US interests increasingly overlapped, at times fostering cooperation and at others generating friction. As the threat of a global nuclear disaster receded with the end of the Cold War, the US became more concerned with the proliferation of weapons of mass destruction (WMD) to unfriendly or unstable nations and non-state actors. The March 1995 Sarin gas attack by a Japanese doomsday cult on the Tokyo subway, along with the bombings of the World Trade Centre in New York two years before by Middle Eastern terrorists, made the Americans feel vulnerable. Consequently, Beijing's sale of weapons and sensitive technology became of ever-greater concern to Americans. Changes were occurring in Taiwan that made the islands more attractive to the Americans and, at the same time, more assertive in seeking a role of dignity in the world community. Both considerations alarmed the PRC. Consequently, as the 1990s unfolded, it became increasingly difficult for Beijing and Washington to manage the Taiwan issue in a mutually acceptable way.[54]

The period ensuing China's Tiananmen Square phase witnessed its controversial involvement in nuclear exports, provoking further debate as well as casting a spell of doubt on the viability of the non-proliferation regimes in place. In addition, the proliferation of ballistic missiles became a cause of grave concern in the post-Cold War world. A number of disturbing developments in the area of missile proliferation took place during 1989 and the first half of 1990. One of the most disturbing trends was that of missile transfers—involving complete systems, as well as components and technology—which continued apace, despite the efforts of a number of countries to stem this flow through the Missile Technology Control Regime (MTCR) signed in 1987. The MTCR aimed to slow down missile proliferation by restraining the transfer of technology, components, and complete systems to Third World missile programmes. The regime consisted of parallel export controls adopted by the participating nations. These controls were designed to slow the development of missiles that were capable of hitting a target the size of a small city from a distance of 190 miles (300 km) or further and which were capable of carrying a warhead weighing 1,100 pounds (500 kg) or more.

In 1988, when China had not yet joined the MTCR, it sold Saudi Arabia the intermediate-range CSS-2, the first ever transfer of such a system to a developing country. At about this time, China also began to market a new class of relatively accurate missiles, with ranges up to 375 miles, to Iran and Syria, among other countries. Responding to US demarches, Beijing subsequently assured Washington in late 1988 that it would cease offering the missiles known as the "M" series for sale. In mid-1989, however, reports appeared that Syria had signed an agreement to purchase the "M" series missiles. During his December 1989 visit to Beijing, US senior Chinese officials again assured National Security Advisor Brent Scowcroft that Beijing would not sell medium-range missiles in the Middle East.[55] No subsequent Chinese sales of such systems were known to have taken place, but in March 1990, Press reports indicated that China was readying a shipment of short-range missiles to the region.[56] These developments bring a fact to the forefront in that the MTCR remains an insufficient constraint on the global spread of ballistic missiles owing primarily to the proliferation activities undertaken by China, especially in reference to Pakistan, Iran, North Korea and the Middle East.

In the post-Cold War era, practically every facet of the US-China relationship had a duality. Americans saw growing exports to China as positive; however, they viewed the mounting US trade deficit and leakage of critical technologies to the PRC as negatives. While the strategic relevance of Sino-American security ties came to be challenged in the post Cold War environment, the unprecedented economic success of China created a different logic for the continuation and further improvement of cooperative ties between the two countries. With the considerable growth in the trade and investment relationship between China and the United States, a new business constituency emerged within the US to protect and promote friendly bilateral ties. The champions of democracy and human rights within the governing circles in Washington and in the circles of non-governmental organisations in the US appeared much less influential than the pro-China business lobby groups.[57]

The Pentagon Report on United States Security Strategy for the East Asia-Pacific Region highlighted the fact that the rapid growth in China's military power, well demonstated by its modernisation programme, has raised the importance of Beijing in the Asian security equation. The report emphasised by stating, "China is a nuclear weapon state, a leading regional military power and a global power with a permanent seat on the UN Security Council."[58] The report by the Pentagon has been instrumental in guiding American security policy toward the region ever since. The strategy the report chose was that of balance and integration. Given the fact that the East Asian balance of power rests on the triangle of China, Japan and the US, by strengthening the US-Japan relationship, the report encouraged a favourable regional balance. By simultaneously encouraging China's entry into the World Trade Organisation and other international institutions, it created incentives for good behaviour. By and large, the strategy seems to have delivered, with the George W Bush Administration acknowledging that although China is becoming more powerful in all dimensions, it is not likely to close the gap with the US any time soon. Nevertheless, there is a fair chance that China is likely to challenge American interests in East Asia, particularly over Taiwan.

While this report clearly reflected the intention of the US government, it also provided enough hints about the difficulty of engaging China. Given its growing economic potential and already sizeable military force, it was essential that China did not become a security threat to the region. The report outlined that for peace, stability and economic growth in the Asia-Pacific region, it was essential that "China is stable and continues to develop friendly relations with its neighbors... China's military posture and development have a great impact on the expectations and behavior of other states in the region. Although China insists their military build-up is defensive and commensurate with China's overall economic growth, others in the region cannot be certain of China's intentions, particularly in this period of leadership transition. China's military modernisation, along with potential long-term goals, is unclear. Moreover, given the fact that Beijing's territorial disputes with several neighboring states remain unresolved, in the absence of a better understanding of China's plans, capabilities and intentions, other Asian nations may feel the need to respond to China's growing military power."[59]

This, in fact, was reflected in the East Asian Strategy Report which reaffirmed Washington's policy of engagement: "In thinking about the Asia-Pacific region, security comes first and a continued US military presence will continue to serve as a bedrock for America's security role in this dynamic area of the world. US interests in Asia have been remarkably consistent over the past two centuries: peace and security;

commercial access to the region; freedom of navigation; and the prevention of the rise of any hegemonic power or coalition."[60] While the US was the most 'complete' power in terms of military, economy, technology and even cultural capabilities and resources, China's vast conventional military forces, its increasingly large and sophisticated nuclear forces and the overall size and growth of its economy made it the second power centre of Asia.

According to Joseph S Nye, there was a raging debate between those who wanted to contain China before its strength increased and those who urged China's integration into the international system. But the containment option was never feasible because, unlike the Soviet Union during the Cold War, China's neighbours did not see it as a clear and present danger. Also, treating China, as an enemy would guarantee future enmity, thus, unnecessarily discarding the possibility of a more benign outcome.[61] Hence, a policy of "constructive engagement" was the kind of approach that the US appeared to adopt. That is not to deny that the key strategic issue facing America in East Asia certainly remains the rise of Chinese power. For nearly three decades, the Chinese economy has grown at 8 percent to 9 percent annually. In 2005, China announced a 12.6 percent increase in its defence spending and Central Intelligence Agency (CIA) Director Porter Goss warned about a worsening military balance in the Taiwan Strait.

Moreover, as Chintamani Mahapatra adroitly states, in the post-Cold War scenario, the US would not react in any different way than it would have done in the event of a military confrontation between China and Taiwan after 1979 in the Cold War setting. The added dimension, according to him, however, would be the economic leverage of the US vis-à-vis China. Given the huge trade surplus enjoyed by China in its trade with the US, China would obviously suffer more than the US in case of imposition of trade sanctions. The Taiwan issue too, would keep coming up in the foreseeable future and would not only determine the political temperature in Sino-US relations but also create regional tension in the Asia-Pacific.[62] While the US strategy of "comprehensive engagement" of China of the 1990s had certain positive elements in it, the limitations were many. If the protracted Taiwan Strait missile exercise confrontation that culminated in the US dispatching two aircraft carrier battle groups (16 ships), to the area near Taiwan in March 1996 was any indication, the speed with which events drew in the United States had a sobering effect on Beijing.[63] As stated by then Secretary of Defence William Perry, "We realised that things, if not attended to, could go quickly and seriously wrong." Taiwan had been the key stumbling block in Sino-US relations from the beginning of the Cold War through the 1970s, but it had temporarily receded as a prominent irritant after late 1982.[64] In the mid-1990s, the issue once again surged to the top of the Sino-American agenda and it remains the most dangerous flashpoint in US-China ties as we enter the 21st century.

Finally, China was fast evolving as an active member of the international community and multilateral organisations, thereby addressing both American desires for integration of the PRC and Chinese aspirations for recognition and international dignity.[65] Significantly, China's rapid economic growth attracted worldwide attention. Since starting to open up and reform its economy in 1978, China averaged 9.4 percent annual Gross Domestic Product (GDP) growth, one of the highest growth rates in the world. In 1978, it accounted for less than one percent of the world economy, and its total foreign trade was worth $20.6 billion. During the early years of the 21st century, it accounted for 4 percent of the world economy. China also attracted hundreds of billions of dollars in foreign investment and more than a trillion dollars of domestic non-public investment.[66] China's total value of foreign trade reached approximately $1.482 trillion by August 2008, growing by 26.4 percent over the same period of the last year, according to statistics issued by Chinese customs on August 12, 2008.

According to the figures provided by the Chinese government, the trade volume between China and the US increased from US $ 500,000 in 1972 and US $ 2.7 billion in 1979 to US $ 80.48 billion in 2001. China and the US became each other's hot spot for investment.[67] As per a Morgan Stanley Report, trade with China in 2004 alone saved

American consumers $100 billion and created four million new jobs. China's imports from the US have added new momentum to the US economy. Since 2002, for five consecutive years, China has been the fastest growing market of American exports. And over the past decade, US exports to China increased more than 350 percent, which is about six times the growth of US exports to other regions. Whereas China was the 13th largest export market for US products in 1995, it is now the US' fourth largest market. US investments in China have yielded high returns. As of November 2007, US investors had poured in a total of $56 billion into 51,555 enterprises in China. These investments have obtained high returns and shared China's economic success. A study by the US-China Chamber of Commerce showed that 70 percent of American companies operating in China profited from their local businesses, and 42 percent of them reported profit margins in China higher than their global average. A study by the US-China Chamber of Commerce showed that 70 percent of American companies operating in China profited from their local businesses, and 42 percent of them reported profit margins in China higher than their global average.

Therefore, it appears increasingly clear that economic imperatives bind America to China (Asia) and vice-a-versa. Knowing that economics was the key to the new twists and turns in the relationship between Washington and Beijing, it also could not be denied that US-China relations contained considerable distrust and ferocity. Another example of this could be seen during the time of the Clinton Administration when it was acknowledged that improved security was needed as far as the United States weapon labs were concerned amidst growing concerns on Chinese espionage activities. Washington was beginning to get convinced that it was the victim of a sustained Chinese espionage campaign aimed at acquiring classified information on US thermonuclear weapons. This raised the suspicion whether US weapons technology could be used in China's strategic modernisation plans as well as widespread Chinese efforts to acquire US dual-use technology through legal and illegal channels.

The Cox Committee Revelations

On April 21, 1999, Director of Central Intelligence (DCI) George Tenet, reported the intelligence community's damage assessment (reviewed by an independent panel led by Admiral Jeremiah) to Congress and the White House. The assessment confirmed that "China obtained by espionage classified US nuclear weapons information that probably accelerated its programme to develop future nuclear weapons." It also revealed that China obtained information on "several" US nuclear reentry vehicles, including the Trident II submarine-launched missile that delivers the W88 nuclear warhead as well as "a variety of" design concepts and weaponisation features, including those of the neutron bomb.[68]

Subsequently, the House Select Committee on US National Security and Military/Commercial Concerns with the People's Republic of China, headed by Christopher Cox followed this with the revelations that were issued in declassified versions of its report (the Cox Report) on China's acquisition of US technology in a number of sensitive areas, including nuclear weapons, high-performance computers and missile and space systems. The declassified version of this report released on May 25, 1999, included classified information on seven warheads, including "every currently deployed thermonuclear warhead in the US ballistic missile arsenal;" on the neutron bomb; and on "a number of" reentry vehicles of US missiles.[69] The PRC acquired information on seven US nuclear warheads, including the W88, the most advanced, miniature US nuclear warhead deployed on the Trident D-5 submarine -launched ballistic missile (SLBM):

- W88; deployed on the Trident D-5 SLBM
- W87; deployed on the Peacekeeper ICBM
- W78; deployed on the Minuteman III ICBM
- W76; deployed on the Trident C-4 SLBM
- W70; previously deployed on the Lance SRBM
- W62; deployed on the Minuteman III ICBM
- W 56; previously deployed on the Minuteman II ICBM

The committee focussed on the potential implications for US national security, judging "that the PRC will exploit elements of the US design information on the PRC's next generation of thermonuclear weapons." The PRC successfully tested smaller thermonuclear warheads from 1992 to 1996, prior to its July 1996 announcement of a moratorium on nuclear testing and its September 1996 signing of the CTBT .[70] The Cox Committee went on to postulate that "the PRC could begin serial production of its next generation of nuclear weapons during the next decade in connection with the development of its next generation of solid-fuel mobile ICBMs, including the DF-31."[71] Regarding whether the PRC's nuclear programme required continuing testing, the committee judged that if the PRC successfully stole US nuclear test codes, computers models and data so as to use them with the US high-performance computers already imported, China "could diminish its need for further nuclear testing to evaluate weapons and proposed design changes."[72] With reference to the strategic balance, the Cox Committee Report stated that "the United States retains an overwhelming qualitative and quantitative advantage in deployed strategic nuclear forces" over the PRC's up to two dozen CSS-4 ICBMs. Nonetheless, the report stated, "In a crisis in which the US confronts the PRC's conventional and nuclear forces at the regional level, a modernised Chinese strategic nuclear ballistic missile force would pose a direct credible threat against the United States." At the same time, though, the committee accepted that it had no information on whether the PRC intended to develop and deploy multiple independently targetable reentry vehicles (MIRVs) for its nuclear missile force.[73]

The disclosures of the Cox Committee dealt a serious blow to the US-Chinese relations with the report's implicit message that the United States should not do business with a country that presents a serious threat to US security and engages in espionage against the US nuclear establishment. The findings of the Cox Report came under severe criticism within China, with Beijing vigorously denying that it engaged in any nuclear espionage and argued that ample information on US nuclear weapons was available from open sources. In an official response on May 27, 1999, Chinese Foreign Ministry spokesman, Zhu

Bangzao, stated, "We have no policy of stealing from other nations and China has never stolen any nuclear secrets from any country, including America."[74] On July 15, 1999, the PRC government issued a response denying the Cox Committee's charges that China stole US secrets. Moreover, the report contained a short paragraph acknowledging that China had the neutron bomb. The statement said China had mastered "in succession the neutron bomb technology and nuclear weapon miniaturisation technology." In addition, "since China already possessed the atom bomb and H-bomb technologies, it is quite logical and natural for it to master the neutron bomb technology through its own efforts over a reasonable period of time."[75] However, various analysts believed that with little evidence and flawed logic, the assessment of the Cox Committee was misleading to a high extent and threatened the rational US diplomatic and defence policy toward Beijing. As a matter of fact, the Cox Report gave added impetus to the already considerably large community of foreign policy watchers in the US who were increasingly cagey of the 'China threat'.

The 'China Threat' Debate

China's growing economic and military weight and widespread uncertainty and apprehension about its immediate intentions and long-term ideas about the regional and world order[76] led to a central query: how should the US and the regional players react to the rise of Chinese power? The future of China is perhaps the most pressing question in what is widely perceived as becoming the world's most important region and the possibility of a 'China threat', therefore, became a hotly debated topic. The 'China threat' argument maintained that an increasingly powerful China was likely to destabilise regional security in the near future. This idea became highly topical as China's economy posted exceptional growth in the early 1990s, as has been discussed earlier. Analysts have noted that a developed economy could potentially turn China's huge population from a weakness into a strength and give Beijing the basis for world-class military and technological capability, a possibility by means of which China could well be poised to be a superpower in the coming decade.

The US appeared to have a strategic option, namely, preemptive containment, which assumed a much more antagonistic world ahead of it. In the regional context, this focussed attention on China, the only state with the ambition, long-term potential, national autonomy and prospective military power that would make it an even remotely possible strategic challenger to America. The trepidations of those who advocated this option were reinforced by the fact that China's ambitions were nuclear, maritime as well as continental; and by the degree to which Beijing's territorial claims in Asia and the Pacific appeared to conflict with those of its neighbours.[77] Advocates of a containment strategy asserted that China's military power and its ambitions and interests would be such that America and its regional security partners would need countervailing capabilities to preclude Chinese domination or coercion of neighbouring states.[78] In order to play down the conflict and bring peace and stability, the need for an enhanced strategic dialogue between the US and China was self-evident. Sustained high-level interaction between Washington and Beijing would have unambiguously conveyed America's strategic stake in the region and signalled to Beijing that a viable long-term security order in Asia was not possible without the full and constructive participation of both China and the US.[79] In a volatile article published in *Time,* American journalist Charles Krauthammer took an extreme position and characterised China as a "bully" that "tries relentlessly to expand its reach," and proposed a two-pronged strategy.[80] He asserted that the United States should strive to "contain" China by cultivating and maintaining a strong alliance with Japan and, at the same time, the US should work to undermine the Communist Party regime and promote political liberalisation by supporting Chinese dissidents, publicly criticising China's human rights abuses and opposing Beijing's efforts to accumulate international prestige.[81]

The heart of the containment strategy, as Krauthammer's article made clear, was the recruitment of allies to join a coalition to balance Chinese power. An anti-Chinese containment strategy would also provide a new rationale for the maintenance of US forces in East Asia. However, what effect this arrangement would eventually have on the existing strategic situation in the Asian continent is anybody's guess. The views of former Secretary of State Henry Kissinger, however, were diametrically opposite as he deftly pointed out, "... stability in Asia is most likely if China and the US cooperate. It is certainly desirable that Washington and Beijing reach broad understanding on the strategic, economic and political issues that divide them."[82]

Going by the trends of Beijing's defence spending that rose significantly in the post-Cold War years (a 21 percent increase was budgeted for 1995), many analysts questioned the increase in China's military funding when external threats to the PRC's security were seen to be at an all time low. A RAND study, for example, used the purchasing power-parity approach to arrive at the stunning figure of $140 billion for China's 1994 defence expenditures. Masashi Nishihara of Japan's National Institute for Defence Studies accused China of "increasing its military power and trying to establish a militarily dominant position in Asia by taking advantage of the current situation when the US and Russia have cut back their armed forces and defence budgets."[83] Furthermore, Singapore, which became outspokenly pro-China after its normalisation of relations with Beijing, expressed similar concern when Prime Minister Goh Chok Tong stated in a 1995 interview, "...In Asia, China's rising power and arms build-up has stirred anxiety... It is important to bring into the open this underlying sense of discomfort, even insecurity, about the political and military ambitions of China."[84]

Arguments for viewing China as a 'threat' believed that Beijing had a poor human rights record, resisted any multilateral discussion of expansive Chinese claims in the South China Sea, and persistently threatened to use force against Taiwan. China's missile tests off the coast of Taiwan, and continued sales of nuclear-capable missile technology to Pakistan hardened these views and China appeared to be swimming against the tide. A *Far Eastern Economic Review* editorial carped, "Too often, China's actions appear founded on the assumption that its neighbours are, if not enemies, at least obstacles... In short, China needs to learn what it makes to be a good neighbour."[85] Adding to this, Larry M Wortzel opined that Beijing "seems locked in pre-Cold War, almost turn-of-the-century modes of quasi-imperial competition for regional hegemony."[86] On the flip side, there were strong arguments against viewing China as a threat. The anti-China threat position began with the argument that China might not be able to develop into a 'threat' even if it wanted to since externally the Chinese were bound by interdependence with their markets and suppliers. In addition, Denny Roy says that the Chinese Communist Party (CCP) was convinced that strong links with the outside world would best facilitate the all-consuming goal of economic development. For instance, Yan Xuetong asserted that traditional Chinese morality guaranteed that a strong China would be a benign China since "China's traditional culture regards it as a shame to grab economic interests by force." Xuetong further said that when Chinese leaders "make a decision on whether to use force, they are to a great extent restrained by...the norm of righteousness."[87] Similarly, Chinese Foreign Minister Qian Qichen also relied on Chinese tradition for evidence of Beijing's pacific intentions, using the Confucian adage 'do not do unto others that you do not like others to do unto you' to strengthen his claim that "China will never threaten or invade others countries."[88]

While many China-watchers were disturbed by its rapid military improvements, anti-threat advocates were quick to note several mitigating points. They stressed that CCP leaders gave military modernisation a relatively low priority prior to the 1990s and asked the People's Liberation Army (PLA) to be patient. As a result, the bulk of China's current weapons stockpile was considered outdated. Now that the Chinese economy has taken off, coupled with the lessons of the Gulf War that brought about the entire concept of "high technology warfare" to the forefront, Beijing was all set to shore up a rather neglected area. According to the prevalent view in Beijing, the US wants to keep Asia under its domination that called for a relatively weaker China. Rallying support among China's neighbours for an anti-China alliance was another tactic—along with human rights criticism, "peaceful evolution," and the campaign that was launched to prevent Beijing from winning the right to host the 2000 Olympic Games—to "pin down the development of China." Mocking the "China threat" in the US news media, a commentary by the official *Xinhua News Agency* said, "It seems that only the United States has the right to development, while China does not. China has to remain permanently poor and backward and bow to the subjugation and exploitation of big Western powers."[89]

It was widely viewed that three discernable images of the US and its role in the post-Cold War era coexisted in China. The first, derived from an ideological perspective, casts the US as a rival value system; the second came out of a realist perspective, thereby casting the US as a hegemonic power; and the last was a product of an interdependence perspective that saw the US as a necessary and even preferable world leader.[90] There was growing belief that the only challenge that was posed to the US' formidable presence in the Asia-Pacific stems from China. In fact, China seeks to emerge as a superpower in its own right and, therefore, questioned the US "posture" of "hegemony" in the global context. This was the result of China's remarkable growth over the past nearly two decades, its ability to develop nuclear weapon deterrence vis-à-vis both the US and Russia and its sustained programme of military modernisation.[91] So, China envisages a greater political role for itself in Asia as a counter-challenge to the US. China-watchers predict that its policy of restraining Japan, constraining India and befriending Southeast Asia with a view to firmly bringing it under its larger political influence, would continue to be the principal objective of its government for the coming years. Like other countries, China has had to adjust its foreign and security policies in the wake of the onset of the post-Cold War world order. Its immediate response could be summed up in two initiatives: *zhoubian* (circumference) diplomacy and defence modernisation. The former was a good-neighbour policy initially aimed at breaking out of Beijing's diplomatic isolation after Tiananmen. The diplomatic realignment, thus, launched, however, was soon to flower into a global strategy in response to the demise of the Soviet Union. Later on, following the low tide of Sino-US relations in 1993, the globalised good-neighbour diplomacy became an instrument with which the Chinese fought back against the perceived continuing US attempt to vilify Beijing as a pariah regime.[92]

The *zhoubian* diplomatic realignment, though later globalised, and defence modernisation were two mutually complementary prongs of the overall Chinese policy response. The PRC diplomatic initiative, which resulted from an assessment of the post-Cold War world order, was also a reaction to Washington's characterisation of the new order as trumpeted by President George HW Bush after Desert Storm. Three points stood out in the Chinese definition of what the new order was or should be: (1) all countries, big and small, should be equal and no one power should dictate the affairs of others; (2) a "unipolar" (read: US) monopoly of power should be checked and countered by a collegial sharing of power among nations, with the United Nations playing a leading role; and (3) the new order should also contain a "new economic world order" in which the developed countries help the developing countries on their path to development.[93]

To the PRC, the new world order posed at least three challenges: (1) the declining importance of nuclear weapons; (2) the rising paramountcy of economic power (as distinct from military prowess); and (3) the loss of China's strategic leverage in the erstwhile US-Soviet rivalry. In the post-Cold War era, American and Chinese conceptions of their security were neither identical nor entirely divergent. Both nations sought stability in the Asia-Pacific region and the world so that they could pursue their respective domestic priorities. China and the United States wished to avoid conflict over Taiwan, though both may have been willing to enter into a conflict if required under certain conditions. Neither country wanted to be witness to a remilitarised Japan that would set off an Asian arms spiral. On the Korean Peninsula, both Washington and Beijing have not only desired stability but also have had reasonably compatible approaches to achieving it—nonetheless, it is true that China has played a major role in deterring the US from using force as well as keeping the North Korean regime afloat.

A terse analysis by Harry Harding suggested that for decades, the US sought what many Americans described as a "special relationship" with China. This special relationship had a strongly cyclical character. In its positive phase, it joined America's "dreams of influence and uplift" to China's hope of securing wealth and power from a foreign patron. In its negative phase, it saw China rejecting American influence as disruptive and demeaning and the US turning away from China.

This cycle, by which hostility gave way to reconciliation and euphoria yielded to disenchantment, was repeated several times in the history of Sino-US relations. The relationship between Washington and Beijing in the post-Cold War period was seen likely to be a less central one for the United States as the result of a more diverse and multipolar world. With the collapse of the Soviet empire and the end of the Cold War, China was no longer regarded simply as one corner of the strategic triangle, the shape of which would determine the global geo-political balance.

Rather than portraying Sino-US relations as a case of pure convergence or a complete divergence of interests, it would be appropriate to portray them as a mixture of complementary and competitive objectives, which would be chiefly characterised by hard bargaining within and between numerous outstanding issues. For instance, US policy-makers could link US accommodation of Chinese interests in areas such as trade policy in return for more Chinese cooperation on nuclear arms control initiatives favoured by the US. Issues relating to proliferation and China have perennially been highly charged issues on the Capitol Hill. China's nuclear and missile exports have threatened existing regimes on nuclear non-proliferation and the next chapter identifies the policies and trends in non-proliferation and the Chinese involvement in the same.

Notes

1. John Wilson Lewis and Xue Litai, *China Builds the Bomb* (Stanford, California: Stanford University Press, 1988), p. 6.
2. For more details, see Ibid., pp. 11-34.
3. Mc George Bundy, *Danger and Survival: Choices About the Bomb in the First Fifty Years* (New Delhi: East West Press Pvt. Ltd., 1988), pp. 526-527.
4. For more details, see Sarah J Diehl and James Clay Moltz, *Nuclear Weapons and Nonproliferation* (California: ABC-CLIO Inc., 2002), p. 75.
5. Bundy, n.3, p. 526.
6. Quoting Mao's 1956 Statement from *Peking Review*, no. 1, January 1, 1977, p. 13.
7. As cited in Bundy, n. 3, p. 528.
8. Diehl and Moltz,n.4, p. 76.
9. Bundy, n. 3, pp. 527-528.
10. Chinese Statement cited in *China Daily*, August 15, 1963.

11. For details, see John W Garver, *Foreign Relations of the People's Republic of China*, (New Jersey: Prentice-Hall, Inc., 1993), p. 55.
12. CRS Report for Congress, "Chinese Nuclear Weapons and Arms Control Policies: Implications and Options for the United States," March 25, 1994, p. 4.
13. Communist Chinese Announcement, *Peking Review,* Supplement, October 16, 1964.
14. Ibid.
15. Ibid.
16. Ibid.
17. Richard P Stebbins, *The United States in World Affairs 1966* (New York: Council on Foreign Relations, Harper and Row Publishers, 1967), pp. 280-281
18. Initially, China did not sign the NPT in 1968 and denounced the treaty as a "conspiracy concocted by the USSR and the US to maintain their nuclear monopoly." China viewed the NPT as a way for the nuclear powers, mainly the US and Soviet Union, to perpetuate their power by limiting the military capabilities of other countries. China maintained that it stood for the complete abolition of nuclear weapons and did not advocate or encourage nuclear proliferation, but the nuclear superpowers had no right to prevent non-nuclear weapons states from acquiring nuclear weapons until the nuclear superpowers committed themselves to complete disarmament. However, in the 1980s, China's position on nuclear proliferation started to change. Beijing continued to criticise the NPT as an imbalanced, discriminatory treaty, but also indicated that it accepted in principle the norm of nuclear nonproliferation. For more details see, http://www.nti.org/db/china/nptorg.htm
19. *Peking Review,* Supplement, October 16, 1964.
20. Ibid.
21. Ibid.
22. US Department of State Bulletin, October 19, 1964, pp. 542-543.
23. US Department of State Bulletin, November 2, 1964, p. 612.
24. Ibid.
25. Avery Goldstein, "Understanding Nuclear Proliferation: Theoretical Explanation and China's National Experience", in Zachary Davis and Benjamin Frankel, eds., *The Proliferation Puzzle: Why Nuclear Weapons Spread and What Results* (London: Frank Cass, 1993), p. 226.
26. The Sino-Soviet treaty of alliance signed in 1950 was mainly China's attempt to protect itself from the threat posed by the other superpower, namely the United States.
27. Stebbins, n. 17, p. 296.
28. Paul HB Godwin, "China's Nuclear Forces: An Assessment," *Current History,* vol. 98, no. 629, September 1999, pp. 263-64.
29. Bundy, n. 3, p. 528.
30. For more details, see Maurice Meisner, *Mao's China and After: A History of the People's Republic* (New York: Free Press, Inc., 1986), p. 399.

31. For more details, see Henry Kissinger, *White House Years* (Boston: Little, Brown and Co., 1979), pp. 183-186.
32. Bundy, n. 3, p. 530.
33. Ibid., p. 535.
34. Meisner, n. 30, p. 400.
35. Chintamani Mahapatra, "The Eagle and the Dragon: After the Cold War," *Strategic Analysis,* vol. 19, no. 2, May 1996, p. 231.
36. Kissinger, n. 31, p. 164.
37. Ibid., p. 1062.
38. David M Lampton, *Same Bed Different Dreams: Managing U.S.-China Relations, 1989-2000,* (California: University of California Press, 2001), p. 67.
39. Ibid.
40. Ibid., p. 68.
41. For details, see Warren Donnelly, "Implementation of the US-Chinese Agreement for Nuclear Cooperation," CRS Report for Congress, Issue Brief 86050, September 28, 1989.
42. Judith Miller, "US Is Holding Up Peking Atom Talks," *The New York Times,* September 19, 1982.
43. Cited in Jennifer Weeks, "Sino-US Cooperation at a Crossroads," *Arms Control Today,* vol. 27, no. 4, June/July 1997, p. 92.
44. Ibid.
45. Leonard S Spector, *Nuclear Ambitions: The Spread of Nuclear Weapons 1989-1990* (Boulder, CO: Westview Press, 1990), p. 61.
46. Cited in Daniel Southerland, "US, China Sign Accords," *The Washington Post,* August 28, 1985.
47. Weeks, n. 43, p. 8.
48. For details, see Spector, n. 45, pp. 38-43.
49. General Accounting Office, Nuclear Agreement: Cooperation Between the United States and the People's Republic of China, NSIAD-86-21BR, November 1985.
50. Byung-joon Ahn, "The United States in Asia: Searching for a New Role," in James Shinn, ed., *Weaving the Net: Conditional Engagement with China,* (New York: Council on Foreign Relations Press, 1996), p. 191.
51. CRS Report for Congress, n. 12, p. 87.
52. Ibid., p. 82.
53. Sujit Dutta, "Transition to Cooperative Peace," in Jasjit Singh, ed., *Reshaping Asian Security"* (New Delhi: Knowledge World, 2001), pp. 345-346.
54. Lampton, n. 38, pp. 65-66.
55. Spector, n. 45, pp. 24-25.
56. Michael Gordon, "Beijing Avoids New Missile Sales Assurances," *The New York Times,* March 30, 1990.
57. Mahapatra, n. 35, p. 231.
58. "US Security Strategy for the East Asia-Pacific Region," Department of Defense Report, Office of International Security Affairs, (Washington, DC, February

1995), pp. 2-5.
59. Ibid.
60. Ibid.
61. Joseph S Nye, "Advancing US Strategy for East Asian Security", *Asian Wall Street Journal,* May 5, 2005.
62. For more details, see Mahapatra, n. 35, pp. 242-43.
63. Lampton, n. 38, p. 46.
64. Ibid.
65. Ibid., p. 68.
66. Bijian, "China's 'Peaceful Rise' to Great-Power Status," *Foreign Affairs,* vol. 84, no. 5, September/October 2005, p. 18.
67. Li Jianying and Zhang Yijun, "Ups and Downs in Sino-US Relations," *Foreign Affairs Journal,* no. 63, March 2002, p. 44.
68. For details see, CRS Report for Congress, "China: Suspected Acquisition of US Nuclear Weapon Data," by Shirley A Kan, September 14, 2000.
69. US House of Representatives Select Committee, 105-851, US National Security and Military/Commercial Concerns with the People's Republic of China, [Declassified Version] May 25, 1999.
70. For details, see, CRS Report for Congress, "Chinese Nuclear Testing and Warhead Development", by Jonathan Medalia, 1997.
71. Cox Committee Findings, n. 69.
72. Ibid.
73. Ibid.
74. *Xinhua News Agency,* May 27, 1999.
75. PRC, Information Office of the State Council, "Facts Speak Louder Than Words and Lies Will Collapse by Themselves—Further Refutation of the Cox Report," July 15, 1999, quoted in CRS Report for Congress, "China: Suspected Acquisition of US Nuclear Weapon Data," by Shirley A Kan, September 2000, p. 46.
76. Paul M Evans, "The New Multilateralism and the Conditional Engagement of China," in Shinn, ed., n. 50, p. 252.
77. Jonathan D Pollack, "Asia's Shifting Strategic Landscape: China and the United States Post-9/11," *Orbis,* vol. 47, no. 4, Fall 2003, p. 109.
78. Ibid.
79. Pollack, n. 77, p. 127.
80. Charles Krauthammer, "Why We Must Contain China", *Time,* July 31, 1995, p. 72.
81. Ibid.
82. Kissinger, n. 31, p. 167.
83. Masashi Nishihara, "Japan has Cause to Worry About Chinese Ambition," *International Herald Tribune,* July 12, 1994, p. 3.
84. Quoted in Michael Richardson, "A Resurgent China Sets Off Alarms Over 'Containment'," *International Herald Tribune,* July 7, 1995, p. 1.
85. For details, see "China Complex," *Far Eastern Economic Review,* July 20, 1995, p. 5.

86. Larry M Wortzel, "China Pursues Traditional Great-Power Status," *Orbis*, vol. 38, no. 2, Spring 1994, p. 157.
87. Yan Xuetong, "China's Post-Cold War Security Strategy," *Contemporary International Relations*, vol. 5, no. 5, May 1995, pp. 6-7.
88. "Give China Time and Space," *Far Eastern Economic Review*, May 25, 1995, p. 30.
89. Xinhua quoted in *International Herald Tribune*, August 24, 1995, p. 4.
90. Jianwei Wang, "Coping with China as a Rising Power," in James Shinn, n. 76, p. 135.
91. SD Muni, "An Asian Balance of Power?" in Jasjit Singh, ed., *Reshaping Asian Security* (New Delhi: Knowledge World, 2001), p. 5.
92. James C Hsiung, "China's Omni-Directional Diplomacy: Realignment to Cope with Monopolar US Power," *Asian Survey*, vol. 35, no. 6, June 1995, p. 573.
93. Ibid., pp. 574 -575.

2

Non-Proliferation,China and the US Policy

One of the major thrusts of US foreign policy in the post-Cold War era has been on proliferation of weapons of mass destruction (WMD), which impinge upon US strategic interests across the globe. The US has undertaken many measures, including strengthening the international nuclear non-proliferation regime and threatening/applying sanctions to punish/deter proliferation attempts by nations that are considered to be of significant 'proliferation concern'. However, Washington has been unsuccessful in achieving this goal and there has been a consistent spread of WMD along with their means of delivery. With the end of the Cold War and the disappearance of the strategic Soviet threat, US policy-makers were able to give greater attention to the potential use of nuclear, biological, and chemical weapons by less powerful countries or terrorist groups. For these reasons, there is concern in Congress about the countries and groups that have these weapons or are developing them, or trying to acquire them. The international community is also involved in debates on the growing threats posed by the continuing trade in transfers of dangerous technology. One of the ever growing concerns in the US and elsewhere is China's involvement in proliferation of weapons of mass destruction, especially in Asia.

The US approached the problem of proliferation by unilaterally putting in place legal measures through Congressional Acts or addition of numerous amendments to existing Acts. Secondly, the US took special measures to prevent proliferation as and when it established bilateral cooperation with several countries around the world in the fields of civilian, nuclear and space programmes. Thirdly, the US was the leader in the movement leading to international WMD control regimes such as the Nuclear Suppliers' Group, Australia Group, Missile Technology Control Regime, Wassenaar Arrangement and Zangger Committee, to name a few.

Multilateral Export Control Regimes

The Nuclear Suppliers Group (NSG) - is an informal institution comprising 40 states, more than half of which are nuclear technology suppliers. It established common guidelines governing nuclear transfers in an effort to ensure that civilian nuclear trade did not contribute to nuclear weapons acquisition. NSG guidelines on nuclear exports were first published in 1978 and fourteen years later, the NSG established additional guidelines for transfers of nuclear-related dual-use equipment, material, and technology. At the 14th plenary meeting of the NSG held in May 2004, the People's Republic of China was approved as a participating government in the export control group. China's addition was regarded as a positive step for the NSG in its endeavours to halt the proliferation of nuclear weapons technology.

As part of its export control policy, China aims to strike a balance between its non-proliferation objectives and its efforts to provide the developing world with access to emergent nuclear technologies for peaceful purpose — a tool to realise its broader foreign policy goals. China's reformulated non-proliferation policies, measures and practices in the Chinese government and its stance on non-proliferation were described in a White Paper titled "China's National Defense in 2002." The paper described how access to nuclear technologies for peaceful purposes is part of the three principles governing China's nuclear exports. These principles state that a client must: (1) guarantee that any technology transferred from China must be intended for peaceful purposes only; (2) accept International Atomic Energy Agency (IAEA) safeguards and; (3) agree not to retransfer technology to a third party without China's approval.[1] The Chinese government has acknowledged that it must take the steps necessary to ensure that nuclear and dual-use technology supplied to client states is not used in an illicit manner. In the aforementioned White Paper, China discussed the challenges of relying on administrative measures to regulate export controls in an economy that has become more open.

The Australia Group (AG) - is an informal arrangement that aims to allow exporting or trans-shipping countries to minimise the risk of assisting chemical and biological weapon (CBW) proliferation. The group was formed in 1984 with 15 members at Australia's initiative, as a response to evidence about chemical weapon use in the Iran-Iraq War. It is also among the few regimes wherein members agreed to adopt 'catch all' controls as a means for ensuring greater government-industry partnership in controlling sensitive exports to suspect end-users. To control the export of chemicals, in June 1996, China issued a list of chemicals subject to supervision and control, and in January 1998, the Chinese media reported that the government had issued instructions requiring a licence for the export of chemicals and related technologies.[2] China now prohibits the export of 10 of the 20 chemicals banned by the Australia Group. China has not joined the Australia Group, and has consistently opposed its existence, holding that the membership is not universal and the trade restrictions that it imposes are discriminatory and in violation of the Chemical Weapons Convention (CWC). Additionally, a significant problem China has with joining the Australia Group is that China had no control over which items were included on the AG's list of chemical precursors and CW-related production equipment. In fact, according to its official stance, "China holds that the Chemical Weapons Convention which has entered into force should constitute the sole legal basis for governing the international chemical trade. Those export control regimes incompatible with the convention should be transformed or abolished. China strongly opposes the actions by the member states of the Australia Group in obstructing the normal chemical trade between States Parties to the convention under the pretext of non-proliferation."[3]

The Missile Technology Control Regime (MTCR) - is an informal and voluntary association of countries sharing the goals of non-proliferation of unmanned delivery systems for WMD and seeking to coordinate national export licensing efforts aimed at preventing their proliferation. The group was originally established in 1987 and the membership stands at 33 nations. In addition, while not members, China, Israel, and Ukraine have agreed to abide by the MTCR guidelines. The MTCR controls exports of missiles (and related technology) whose performance in terms of payload and range exceeds stated parameters. The regime's guidelines divided missile-related exports into two categories—one with a "strong presumption of denial" [complete rocket systems and unmanned aerial vehicles (UAVs), major sub-systems, and critical production equipment], and another comprising dual-use items that may or may not be intended for use in missile systems. In other words, Category I included complete systems and sub-systems capable of carrying a payload of a 500 kg (1,100 lb) warhead over a range of at least 300 km (186 miles) and specially designed production facilities for such systems. Category II included missile-related components such as propellants, avionics equipment, and other items used for the production of Category I systems.

The initial agreement called on member states to coordinate domestic export policies to restrict sales of ballistic and cruise missiles (and related technologies) that could deliver nuclear weapons, defined as those missiles with ranges greater than 300 km and payloads over 500 km. The regime was modified in 1993 to include missiles capable of carrying chemical/biological weapons (CW/BW) as well. Because CW/BW payloads are lighter than nuclear warheads, the missile payload requirements were removed. At its most recent meetings in October 1995, MTCR members updated the guidelines to accommodate technological advances. The MTCR is not a treaty, and is not binding under international law. Further, penalties for violations vary between members, and the lack of an agreed-upon enforcement mechanism further led to internal disagreements. However, the MTCR has proven successful in blocking some sales of the potentially destabilising and threatening missile systems or components, and has slowed the pace of missile proliferation worldwide.[4]

The Wassenaar Arrangement (WA) - is an informal agreement of 33 states established in 1996 to prevent countries from acquiring large and dangerous stockpiles of conventional weapons and sensitive technologies by encouraging members to share information on their exports to non-members. There were two agreed lists of items: a munitions list, which comprised conventional weapons almost exclusively designed for war-fighting such as tanks and fighter aircrafts, as well as military explosives; and a dual-use technology list that was broken into two tiers: Tier 1—the basic list—was made up of sensitive items and technologies, and Tier 2 consisted of very sensitive items that were subject to more stringent monitoring. The Wassenaar Arrangement was widely viewed as an evolving part of US foreign and defence policy that sought to restrict exports of destabilising weapons through a broad consensual process among potential suppliers. While laudable in both aims and means, its status and modest progress raised questions about whether and how it would be able to reach binding control over proliferation of advanced systems. An essential limiting factor is that some major arms exporters such as China, Belarus and Israel are not members.

Under the evolving Wassenaar Arrangement, arms proliferation (both weapons and most dual-use technologies) to the specified pariah states would be effectively denied. It was anticipated by the arrangement's advocates that exports of some dual-use technology to these states might occur in special cases if the end user were non-military and could be reliably monitored (e.g. machine tools for civil uses). Apart from the pariah states, control of arms proliferation in the rest of the world would depend on when and how the small group establishes binding criteria for allowing or proscribing weapons exports. On the other hand, if these defining criteria were delayed, or if they failed to be agreed upon, controlling proliferation would be less a reality and more a velleity.

Enforcement of the Wassenaar Arrangement's protocols largely depended on arriving at a consensus among members of both the large and small groups. It was arguable whether this consensus would be robust enough to offset the incentives for breakout among current arms sellers, or among potential new sellers who might be attracted to the newly restricted market. The advocates of this regime argued that the Wassenaar Arrangement would not have discernible economic effects on the US defence industry, nor would it in any appreciable way affect current and expected reductions in US defence procurement. Finally, the administrative practicability of implementing the arrangement's procedures and agreements inevitably presented a formidable challenge. With 28 member-countries in the full group, and six members in the small group, delays, misunderstandings, and periodic miscarriages were hard to avoid.[5]

The Zangger Committee (ZAC) - is also known as the "NPT Exporters Committee", and was established in the early 1970s. It is a 35-member group of nuclear suppliers that produced the so-called 'trigger list' of nuclear materials, equipment and technology requiring IAEA safeguards. The Zangger Committee essentially contributed to the interpretation of Article III, paragraph 2, of the NPT and thereby offered guidance to all parties to the treaty. The main significance of this paragraph was that parties to the treaty should not export directly or indirectly, nuclear equipment and material to non-nuclear weapon states unless the export was subject to IAEA safeguards. China officially joined the committee on October 16, 1997, and stated, "China supports the general goals of the Committee, appreciates the positive role the Committee has played in preventing nuclear proliferation and stands ready to conduct regular consultations with other member countries of the Committee on issues of nuclear non-proliferation and export control with a view to making joint efforts to prevent proliferation of nuclear weapons."[6] Although China has accepted the principle of the international trigger list and has joined the NSG, it still objects to the requirement of full-scope nuclear safeguards. China's membership in ZAC could complicate plans to add full-scope safeguards to the committee's export requirements in the future.

Most of China's most sensitive arms deals (as opposed to the sales of military-related technologies and dual-use items) have been conducted by Poly Technologies, which gets approval directly from members of the Central Military Commission (CMC). Other corporations are authorised to sell less sophisticated conventional weapons and equipment, but if they wish to sell arms to sensitive regions or to sell more sophisticated weapons and equipment, they are required to consult with the Ministry of Foreign Affairs (MFA) and other organisations. If the MFA believes that a sale will adversely affect China's foreign relations, it will bring it to the attention of China's top leadership.[7] However, still remaining a cause of concern to the US and the rest of the international community, is the significant role played by China in the realm of nuclear and missile proliferation across Asia and beyond. Despite its international pledges and growing commitment to arms control, Beijing still lacks the procedures to effectively implement many agreements. It is likely that most sensitive weapons sales have occurred with the knowledge and approval of the central government. The argument that China has no control over its arms industries is also undermined by the observation that Chinese arms have not been sold to potential military adversaries, such as Vietnam, India or Taiwan for that matter.[8] It would be inappropriate to state that the digest of China's nuclear posture is showered with adjectives such as "reported", "rumoured", "alleged", "possible" among a few. This is primarily because China has put almost next to nothing on the public record regarding transparency of records on WMD, which continues to remain dismal. Moreover, the post-Cold War environment of the 1990s saw new challenges in the so-called Chinese arms control policies. For one thing, the US-Russian arms reduction efforts and agreements, nuclear test ban treaty and a few other arms control initiatives clearly contrast with China's quest for an expanded nuclear arsenal and its suspected role in proliferation. The attitude of China toward nuclear proliferation has been a major national security concern for the US ever since China became a nuclear-weapon state in 1964. A year prior to China's first nuclear explosion, the *Peking Review* declared that "[s] o long as the imperialists refuse to ban nuclear weapons, the greater the number of socialist countries possessing them, the better the guarantee of world peace."[9]

The non-proliferation concerns of the US involving the inscrutable Chinese were considerably influenced by the indiscriminate arms export policy of China. Beijing, meanwhile, continued to be the largest exporter of arms in Asia. An important trend emerging in its arms transfers in the future appeared to be the import, and subsequent export, of sophisticated high-technology weapon systems and equipment.[10] China's arms exports was an issue that, time and again, generated considerable amount of concern in the international community, especially in the non-proliferation circles, since there were imminent dangers of the spread of WMD and their respective means of delivery. The total of China's contracts for arms exports for the year 1993 registered considerable growth, three times from the lowest $100 million in 1992 to $300 million for 1993. China's market was primarily confined to the Middle East, South and Southeast Asian nations.[11] What was more disquieting was that China displayed an apparent willingness to sell weapons to countries in unstable regions, posing concerns for the international community.

In an article published in *Orbis,* Denny Roy argued that China's rapid economic development raised the prospect of a serious PRC-US rivalry, with global ramifications comparable to the last century's Cold War. In recent years, the notion that a stronger China threatened the interests of the United States and some of its allies became commonplace. The central argument here was that a stronger China potentially posed new types of hazards to US interests.[12] In this respect, Chinese proliferation of WMD technology was best understood as a contingent hazard. This proliferation served several purposes in the past, including revenue-raising, strengthening Pakistan's capability to counter-balance India, and retaliating against US policies of which Beijing disapproved. For the purposes of bringing in hard currency and strengthening Pakistan, a stronger China of the future was no more likely to proliferate WMD technology, and may be less so, than China today. Furthermore, there was a possible upside to China's evolving from a regional power into a great power with a global outlook. Although this did not necessarily mean that a stronger China would have abandoned its long-standing relationship with Islamabad, the strategic rationale for WMD transfers to Pakistan would be no greater than in the past—unless the real target of such transfers was not India but the United States. Chinese involvement in the proliferation of WMD was seen many a times as a tool that could be employed to imperil US interests outside the Asia-

Pacific or as a bargaining chip to counter US policies the Chinese find threatening (e.g. arms sales to Taiwan).[13]

During the Iran-Iraq War, China sold weapons to both participants, and throughout the decade China made significant arms transfers throughout the developing world. It did not offer a large technological advantage to its clients, but emphasised less expensive major systems such as the F-7 fighter to cash-strapped or isolated countries like Iran, Pakistan and Burma. While other countries' military expenditures had been falling, defence spending per person in China remained at about the same level over the last ten years.[14] According to US intelligence sources, China reportedly sold around 36-40 liquid-fuelled IRBMs, the DF-3A, also known as the CSS-2, to Saudi Arabia in 1987. This ballistic missile had an estimated range of up to 2,800 km and fetched China an estimated $3-3.5 billion. It was this deal with Saudi Arabia that propelled China high in the international arms market, compelling the great powers to take notice of the potential of the PRC's arms exports.[15]

It appears palpable that China's approach to non-proliferation is fundamentally at odds with the arms control agenda of the United States and its European and Asian allies. Beijing's initial refusal to support and adhere to the international non-proliferation regimes could be seen as a byproduct of its strategic outlook. The PLA perceives the US as a regional bully that employs arms control agreements to handcuff its potential adversaries.[16] Below is a brief account of the existent international regimes to prevent the spread of WMD and their respective means of delivery.

China's Compliance with International Arms Control Agreements

During the Cold War era, the Chinese stayed away from the arms control initiatives and agreements, but modified their behaviour and attitude after the Soviet disintegration. The only exception was perhaps the Chinese accession to the Biological Weapons Convention (BWC) signed in 1984. Months after the Soviet collapse, China announced its decision to accede to the NPT and adhere to the principles of the MTCR.

The post-Cold War world witnessed the US and Russia continuing to work towards efforts to try and achieve a new breakthrough that could undercut China's nuclear strategy. China opted to accommodate US-backed international arms control pressures by joining the NPT in 1992, and agreeing to abide by the missile export guidelines of the MTCR.

China, in February 1992, unilaterally promised to abide by the MTCR and acceded to the NPT on March 9, 1992. In September 1996, China signed the CTBT. Beijing then became a signatory to the CWC in 1997. It sat as an observer at the meeting of the Zangger Committee in May 1997, and formally joined it as a full member in October 1997. It is important to note that the international arms control agreements to which China committed have more relevance to the non-proliferation of WMD than to controls over China's weapon programmes.[17] While Beijing refused to cut down the size of its nuclear forces and continued its ballistic missile development programme, it was suspected of involvement in exporting nuclear related equipment and ballistic missile technology to various nations that were considered unstable and unfriendly by the US and its allies.

Although China acceded to the NPT on March 9, 1992, its nuclear export policies have been a source of concern. While the NPT does not ban nuclear exports to non-NPT countries, nearly all nuclear exporting nations have adopted common export standards, including a requirement that any nation that imports nuclear technology must allow IAEA safeguards on all of its nuclear activities. China did not follow this standard. Beijing's exports of nuclear technology and components to Pakistan, Iran, Syria and Algeria, and missile exports to various countries raised suspicions about its non-proliferation credentials. Despite assurances that it would take measures to advance its non-proliferation commitments, China's actions did not live up to its words. Moreover, Washington repeatedly expressed concern about China's failure to live up to its non-proliferation assurances.[18]

However, Beijing had its own interpretations, which were meant to counter American allegations that it was a violator of international agreements. China maintained that it did not violate any international non-proliferation or arms control agreements by exporting nuclear technology or equipment. Moreover, it claimed that it could not be accused of violating the agreement since the MTCR was not an international treaty. The US concerns went beyond China's compliance or non-compliance of agreements. The Director of Central Intelligence (DCI), in June 1997, submitted a required report to Congress stating that during July-December 1996, "China was the most significant supplier of WMD-related goods and technology to foreign countries."[19]

Compliance with the BWC and CWC: China acceded to the BWC in 1984. The BWC banned the development, production, and stockpiling of biological agents or toxins which had no justification for peaceful purposes. China signed the CWC on January 13, 1993, and deposited its instrument of ratification on April 25, 1997. The CWC banned the development, production, stockpiling, and use of chemical weapons and required the destruction of all chemical weapons and production facilities. The CWC entered into force on April 29, 1997. However, there continued to be concerns about China's compliance with the BWC. Questions about China's chemical transfers and chemical weapon capability became serious since the CWC entered into force. The secretary of defence reported in April 1996, "China has a mature chemical warfare capability and may well have maintained the biological warfare programme it had prior to acceding to the BWC in 1984. It funded a chemical warfare programme since the 1950s and has produced and weaponised a wide variety of agents. Its biological warfare programme included manufacturing infectious micro-organisms and toxins."[20]

US government reports repeatedly noted China's violations in the area of chemical and biological weapons programmes. The Annual Compliance Report to the Congress issued by the president and the Arms Control and Disarmament Agency (ACDA) in 1994, noted, "China's CBM-mandated declarations (Confidence Building-Measures of the Chemical and Biological Weapons Convention) have not resolved US concerns about this programme and there are strong indications that China probably maintains its offensive programmes." The classified version of this ACDA Report reportedly was even more explicit in condemning these treaty violations.[21] An April 1996 proliferation report issued by the office of Secretary of Defence, William Perry, described China's programmes as follows:

> China has a mature chemical warfare capability and may well have maintained the biological warfare programme it had prior to acceding to the Biological Weapons Convention in 1984. It has funded a chemical warfare programme since the 1950s and has produced and weaponised a wide variety of agents. Its biological warfare programme included manufacturing infectious microorganisms and toxins. China has a wide range of delivery means available, including ballistic and cruise missiles and aircraft, and is continuing to develop systems with upgraded capabilities.[22]

In May 1997, the United States imposed sanctions on two Chinese companies and five Chinese individuals for knowingly assisting Iran's chemical weapons programme. The two companies were not state-owned.[23]

Compliance with the MTCR: China, in February 1992, unilaterally promised to abide by the MTCR. In addition, in return for a waiver of US sanctions, China committed, in a statement made on October 4, 1994, not to export surface-to-surface missiles "inherently capable" of delivering a 500 kg warhead to 300 km. This seemed to be a curt response to the incident of June 1991, when the George HW Bush Administration first imposed sanctions on China for transferring M-11 missile-related technology to Pakistan, since the M-11 short-range ballistic missile (SRBM) was covered by the MTCR guidelines. China promised in February 1992 to abide by the MTCR, and after that, the sanctions were waived, China later violated that commitment. President Clinton publicly acknowledged US concerns that China may have transferred complete M-11 missiles to Pakistan. Furthermore, he reported to Congress on May 28, 1993, "At present, the greatest concern involves reports that China in November 1992 transferred MTCR-class M-11 missiles or related equipment to Pakistan." Some believe that the Chinese missiles were transferred in retaliation for President Bush's sale of F-16 fighters to Taiwan.[24]

On August 24, 1993, the United States again determined that China had shipped to Pakistan equipment related to the M-11 SRBM and imposed sanctions in accordance with Section 73 (a) of the Arms Export Control Act and Section 11 B (b)(1) of the Export Administration Act. On October 4, 1994, Secretary of State Warren Christopher and Chinese Foreign Minister Qian Qichen signed a joint statement in which the United States agreed to waive the August 1993 missile sanctions and China agreed not to export "ground-to-ground missiles" which were "inherently capable" of delivering at least 500 kg to at least 300 km.[25]

Nevertheless, reports continued to allege that China had contravened its commitments to the MTCR. A June 1995 report said that the CIA found that China delivered "in the last three months" missile parts to Pakistan that could be used in M-11s.[26] According to the same report, the CIA found that China delivered dozens or perhaps hundreds of missile guidance systems and computerised machine tools to Iran some time between mid-1994 and mid-1995.[27] Senior Administration officials confirmed that there were concerns about Chinese missile-related transfers, while arguing that sanctions had not been warranted. The secretary of defence's April 1996 report, *Proliferation: Threat and Response,* stated, "China remains Pakistan's most important supplier of missile-related technologies." The report did not, however, say that China was in violation of its commitment to the MTCR.[28] China, on the other hand, called the regime "unfair, irrational and also ineffective," criticising the state parties for demanding that developing nations abandon their missile development programmes and join the MTCR while those member states "practise hegemonism to the extreme by dumping a huge amount of advanced missiles on the territories of other countries."[29]

Compliance with the CTBT: During negotiations on the CTBT, China, on July 30, 1996, became the last of the five declared nuclear powers to begin a moratorium on nuclear testing. Although the CTBT has not entered into force, in September 1996, China signed the treaty that banned nuclear testing. In spite of all the numerous mentioned arms control regimes, according to a recent assessment by the Arms

Control and Disarmament Agency, China was still not fully committed to international non-proliferation regimes:

> Problems have arisen primarily in the area of non-proliferation export controls, where China has failed to adopt an effective national system and has proven reluctant to embrace completely the norms established by the multilateral regimes, i.e. the Australia Group (CBW exports), the Nuclear Suppliers Group, the Missile Technology Control Regime and the Wassenaar Agreement (conventional arms exports and related dual-use items).[30]

Going by the above discussion, it does become unambiguous that there is considerable uncertainty in the international security environment combined with increased diffusion of dual-use technologies throughout the world, which, in turn, has created an environment in which it is critical that the regulatory framework integrate technology and weapons controls. At the same time, the regulatory framework must be flexible enough to accommodate changes in policies and in weapons and technology controls. An integrated legal framework and list of weapons and associated technologies, and an independently managed licence review process would provide better support for implementation of arms proliferation policies.

US Non-Proliferation Policy: The Post-Cold War Set-Up

Once in the Oval Office, President Clinton reversed his anti-Chinese rhetoric and adhered to *real politik*. US-China tension arose over several traditional issues such as human rights, Taiwan, Tibet, Hong Kong and trade-related disputes during the Clinton Administration. Both Beijing and Washington used high-sounding rhetoric to express their views more strongly. However, the post-Cold War period witnessed a turning point in Sino-US relations, when, in the summer of 1993, the *Yinghe* incident enraged Beijing. This incident cropped up amid Washington's suspicions that China was exporting WMD. The *Yinghe* (galaxy) was a Chinese ship that US intelligence concluded was transporting components of poison gas to Iran. US agents who boarded the ship conducted a search, but not before it had been kept adrift on the high seas for several days. Washington even prevented it from making port calls. It was finally allowed to dock at Port Dammam, in Saudi Arabia on August 24, 1993, and despite the high suspense, the search failed to find any trace of the components that the US insisted the ship was carrying. This incident infuriated Beijing and caused much embarrassment to the Americans. On another front, in October 1993, China conducted a nuclear test, further frustrating continuing US efforts to create an international agreement on a permanent test ban.

Significantly, this was one of the many drivers for the Clinton Administration to put forth the agenda of nuclear arms control and non-proliferation at the top of the US foreign policy priorities. There were strong efforts to curb the proliferation of advanced missile systems used to deliver nuclear, chemical and biological weapons. The Administration focussed on deep cuts in nuclear weapons by the US and Russia and ending the production of fissile material. China, possessing a large capacity to produce fissile material, was also a target for selling Pakistan and Iran civilian nuclear reactors and technology that could lead to clandestine efforts to produce fissile material.

The Clinton Administration developed an explicit policy not just for dual-use goods but also for the sale of certain conventional arms with implications for WMD use. This policy emphasised regional security and stability, helping allies to deter potential threats, promoting interoperability with US defence equipment, and preserving the US defence industrial base. It pledged government support in implementing sales once exports were approved, and it acknowledged the continuation of the policy of case-by-case licensing decisions. Features that distinguished the Clinton White House's policy from those of prior Administrations are given below.

Regional Focus

The Clinton Administration policy weighed arms transfer decisions primarily in their regional, rather than global, security and stability context.

Efforts to Promote Inter-Allied Cooperation: The Clinton policy highlighted the importance of multilateral consensus and cooperation in limiting arms sales, and reserved unilateral efforts for the smallest possible number of cases. To this end, the Administration continued to negotiate the final form of the recently agreed to multilateral Wassenaar Arrangement, which replaced the expired Coordinating Committee for Multilateral Export Control (CoCom) regime. The goals of the arrangement were said to increase transparency and promote responsibility in sales of both conventional arms and dual-use technologies, again concentrating on regional security threats.

Rogue States Prohibitions : A key component of the Wassenaar Arrangement was its focus on preventing sales of arms and sensitive technologies to "countries of concern" (Iran, Iraq, Libya and North Korea), rather than to the Communist bloc countries.

Decontrol of Dual-Use Technologies: The Clinton Administration took an aggressive stance toward removing controls on dual-use technologies it believed were outdated or ineffective. The policy attempted to tighten export restrictions on 'chokehold' technologies—technologies that would make a critical difference in the capability of the recipient to produce or deliver WMD. Simultaneously, the Administration sought to loosen controls on items that are widely available on the international market.

More Explicit Recognition of Economic Contributions of Arms Exports : The Clinton Administration's conventional arms transfer policy accorded a more explicit level of recognition of the preservation of the defence industrial base and to domestic economic considerations associated with arms exports. This policy was developed both as a response to, and a strategy for, a rapidly changing world underscored by the uncertain future that US policy confronted.[31]

Dual-Use Technology Controls

The Export Administration Act (EAA), whose antecedents date to the 1940s, statutorily regulates dual-use technology exports. This law's initial purpose was to ensure that sufficient quantities of critical technologies remained at home to support US consumption needed during World War II. The law and associated regulations have since been expanded to support efforts to keep certain enabling technologies out of the hands of hostile states. The MTCR, nuclear non-proliferation, chemical and biological regime are all supported through this law, as was the CoCom regime. The law was implemented through regulations that identified the commodities to be controlled through the commodity control list (CCL)], the countries for which certain items were controlled, and the justification for the control (national security or foreign policy grounds). Although the EAA expired, the law and associated regulations continued to be enforced under the International Emergence Economic Powers Act (IEEPA).[32]

On the flip side, however, the staunch detractors claimed that there was a major flap about the Clinton Administration's cockeyed National Intelligence Estimates (NIEs) on proliferation threats and about President Clinton's use of those estimates in vetoing national missile defence deployment programmes. The president and his team were accused of having downplayed proliferation dangers from China, Russia and various "states of proliferation concern" and invariably trumpeting "successes." The Administration's proliferation and arms control policies were criticised as policies of "illusion, denial, cover-up, and high-risk gambles."[33]

Nonetheless, President Clinton was conscious of the real-world dangers that proliferation of WMD posed to his Administration's defence policies. On November 9, 1995, following the wording of a similar directive issued a year earlier (November 14, 1994), President Clinton issued an Executive Order in which he declared:

> I, William J Clinton, President of the United States of America, find that *the proliferation of nuclear, biological and chemical weapons ("weapons of mass destruction") and the means of delivering such weapons,* continues to pose an unusual and extraordinary threat to the national security, foreign policy, and economy of the United States, and hereby, declare a national emergency to deal with that threat.[34] (Emphasis added.)

If taken literally, and seriously, the 1995 and 1994 Executive Orders acknowledged grave strategic threats to the United States from the proliferation of WMD and the means of delivering them. These threats needed to be matched by requisite policies and programmes to fulfill the constitutional imperative "to provide for the common defence."[35]

A special proliferation emphasis was warranted on China. In his statement before the House of Representatives, Sven F Kraemer argued that there seemed to be an urgent need to review the proliferation problems and the vote on China's most favoured nation (MFN) status, and there was indeed a strong strategic connection between these two issues. He stressed that if the United States was serious about proliferation, then in that case, it should not reward China with MFN status, given its poor record in proliferation, in trade, and in its aggressive behaviour toward its neighbours. Kraemer testified on these issues to the US Senate Committee on Foreign Relations in June 1996 and went on to state:

> Within the next decade or two, China will be one of the world's two or three most powerful nations. It already has the world's third ranking economy and is increasing its national assertiveness as it builds regional and strategic military might. What America does, or fails to do—what we stand for as a nation—will have considerable influence on whether or not China's national assertiveness will be aggressive and whether China can turn from its reactionary Communist ideology to the path of democracy and peace.[36]

Giving impetus to Kraemer's testimony, a Central Intelligence Agency (CIA) report too concluded that, in the second half of 1996, "China was the single most important supplier of equipment and technology for WMD" worldwide.[37] This dubious honour reflected a pattern of Chinese export misbehaviour that continued for decades. Subsequently, President Clinton reported to Congress, "Weapons of mass destruction pose the greatest potential threat to global stability and security. Proliferation of advance weapons and technologies threatens to provide rogue states, terrorists and international crime organisations with the means to inflict terrible damage on the United States, our allies and US citizens and troops abroad."[38] In October 1996, President Clinton described the situation as follows:

> We have worked patiently and pragmatically to reduce the threat of weapons of mass destruction, to take on the challenge of terrorism, to build an open trading system for the 21st century, to help secure the gains that peace and freedom are making around the world. We are making the

future more secure by lifting the danger of WMD.[39]

By the end of 2000, the Clinton Administration agreed to waive missile proliferation sanctions, resume processing licences to export satellites to China, and discuss an extension of the bilateral space launch agreement, in return for another promise from China on missile non-proliferation. However, the ongoing PRC proliferation activities again raised questions about sanctions. In contrast to the Clinton Administration, the George W Bush Administration repeatedly imposed sanctions on PRC "entities" for troublesome transfers. Among those sanctions, in September 2001, the Administration imposed missile proliferation sanctions that effectively denied satellite exports (for two years), after a PRC company transferred technology to Pakistan, despite the November 2000 promise. In September 2003, the State Department imposed additional sanctions on the China North Industries Corporation (NORINCO), a defence industrial entity, effectively denying satellite exports to China. Disbelievers still question whether China's cooperation in weapons non-proliferation has warranted President Bush's pursuit of closer bilateral ties. In this relationship, some observers say that President Bush has not forcefully pressed China's leaders on weapons non-proliferation as a priority issue, even while imposing numerous US sanctions. On as many as 19 occasions, the Administration has imposed sanctions on 32 different PRC "entities" (not the government) for transfers (related to missiles and chemical weapons) to Pakistan, Iran, or another country, including repeated sanctions on some "serial proliferators." Successive Administrations have pursed the "engagement" policy with Beijing while stressing the "comprehensive engagement" approach. President George W Bush has been unsuccessful in pressing the Chinese leadership on weapons non-proliferation as a key issue that threatens to undermine world security. Although the Bush Administration followed the Clinton Administration and imposed sanctions time and again against China, the sanctions turned counter-productive and simply too broad. China's export controls have always been under a cloud of suspicion given its role in proliferation of WMD in the case of both Pakistan and Iran. These cases also provide the window to the larger issue of the nuclear proliferation ring that ran through Asia. The following chapter analyses the US response to China's collaboration with Pakistan and Iran, giving particular emphasis to Beijing's nuclear and missile proliferation activities in the said countries.

Notes

1. PRC Information Office of the State Council, "China's National Defense in 2002," White Paper, December 9, 2002, http://www.china.org.cn/e-white/20021209/I.htm
2. PRC State Council, "China's National Defense," cited in "China Clamps Down on Its CW Trading," *Jane's Defense Weekly*, January 7, 1998, p. 5.
3. Ministry of Foreign Affairs, People's Republic of China, "The Australia Group," 2000, http://www.fmprc.gov.cn/eng/5254.html
4. Marcy Agmon, James L Bonomo, Michael Kennedy, Maren Leed, Kenneth Watman, Katherine Webb and Charles Wolf, Jr., "Arms Proliferation Policy: Support to the Presidential Advisory Board", A Report by the RAND National Defence Research Institute, (CA: Santa Monica, 1996), p. 30.
5. Ibid., pp. 64-65.
6. Statement by Ambassador Li Changhe, Chinese Permanent Mission in Vienna at the Meeting of the Zangger Committee, October 16, 1997.
7. John W Lewis, Hua Di, and Xue Litai, "Beijing's Defense Establishment: Solving the Arms-Export Enigma," *International Security*, vol. 15, no. 4, Spring 1991, pp. 93-96.
8. For more, see Daniel Byman and Roger Cliff, "China's Arms Sales: Motivations and Implications," Monograph by RAND Corporation, 1993-2003.
9. Statement by Senator William Proxmire to the US Senate Committee on Foreign Relations quoting the August 16, 1963 *Peking Review,* October 9, 1985.
10. Rahul Roy-Chaudhury and Swaran Singh, "Post-Cold War Trends in Arms Transfers," *Strategic Analysis*, vol. 17, no. 12, March 1995, p. 1512.
11. Swaran Singh, "China's Arms Trade: Taking off Again," *Strategic Analysis,* vol. 17, no. 7, October 1994, p. 808.
12. For more details, see Denny Roy, "Rising China and US Interests: Inevitable vs. Contingent Hazards," *Orbis,* vol. 47, no. 1, Winter 2003, p. 125.
13. Ibid., p. 129.
14. RAND Study, n. 4, p. 12.
15. Paul Godwin and John J Schulz, "Arming the Dragon for the 21st Century: China's Defense Modernization Program," *Arms Control Today,* vol. 23, no. 10, December 1993, p. 4.
16. Justin Bernier, "Asia's Shifting Strategic Landscape: China's Strategic Proxies," *Orbis,* vol. 47, no. 4, Fall 2003, p. 632.
17. For details, see CRS Issue Brief, Chinese Proliferation of Weapons of Mass Destruction: Current Policy Issue, 92056, September 13, 1996.

18. CRS Report for Congress, "The 1985 US-China Agreement for Nuclear Cooperation: Moving Towards Implementation?" April 10, 1997, pp. 2-3.
19. CRS Report for Congress, "China's Compliance with International Arms Control Agreements," September 16, 1997, p. 2.
20. US Department of State, "Proliferation of Missiles and Essential Components of Nuclear, Biological and Chemical Weapons," Annual Report, September 1996.
21. "Review of the Clinton Administration Nonproliferation Policy," Hearing Before the Committee on International Relations, House of Representatives, One Hundred Fourth Congress, Second Session, June 19, 1996, pp. 97-98.
22. Ibid., p. 98.
23. For more, see the Subcommittee on Security, Proliferation and Federal Services, *The Proliferation Primer*, 1997, p. 8.
24. CRS Report for Congress, n. 19, p. 3.
25. Ibid.
26. *International Herald Tribune,* June 23, 1995.
27. Ibid.
28. US Department of Defense Report, *Proliferation: Threat and Response,* January 2001, p. 38.
29. Chinese statement cited in, Ministry of Foreign Affairs of the People's Republic of China, available at http://www.fmprc.gov.ca/eng/5039.html
30. Steven Dolley, "China's Record of Proliferation Misbehaviour", CRS Issue Brief for Congress, at http://www.nci.org/nci/
31. RAND Study, n. 4, pp. 27-28.
32. Ibid., p. 91.
33. Sven F Kraemer, "Global Proliferation Threats, China, and MFN," Statement before the Committee on International Relations, US House of Representatives, June 19, 1996.
34. Ibid.
35. Ibid.
36. Kraemer, n. 33.
37. CIA, "The Acquisition of Technology Relating to Weapons of Mass Destruction and Advanced Conventional Munitions," Unclassified Report submitted to US Congress, 1997, p. 5.
38. CRS Report for Congress, "Nuclear, Biological, and Chemical Weapons and Missiles: The Current Situation and Trends," October 2, 2000, p. 1.
39. Ibid., p. 3.

3

China's WMD Collaboration with Pakistan and Iran

China's export activities of sensitive nuclear technologies substantiated long-standing fears within the United States and beyond that the advent of new nuclear supplier states could facilitate the spread of nuclear arms. China was instrumental in providing nuclear and missile technology significantly to Pakistan and Iran. Although the Clinton Administration viewed China's export control system and adherence to international non-proliferation norms as a core part of the central issues in US-Chinese relations, it categorised China's non-proliferation record as mixed, stressing the degree to which Chinese policies had progressed over the past few years, while acknowledging continued concerns about Beijing's loose export control policies. There was intense debate as well as concern on the Chinese transfer of sensitive nuclear technology, particularly to Pakistan and Iran.

Beijing: Islamabad's Nuclear Patron

Although China finally declared its support for the principle of non-proliferation in 1982, it nevertheless directly aided Pakistan's nuclear programme throughout the 1980s. Zulfikar Ali Bhutto had pioneered closer relations with the Chinese since the 1960s when he was the foreign minister of Pakistan. Bhutto recognised that China was keen to provide crucial help to Pakistan in order to counter India with which it had fought a brief war in 1962 and wanted to take optimum advantage of the ongoing Sino-Indian rivalry. Thus, Bhutto found success in bringing on board his most crucial ally when he paid a number of visits to Beijing, the first in January 1972, again in May 1974, and then a critical visit in the summer of 1976.[1] After its 1976 deal with Bhutto, China proved to be a crucial partner in Pakistan's nuclear programme and went on to become the principal supplier of sensitive nuclear and missile technology to Islamabad.

Since the early 1970s, Chinese tanks and aircraft were increasingly visible at Pakistan's national military parades as its replenished stocks were used up in the 1971 War with India. Economic and technical support also began heading to Islamabad. Bhutto described gaining China's support as "my greatest achievement and contribution to the survival of our people and our nation" and the culmination of eleven years of work. Secretly, Bhutto had also gained China's agreement to help build a nuclear bomb.[2] It was widely apparent that China was expected to assume the role of the "silent partner" in Pakistan's nuclear programme, providing it with crucial technical help in its early years.

Pakistani nuclear scientist Abdul Qadeer Khan, who is considered the founder of Pakistan's nuclear programme and further discredited for running a nuclear black market in Asia, claims he wrote to Gen Zia-ul Haq in 1982 saying he had enriched uranium and now wanted to build a warhead. After receiving the go-ahead (and the instruction to not tell anyone), two years later, he claims, the task was complete as Khan Research Laboratory (KRL) conducted a cold test (a cold test involves triggering the implosion device to check if it works but without using fissile material). Khan maintains that Zia's deputy stole the papers and handed them over to the Pakistan Atomic Energy Commission (PAEC) which then claimed it had done the work. Therefore, Khan claims the 1998 tests were based on his design.[3] Meanwhile, PAEC officials claim that as far back as 1974, they had been given the task of warhead design and were the first to do cold tests in 1983. The likelihood is that Zia became impatient by 1981 at the pace of PAEC's work (nearly sacking Munir Khan) and so took the expensive decision of creating two parallel weaponisation programmes to introduce an element of competition so as to accelerate the process towards realising their nuclear ambitions.

PAEC probably did get there first but Zia ensured that material flowed back and forth between the teams without them knowing it, leading to accusations of copying, which inflamed tensions.[4]

Interestingly, Khan had a strange habit of carrying around documents relating to a weapons design in his briefcase, a habit that persisted until intelligence officers reported it to Zia who told him to keep them in a safe. But, according to one account, before this happened, US intelligence officers managed to access AQ Khan's luggage in a hotel room during one of his trips abroad in the early 1980s.[5] Rifling through his papers, they reportedly found a document proving Pakistan was in receipt of outside help: a drawing of a simple but effective nuclear bomb and the steps needed to make it. It was clear that the design had come from China. Beijing had handed over a full, proven weapon design, thought to be based on a Chinese test conducted way back in 1966.[6] In fact, it was the same Chinese design that would be found in another bag in Libya two decades later—and the question of where else it might have gone is one of the great mysteries, and worries surrounding Khan's activities.[7]

In some ways, China is the first example of Khan trading nuclear secrets, long before his other deals came out in the open. From the 1970s to the early 1980s, China was keen to get its hands on Western nuclear technology, even asking the Iranians to pass on copies of contracts with the West. Khan knew that in the URENCO designs, he had something valuable that could be offered to other countries and that he had a global niche in the market that he could exploit. China was keen to see a nuclear-capable Pakistan and thereby see its rival India kept at bay. Pakistan arguably received more than it gave in the deal. As well as help with reactors and the weapons design, Pakistan also received nuclear material—either weapons-grade uranium or uranium hexafluoride according to different accounts, which allowed Khan to test his centrifuges at the early stages.[8] Chinese scientists were also present at Kahuta, possibly helping out or observing. Khan continued travelling to China until the end of his career, although, since he was dealing with state corporations, it was hard to know whether the Chinese government was involved in his activities.[9]

According to nuclear proliferation analyst Gary Milhollin, "If you subtract Chinese help, there wouldn't be a Pakistani programme." The relationship continued under Zia, with the Chinese president paying a visit to Pakistan in April 1984. In the 1970s and 1980s, there was no doubt that this was a state-to-state deal and that Khan was a key intermediary. "It was a China-Pakistan relationship but Khan was the guy with the contacts. He opened the door... China was absolutely instrumental in assisting Pakistan's nuclear programme through Khan," according to Richard Barlow. Khan made many visits to China during the 1980s, including one for weapons design training in the early 1980s and again in November 1988.[10]

All this while, the US Administration had been keeping a tab on these developments brewing between Beijing and Islamabad and there were growing concerns about Beijing's nuclear assistance to Pakistan and its unsafeguarded nuclear sales. The Reagan Administration decided in 1982 to suspend talks it had initiated with Beijing on an agreement for cooperation in the field of nuclear energy.[11] By 1983, the CIA was warning that China had provided crucial assistance to Pakistan's nuclear programme. Initially, this had been seen as largely centred on supporting the Karachi power reactor. But a secret briefing memo from the State Department added, "We now believe cooperation has taken place in the areas of fissile material production and possibly also nuclear device design."[12] This was viewed as a major stymie towards the realisation of a China-US nuclear cooperation deal. Khan's agents had used the Chinese weapons design to tour round Europe procuring elements to put it together, giving US intelligence a good sense of what Pakistan had. In an effort to keep in the game and solidify his status and reputation, having the design would have also helped Khan to keep up the pace in his battle with PAEC, which was trying to develop its own version.

In mid-1983, China began an apparent shift in its position and the US-China talks were resumed. Subsequently, in January 1984, China joined the IAEA and conveyed to the US that in the future it would adhere to the requirement of IAEA safeguards on its nuclear exports to non-nuclear weapon states. In a series of statements beginning that month, top Chinese leaders declared China's firm commitment to non-proliferation. Premier Zhao Ziyang stated in an address to the Sixth National People's Congress in May 1984, for example, that China did "not engage in nuclear proliferation by helping other countries to develop nuclear weapons." Based on these assurances, a nuclear trade agreement was initiated in Beijing during President Ronald Reagan's April 1984 visit.[13]

The Reagan Administration did not submit the accord for the required review by Congress until July 1985, over a year later, reportedly because of concerns that Chinese nuclear aid to Pakistan was continuing. After further bilateral talks, however, China finally agreed to implement its non-proliferation policy, "in a manner consistent with basic non-proliferation practices common to the United States and other suppliers," a circumlocution apparently intended to signify that any Chinese assistance to Pakistan had been halted, although China always officially denied that anything beyond normal scientific exchanges ever took place. In the fall of 1985, China also announced that it would voluntarily place some of its civilian nuclear installations under IAEA safeguards, matching a step previously taken by all other nuclear weapon states.[14]

The US-China agreement went into effect in December 1985 after a lengthy Congressional review. Through a joint resolution, however, Congress required that before a licence could be issued for any nuclear exports to China under the agreement, the president would have to certify to Congress, after further negotiations with Beijing, that China was not assisting other states to develop nuclear weapons; that the provisions of the accord would be "effective" in ensuring that US nuclear exports were used exclusively for peaceful purposes; and that the United States would retain certain controls over China's extraction of plutonium from spent fuel from US-supplied fuel or in a US-supplied reactor.[15] Till mid-1990, these certifications had not been made, principally because of US concerns that China was continuing to provide assistance to Pakistan's nuclear weapons programme.

China was also believed, however, to have provided essential weapons-related nuclear aid directly to Pakistan, including the design of the nuclear device detonated in China's fourth nuclear test, uranium enrichment knowhow, and—according to various reports—quantities of weapons-usable highly enriched uranium sufficient for Pakistan to build two nuclear devices in the early 1980s.[16] Although China pledged publicly in 1984 that it would not contribute to the spread of nuclear weapons and agreed to IAEA safeguards on its nuclear exports, there was evidence that China continued providing weapons-related aid to Pakistan and exported unsafeguarded nuclear material to other nations as late as 1987.[17] Moreover, it was widely believed that China provided Pakistan with the design for a nuclear weapon in the 1980s, and probably enough highly enriched uranium (HEU) for one to two bombs. In addition, China reportedly gave Pakistan enough weapons grade uranium to manufacture two nuclear explosive devices.[18] It also assisted Pakistan in the construction of an unsafeguarded plutonium production reactor at Khushab, and possibly a reprocessing plant at Chasma.[19] In 1986, China sold Pakistan tritium, an element used in the trigger of hydrogen bombs as well as to boost the yield of fission weapons.

By 1987, the United States had gained more intelligence on the China-Pakistan relationship and wanted to confront Pakistan and, thus, Lawrence Livermore National Laboratory was asked to mock-up a small model of the weapon based on the Chinese design, using the intelligence picked up from procurement patterns. When Pakistan's foreign minister came to the State Department, he was taken to a room where a sheet was removed to reveal a football size mock-up of the bomb along with a model of the entire Kahuta plant. But the minister still denied any relationship between Islamabad and Beijing or work on the bomb. The United States told the Pakistanis that a Chinese source had provided the information "at great personal risk." However, Pakistani officials were convinced that the Chinese spy story was cover for the fact that the CIA had a highly placed agent within their programme whom Washington was trying to protect.[20]

Extensive investigations were conducted into the subject and senior Pakistani intelligence officials believe that the CIA cultivated and recruited a scientist in the early 1980s who had access to all key locations, including Kahuta, and may even have planned a technical sabotage with the CIA that was foiled.[21] Whether the US acquired the specific intelligence from China, Kahuta or from AQ Khan's luggage, the reality was that the US had multiple sources of intelligence—derived from human spies and technical devices—which gave it an incredibly detailed picture. The level of knowledge within the CIA about Pakistan's nuclear progress would cause increasing discomfort to both politicians and the intelligence community.[22] Along with this, China was believed to have provided assistance to a number of Pakistan's nuclear reactors ranging from the construction of a safeguarded nuclear-power plant at Chasma to supplying it with an advanced-computer control system. Beijing also supplied heavy water to the safeguarded Kanupp reactor (originally supplied by Canada), and provided assistance in the construction of an unsafeguarded plutonium-production reactor near Khushab. The situation with regard to the Kanupp and Khushab reactors continued to remain of particular proliferation significance. A shortage of heavy water was apparently the principal obstacle in the start-up of the nearly completed, unsafeguarded Khushab reactor.

Fig 3.1: Heavy Water Research Reactor at Khushab

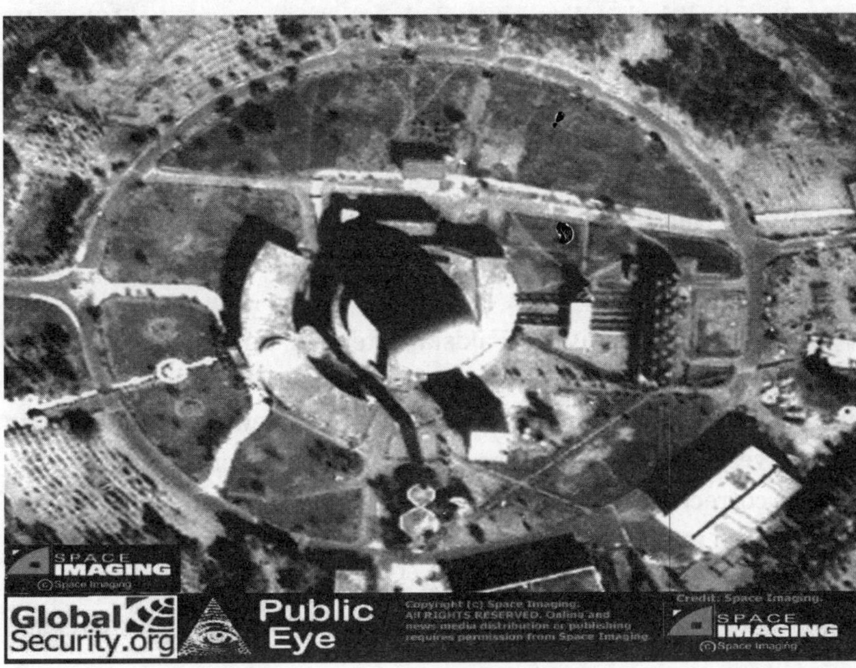

The twists and turns the Administration took to preserve its alliance with Pakistan and turn a blind eye to the nuclear programme became increasingly tortuous. So much so, that Senator John Glenn reckoned that successive Administrations "practised a nuclear non-proliferation policy bordering on lawlessness."[23] In 1985, the US Congress passed the Pressler Amendment, which required that the Administration certify at the start of each fiscal year that Pakistan did not possess a nuclear device. A 1986 National Intelligence Estimate concluded that Kahuta had enriched sufficient weapons-grade uranium and had all the parts for a device. It arrived at the conclusion that Pakistan could have a bomb within two weeks of making a decision and was only "two screwdriver turns" from assembling a weapon.[24]

The Administration continued to certify to Congress that Pakistan did not have a nuclear weapon through the late 1980s, despite this evidence to the contrary. The Administration got around this by saying Pakistan had not stockpiled or put together every single element for a bomb but the justifications bordered on the absurd. "In my view, it was irrefutable evidence," remembers Richard J Kerr who was then deputy director of intelligence at the CIA. "The argument always came down to a political judgment and that judgment was made on the basis of not whether or not there was a weapon but whether that was a convenient time to declare that they had a weapon." The intelligence was fixed to fit the policy that Pakistan was simply too important an ally to lose[25]—a fact that has not changed much in the past decades be it Pakistan's clandestine nuclear and missile programme or providing a safe haven and breeding ground to radical extremist outfits in the present context.

Meanwhile, from 1987, Pakistan stepped up its efforts on the nuclear front and edged closer to the nuclear threshold. AQ Khan himself made one of his occasional public interviews and caused huge shockwaves, "What the CIA has been saying about our possessing the bomb is correct," he said, hoping to send out a signal to the Indians of the Pakistani intent and capability. "They told us Pakistan could never produce the bomb and they doubted my capabilities, but they now know we have it." Khan's boast caused huge embarrassment, not least for the US Administration, which was telling Congress that there was no sign yet of a Pakistani bomb. Khan was soon forced to withdraw his remarks but Pakistani officials would later admit that they possessed the bomb from this year.[26] By the end of the 1980s, Pakistan had the bomb but chose not to make a formal entry into the nuclear club.

All along, numerous reports also indicated that China supplied heavy water (D2O) to the safeguarded Kanupp reactor at a rate to make up heavy-water losses of 2 to 4 per cent a year. Although the Kanupp reactor had large reported losses of heavy water in its early years of operation, the facility was upgraded later to bring the reactor into conformity with industry standards, and reduce the heavy water loss rate to about one percent annually. Thus, China was believed to have supplied Pakistan with up to nearly four metric tonnes more heavy water per year than it needed for its safeguarded power reactor, leaving open the possibility of diversion of surplus heavy water to Khushab, which needed only five tonnes of heavy water to start up and fifteen tonnes to operate at full power.[27]

Heavy water was required to operate certain reactors and some of it could be used in producing plutonium for nuclear weapons. Routine transfers of D2O did occur and Chinese officials insisted that the transfers had taken place to the safeguarded Kanupp facility only. A special industrial furnace could be used to melt plutonium or enriched uranium into the shape of a nuclear bomb core. It was reportedly sold by China to Pakistan at the Khushab facility in 1996. According to a study conducted by the Monterey Institute of International Studies, China reportedly transferred the nuclear weapon design of a 25-kiloton nuclear bomb—possibly a Chic-4 design—to Pakistan way back in 1983. There also were reports of heavily enriched uranium being transferred around the same time.[28]

However, since Pakistan was not an NPT signatory, it refrained the IAEA from conducting inspections of its nuclear facilities. As a matter of fact, the Reagan Administration compiled evidence that China was helping Pakistan operate its Kahuta uranium enrichment plant. It also learnt that China had provided Pakistan with a nuclear bomb design and suspected that China had given Pakistan blueprints for a research reactor constructed in 1989. Several months before becoming an NPT signatory in 1991, China and Pakistan finalised an agreement in which Beijing would construct a 300 megawatt (MW) nuclear power reactor for Pakistan.[29]

During a visit to Islamabad on November 16, 1989, Chinese Premier Li Peng announced that China would sell to Pakistan a 300 MW nuclear power reactor, under a nuclear cooperation agreement the two states had signed in 1986. Although the reactor itself and any plutonium produced from its operation were to be under IAEA safeguards, Beijing did not require as a condition for the sale that Pakistan accept such safeguards on its entire nuclear programme, a step that would effectively have required Islamabad to give up its nuclear weapons programme. Since the mid-1970s, when Pakistan's interest in nuclear arms became apparent, no other nuclear supplier was prepared to make major nuclear sales to Pakistan unless it accepted this condition. Moreover, for much of the 1980s, as the result of a US initiative, no supplier had made a major nuclear sale to any country that had not accepted such "full-scope" safeguards. In 1988, however, the Soviet Union broke this *de facto* embargo, by agreeing to sell two large nuclear power reactors to India, its long-time security partner in the region. This precedent undoubtedly paved the way for Beijing to make a comparable sale to Pakistan— its own regional ally.[30]

The nuclear reactor was said to be a replica of China's first indigenous nuclear power plant, a unit moderated with "light", or ordinary, water and fuelled with low enriched uranium. That Pakistan would purchase such a costly facility from so unproven a supplier leaves little doubt that political factors were dominant in the arrangement. The deal allowed Beijing to cement relations with its regional partner at a time when it was facing increasing international isolation because of its violent repression of the country's pro-democracy movement. Similarly, the agreement allowed Benazir Bhutto to boost her standing with her country's nuclear advocates after her apparent efforts to slow elements of Pakistan's nuclear weapons programme earlier in the year.[31]

The US expressed staid concern that the Chinese had in fact helped Pakistan construct a 50-70 MW research/plutonium production reactor at Khushab and a plutonium extraction plant at Chasma—facilities that had not been subject to IAEA inspection. US officials suspected that once completed, the reactor at Khushab would be used in conjunction with the nearby Chasma plant. US intelligence officials estimated that the two facilities could produce a significant amount of unsafeguarded weapons-usable plutonium. In addition, the State Department on December 3, 1996, urged China not to proceed with the sale of the 300 MW pressurised water reactor (PWR) to Pakistan's Chasma facility. The State Department reiterated its position that the PRC's nuclear cooperation with Pakistan "is a source of friction between China and the US."[32]

Apart from such direct aid for nascent nuclear weapon efforts, each of the *de facto* nuclear weapon states and China were also in a position to offer ostensibly non-military nuclear aid in such fields as uranium enrichment, plutonium extraction, research reactor design and construction, fuel fabrication and uranium production. Comparable assistance was also available from many other countries that had not pursued nuclear weapons capabilities but, at the same time, possessed growing civilian nuclear industries.[33] Pakistan was reported in January 1990 to have begun negotiations with the PRC to obtain a nuclear-powered submarine.[34] Beijing had previously transferred conventional 'Romeo-class' submarines to Islamabad. A transfer of a nuclear-powered submarine would add to another serious breach of norm.

In the early 1990s, the proliferation concerns with respect to China became significantly highlighted, especially given the additional challenge of missile proliferation emanating from Beijing. In October 1990, President George HW Bush finally invoked the Pressler Amendment and cut off American aid, saying he could no longer certify that Pakistan did not have the bomb. Overnight Pakistan went from being the third largest recipient of military aid to getting nothing. Once the Cold War was over, Pakistan appeared to be losing its strategic edge and became far less interesting and useful to policy-makers in Washington. With the US aid tap turned off, Pakistan spent the 1990s teetering on the edge of bankruptcy.[35] Although it remained a targeted recipient of MTCR-controlled technologies, China went on to becoming a supplier of MTCR-restricted missiles, components, and technologies to countries such as Pakistan, Iran, Saudi Arabia and Syria. In other words, it had become an exporter not bound by any missile non-proliferation export control obligations.[36]

'M-11' Missile Issue

China's missile sales had been a continuing source of discord in US-China relations. International concerns doubled when Sino-Pakistan nuclear cooperation in the 1980s got extended to cooperation in the field of ballistic missile development in the 1990s.[37] In the early 1990s, it was revealed that the Chinese had supplied M-11 missiles to Pakistan, the result of a suspected 1987 deal, but these were left in their crates at an air force base west of Lahore to try and avoid sanctions and growing international pressure on China's activities. In 1991, the US objected to Chinese sales of M-11 ballistic missile technologies to Pakistan and, for the first time, imposed sanctions on China in accordance with the newly passed Missile Technology Control Act.

China did apparently violate the MTCR (which it has not formally joined but whose guidelines it has promised to abide by) when it transferred components of M-11 missiles to Pakistan in November 1992. Beijing argued that since the M-11 has a range of only 280 km, it did not violate the MTCR, which prohibits the transfer of missiles capable of carrying 500 kg to a range of 300 km or more. On the contrary, the US took the position that since the M-11 has a payload of 800 kg, by reducing the payload, the M-11 could be modified to carry 500 kg over 300 km and, thus, exceeded the MTCR parameters. The Chinese government may well have been acting in bad faith when it transferred M-11 missiles to Pakistan, but it may have done so in the belief that the M-11 technically did not violate the MTCR, or at least that it could credibly make such an argument. It is noteworthy, for example, that the system in dispute is the M-11 and not the M-9, which, with its 600-km range, clearly would violate the MTCR, despite the fact that the M-9 was originally developed for export.[38] The sanctions were imposed for alleged exports of M-11 ballistic missiles to Pakistan and alleged planned exports of M-9 missile technology to Syria.[39] By April 1991, the Bush Administration denied licences for the export of US parts for a Chinese satellite, the Dongfanghong-3, citing "serious proliferation concerns."[40] On May 27, 1991, President George HW Bush declared sanctions on China for transferring to Pakistan technology related to the M-11 short-range ballistic missiles.

These sanctions required by Sec. 73(a) of the Arms Export Control Act (P.L. 90-629) and Sec. 11B(b) (I) of the Export Administration Act (P.L. 96-72), were intended to strictly enforce the MTCR. The sanctions, which took effect on June 16 and 25, 1991, denied export licences and waivers of sanctions for: (1) high-speed computers to China, which can be used for missile flight-testing; (2) satellites for launch by China; and (3) missile technology or equipment. They affected two Chinese aerospace corporations: the China Great Wall Industry Corporation, and China Precision Machinery Import Export Corporation.[41] The sanctions were lifted on May 23, 1992, only to be reimposed in August 1993. Soon after the US sanctions, Beijing agreed to observe the MTCR guidelines, although in December 1992, reports surfaced yet again that China had transferred 34 complete M-11 missiles to Pakistan and also allegedly built a turnkey missile plant for Pakistan at Tarwanah, a suburb of Rawalpindi, in violation of its 1991 pledge. As a result, in May 1993, the Clinton Administration reimposed MTCR-related sanctions against China.[42] Once again, China, on October 4, 1994, agreed not to export ground-to-ground missiles inherently capable of delivering at least 500 kg at 300 km—an understanding the US side sought to include the M-11 missiles under the MTCR. Following this, on November 1, 1994, the Clinton Administration waived those sanctions.[43]

The Chinese government, however, did raise its strong opposition to the numerous sanctions imposed on it by terming the sanctions groundless and threatening to scrap its promise to abide by the MTCR guidelines. During hectic post-sanctions negotiations with the US, China argued that the deal did not violate the MTCR because the M-11 could deliver a 500 kg payload only over an advertised range of 280 km, within the MTCR's parameters, which only permit transfers of missiles that can fly less than 300 km with that payload size. US experts, however, insisted that the missiles in question could easily fly another 20 km as a result of small shifts or cuts in the payload. China denied having violated the agreement, but it renewed its commitments to MTCR requirements in early 1994. Concerns persisted about possible transfers to both Iran and Pakistan and the US government continued to monitor the situation.[44]

By the mid-1990s, the intelligence leaks became public and consequently there were calls from Congress to sanction either China or Pakistan or both, but the Clinton Administration was desperate to avoid taking such actions as it was trying to improve relations with both countries. Especially in the case of China, the Clinton White House was actively pursuing a policy of engaging containment. Therefore, policy-makers had used "almost any measure" to block judgements that would have led automatically to sanctions, according to Gordon Oehler who ran the CIA Non-Proliferation Centre until 1997.[45] And China too was nervous about going too far and risking US wrath and consequently Beijing began to edge away from its active role in missile proliferation.[46]

Officials in the US intelligence community suspected that the M-11s had been deployed by Pakistan and were operational.[47] Notably, the CIA reported in August 1996, that China was helping Pakistan construct the M-11 production facility within Pakistan. According to the CIA, China provided Pakistan with 30 ready-to-launch M-11 ballistic missiles, capable of delivering nuclear warheads. The Sino-Pakistan cooperation in missile development programmes became an irritant in US-Pakistan ties. In July 1993, the US intelligence sources reported about the secret Chinese supply of M-11 missile components to Pakistan in violation of the MTCR. As a result, Washington imposed a two-year sanction under Category II of the MTCR on China and Pakistan, which prohibited the exports of satellites and other advance technologies to these countries. A few days after the imposition of US sanctions, Pakistan's Foreign Secretary Shahryar Khan visited Washington. The trip was scheduled earlier, but the timing was significant as the most important aspect of Khan's visit was an effort to dilute, if not eliminate, the effect of the Pressler Amendment. In the meantime, US National Security Advisor Anthony Lake had also underscored the need for further dialogue with Pakistan to tackle the ongoing problem arising out of the Pressler Amendment.[48] In less than a month after

Khan's meeting with Lake, the US Senate authorised President Clinton to grant some development assistance to Pakistan by exempting the sale of wheat and soyabean to Pakistan and also funds for welfare programmes from the Pressler Amendment.[49]

Resultantly, Islamabad was left looking elsewhere for a missile with a longer range and which could carry a larger payload. The North Korean 'Nodong' fitted the bill. North Korea was also more likely to be a reliable vendor of ballistic missile technology, in that it was known to be willing to sell pretty much anything for hard cash, of which it was desperately short. This was also the time when Pakistani Prime Minister Benazir Bhutto adamantly declared that the deal with the North Koreans was for cash and said, "When I went to North Korea, AQ Khan told me we can get their (missile) technology (so) that we can compare (it) to our own. So I took (it) up with Kim Il Sung...December '93 I talked to him, he agreed... and it was in cash, they needed money and so it was done for cash, with no exchange of nuclear technology. Exchanging nuclear technology for missiles was never even discussed during my visit."[50] As a result of the deal, Islamabad got the Nodong missile and rechristened it the Ghauri.

Fig 3.2: Official photograph released by the Government of Pakistan showcasing lift-off of the Ghauri medium range ballistic missile on April 6, 1998.

In the years following Benazir Bhutto's visit, between January 1997 and March 1998, North Korea exported components for as many as twelve Nodong missiles to Pakistan. In April 1998, Khan finally test-fired the Ghauri, claiming that his contribution to Pakistan's security extended far beyond mere enrichment of uranium. The money for the missiles was paid in installments, under the cover of conventional arms purchases. It has been estimated that the Nodongs would have cost at least $3 billion.[51] But by 1997, cash was getting harder to come by for the Pakistan government, with foreign reserves nose-diving to critically low levels, almost putting the country on an edge of default. Then arrived the alternative option vis-à-vis the mode of payment. A US government-source leak to *The New York Times* in October 2002 claimed that Pakistan was the likely source of the North Korean gas centrifuge uranium enrichment programme, giving fuel to the notion of an exchange, since by the mid-1990s North Korea was looking for help vis-à-vis its clandestine enrichment programme.[52] Barter was in the interest of both countries, as each had technology the other desperately wanted and neither had the cash to pay for it. The nuclear-for-missile barter trade between Islamabad and Pyongyang probably began in 1997 and continued at least until July 2002.[53] In addition, China's missile exports, although not directly related to its nuclear exports, have affected discussions of nuclear cooperation between the US and the PRC.

Ring Magnets Sale

Since Washington did not want to fray relations with Islamabad, the Clinton Administration decided to reestablish closer ties and it went ahead with the decision of relaxing the Pressler Amendment. Finally, on September 21, 1995, the US Senate passed the Brown Amendment. It proposed the supply of a military package worth $ 368 million to Pakistan through a one-time waiver of the Pressler Amendment. Days after President Clinton signed the Brown Amendment, in February 1996, *The Washington Times* reported a CIA finding that China had sold 5,000 ring magnets to Pakistan for its main plant to enrich uranium in high-speed gas centrifuges. Both Pakistan and China denied the sale had occurred. As a matter of fact, the Clinton Administration's claim that the Brown Amendment would enhance the US non-proliferation goal soon came for a test when the US reports on the Chinese supply of ring magnets to Pakistan were made public. Congressmen questioned the State Department officials as to why they had kept Congress in the dark about the CIA report on the ring magnets issue when the Brown Amendment was under discussion. According to published reports, the officials, including those in the South Asian Bureau of the State Department, had known about the Chinese transfer of ring magnets, but the State Department had exerted so much effort for the passage of the Brown Amendment that it had decided against volunteering the CIA report to Congress for fear of jeopardising its own efforts.[54] With the renewal of the Congressional demands for repealing the Brown Amendment and Senator Larry Pressler commenting, "When faced with a serious violation of the nonproliferation law, this administration blinked at this law and winked at Pakistan,"[55] Clinton's Deputy National Security Advisor Sandy Berger and Deputy Secretary of State Strobe Talbott went to Capitol Hill to brief the senators on the matter at a closed-door session. The Clinton Administration's argument was that Pakistan paid for the F-16 aircraft many years ago while it purchased the ring magnets only in 1995![56]

The US State Department initially believed that the ring magnets deal violated the US Arms Export Control Act, which required the president to impose sanctions on any country that "transfers to a non-nuclear weapon state any design information or component" used in building nuclear arms. Senator Larry Pressler was furious when he came to know about this deal. He remarked, "I am very disturbed that this illegal sale of nuclear technology was taking place at the same time that the government of Pakistan and the Clinton Administration actively were lobbying Congress to pass the Brown Amendment."[57] There was little doubt that the Clinton White House and the State Department also backed Senator Brown and his supporters in Congress. After painstakingly working towards diluting the Pressler Amendment, the Clinton Administration was not prepared to see the ineffectiveness of the Brown Amendment.[58]

To add to the ongoing imbroglio, on April 15, 1996, the *Wall Street Journal* reported that some Chinese officials privately admitted selling 5,000 ring magnets to Pakistan. The Chinese officials, who included the vice-president of the National Nuclear Cooperation of China, argued that the magnets were not magnetised and, thus, did not violate the Nuclear Suppliers Group's trigger list. A US State Department official reacted sharply against the Chinese argument and said that it was not difficult to magnetise the magnets and that it was like "selling a fighter jet to someone and saying we did not fill up the fuel tank."[59]

In some views, the transfer could be interpreted as a violation of Article I of the NPT. The Clinton Administration, however, announced on May 10, 1996, that it would not invoke laws requiring sanctions on China or Pakistan for the sale. In return, Beijing agreed to reaffirm its commitment to nuclear non-proliferation. It was stated by China that it would only provide assistance to safeguarded nuclear facilities.[60] In response to the Administration's decision not to impose sanctions, Congress, in an amendment to the 1997 Defence Authorisation Act (PL 104-201), asserted that "the stability and growth of future relations between the people, the economies and the government of the United States and the PRC will significantly depend upon substantive evidence of cooperation by the government of the PRC in efforts to halt the global proliferation of WMD and their means of delivery."[61] The ring magnets could enable Pakistan, according to *Nucleonics News,* to double its capacity to enrich uranium for weapon purposes. The Clinton Administration, however, went ahead with the Brown package, and resumed military aid to Pakistan.

Crucially, a 1997 CIA report concluded that for the period July to December 1996—i.e. after China's May 11, 1996 pledge to the United States not to provide assistance to unsafeguarded nuclear facilities—China was Pakistan's "primary source of nuclear-related equipment and technology..."[62] Ironically however, China continued to make controversial exports, often in contravention of its non-proliferation commitments. After the Jiang-Clinton Summit of October 1997, when

President Jiang Zemin reportedly promised to refrain from assisting Iran's weapons of mass destruction activities/programmes, President Bill Clinton gave a certification to the US Congress in January 1998 that "China is not assisting and will not assist any non-nuclear weapon state, either directly or indirectly, in acquiring nuclear explosive devices or the material or components for such devices." Less than a month after this certification became official on March 19, 1998, paving the way for the 1985 nuclear cooperation agreement between China and the US, Pakistan test-fired the Ghauri missile. It seemed the United States was following a "policy of constructive engagement rather than punitive actions" as far as Pakistan was concerned. This policy was made clear after the US special diplomat Bill Richardson's visit to Islamabad post the Ghauri test.[63] Pakistan's prime minister announced after meeting Richardson that he had been assured that Washington was not considering action against Islamabad for test-firing the Ghauri missile.

Significantly, after the numerous pledges by China to stop assisting Pakistan's nuclear and missile programme, the post-Chagai phase in the summer of 2001, only months after the Clinton Administration waived penalties against China in return for new assurances that it would stop assisting foreign missile programmes, witnessed US intelligence discovering that China Metallurgical Equipment Corporation, a major state-run arms producer, illegally shipped missile components to Pakistan. The George W Bush Administration subsequently activated sanctions barring US companies from launching satellites on Chinese rockets or providing the growing Chinese satellite industry with US technology.[64] As of June 2003, US intelligence agencies nevertheless continued to believe that Chinese firms remained key suppliers of missile technologies to Pakistan.[65]

Critics also raised questions about a May 2004 Chinese agreement to build a second civilian nuclear reactor at Chasma in Pakistan. Although the agreement predated China's NSG membership and the reactor would be placed under IAEA safeguards, questions remained about the merit of nuclear transfers to a country whose weak export control measures permitted the Khan network to undermine global security and where risks of unauthorised diversion of Chinese technologies and materials to its weapons programme remained high. Further, media reports following Chinese Premier Wen Jiabao's April 2005 visit to Pakistan quoted senior Pakistani atomic energy officials as saying that China wanted to build additional reactors, although doing so would violate its obligations under current NSG guidelines.[66]

There seems to be a misguided policy approach continuing even today, as the Bush Administration is not fully dismantling the Abdul Qadeer Khan network, to the short-term goal of building a relationship with Pakistan in order to wage its war on terror in Afghanistan. The nuclear proliferation ring among China, Pakistan, Iran and North Korea needs to be addressed in the starkest form of reality if the ever-growing peril of proliferation of WMD and their respective means of delivery is to be checked.

China-Iran WMD Axis

With the onset of the Iran-Iraq War in September 1980, China stepped in to becoming one of Iran's closest international partners, both diplomatically and in terms of assisting Iran's war efforts against Iraq. For China, arms sales and improved Sino-Iranian relations served a number of strategic, political and economic interests.[67] China's cooperation with Iran began in the mid-1980s in the field of missile technology and since then, China has assisted Iran in the development of its indigenous ballistic and cruise missile production capability and offered technologies and assistance in the development of its clandestine chemical and nuclear weapons programme.[68]

Tracing the historical roots, China entered into a nuclear cooperation agreement with Iran in 1985. The first nuclear agreement between Beijing and Tehran came in 1989. In 1991, a major nuclear deal was signed when a senior Chinese official visited Iran, touring around facilities near the ancient city of Isfahan, one of Iran's most historic sites situated south of Tehran. That year, China secretly provided Iran with three cylinders, one large and two small, containing 1.8 tonnes of uranium ore, a deal that Iran did not report to the IAEA. This allowed the Iranians to carry out experiments through the 1990s without the IAEA noticing any diversion of existing material that the agency had been monitoring. China also agreed to build for the Iranians a complete uranium conversion plant at Isfahan. In September 1995, the Chinese ambassador to Iran confirmed that China was supplying uranium enrichment and other nuclear technology to Iran. China is Iran's most important supplier of nuclear technology, exporting over $60 million worth annually, and as many as 14 Chinese nuclear experts were reportedly working at Iranian nuclear facilities.[69]

Sino-Iranian nuclear cooperation can be traced to the mid-1980s with most of the nuclear related assistance revolving around the Isfahan nuclear complex. In 1985, the PRC in all probability supplied two sub-critical 'training reactors' to the site [a 27 kilowatt (KW) miniature neutron source reactor and a heavy water zero power reactor]. In the late 1980s, the PRC reportedly sold a small electromagnetic isotope separator called a calutron to Iran for use at the Isfahan facility.[70] (This instrument had the capacity to enrich uranium to weapons grade levels. In fact, calutrons had enriched the uranium in the "Little Boy" bomb that destroyed Hiroshima.) In 1990, China and Iran signed a 10-year nuclear cooperation agreement. Following the enactment of this accord, China agreed to construct a small 27 KW research reactor for the production of radioisotopes at the Isfahan Research Centre. This reactor became operational in 1994. In addition, in September 1992, China agreed to build two 300 MW light water nuclear reactors (LWRs) for Tehran by 2002. While this type of reactor is most suited for civilian use, there were constant suspicions that the technology and expertise could indirectly aid Iran's suspected nuclear weapons programmes. Over the last several years, delays have hampered this project. The two nations have reportedly disagreed over the financial terms, the technical designs and sites for the reactors.[71]

Fig 3.3: Iran's uranium conversion facility at Isfahan, 410 km south of the capital Tehran, as on March 2005. This facility reprocesses uranium ore concentrate, known as yellowcake, into uranium hexaflouride gas. The gas is then taken to Natanz and fed into the centrifuges for enrichment.

As the decade wore on, China grew more wary of Iran's intentions and the United States began to exert more and more pressure on China to halt its support. Eventually, a 1997 deal with the United States led China to cut off the remaining assistance. But Iran already had the plans and continued to build the conversion facility at Isfahan using the Chinese designs. Through the 1990s, as China's support waned, Russia was perceived as the main facilitator of any future development in the Iranian nuclear programme.[72] The Iranians realised that Pakistan's assistance towards their nuclear ambitions would be crucial since the early 1980s. Accordingly, Iranian President Ali Khamenei, who later became the country's supreme leader, a long-time proponent of the nuclear option, paid a visit to Pakistan in February 1986. That year, there were official but secret contacts between Iran and Pakistan in the nuclear field. Iran was looking for help and some Iranian scientists went over to Pakistan.[73] In 1987, a secret technical cooperation agreement was signed covering military and nuclear cooperation at a secret meeting in Vienna between heads of the two countries' Atomic Energy Commissions.[74] This official but clandestine deal between the two countries would help provide the channels of contact for AQ Khan's own work. Scientists began to travel back and forth between the two countries and the Iranians started to inquire about "non-peaceful nuclear matters."[75] Although at the official state level, limited cooperation between Pakistan and Iran continued into the early 1990s, the exact moment of first contact between Khan and the Iranians still remains unclear. Indian intelligence believes it came after a top Iranian scientist visited Pakistan in 1984.[76]

It has also been reported that Khan secretly visited Iran to review the damage at the Bushehr reactor (which had been repeatedly bombed by Iraq) in February 1986 for the first of a number of visits. Some reports claim that in January 1987, Khan was flown in a private jet from Islamabad to Tehran to meet up with top Iranian officials, at an Intelligence Ministry guesthouse in Parchin, south of Tehran, and that during this visit, he pushed the idea of pursuing uranium enrichment as a viable option.[77] The official 1987 nuclear deal would have facilitated and legitimised contacts with Khan, providing him with cover to do his work and for the Iranians to start asking what more Pakistan and Khan could provide to them. Ultimately though, the deal would be driven as much by his network as by Khan himself.

Fig 3.4: Bushehr Reactor

According to Robert Einhorn, a senior non-proliferation official at the State Department until 2001, "It was our assumption that by the early to mid-90s the Pakistani-Iranian cooperation was not a significant factor. We believed through the 1990s that Iran was looking elsewhere—Russia and China, for instance. We spent a lot of time in the 90s trying to turn off Russian and Chinese connections to Iran but Pakistan was just not on our radar screen."[78] A late 1991 US National Intelligence Estimate judged that Iran was committed to developing nuclear weapons. This is based on a US assumption of Chinese help and Iranian procurement patterns. But it was seen as being at an early stage. The efforts to block procurement and to persuade Russia and China not to assist Iran seemed to be bearing fruit and so, by the mid-1990s, US intelligence actually became more optimistic about containing Iran's ambitions and lowered its estimate of Iranian nuclear capability. Today, Iran is widely suspected of possessing a nuclear weapons programme despite its status as an NPT signatory. US intelligence agencies have since drawn a number of conclusions about Sino-Iranian nuclear cooperation. Former CIA Director, James Woolsey told the Senate Government Affairs Committee in 1993, "Iran will probably take 8-10 years to produce its own nuclear weapons, perhaps fewer years if it receives critical foreign assistance for its development effort."[79]

In 1991, China and Iran announced China's agreement to supply Iran's first 20 MW research nuclear reactors. The US concern on the nature of research led to this deal being scrapped as they were suspicious of Iran following a secret nuclear weapons programme, and Iran's heavy reliance on Chinese technology in this regard. In September 1992, Iran and China signed another nuclear agreement where China announced its intent to supply two 300 MW pressurised water reactors to Iran which had to be completed in ten years time.[80] Subsequently, in 1993 and 1994, according to reports that appeared in the Press, China supplied Iran with a research reactor capable of producing plutonium.[81] According to Deputy Assistant Secretary of State for Non-proliferation, Robert Einhorn, China contracted with Iran to construct two nuclear power reactors near Bushehr, though it is not clear whether these plans have been put on hold.[82] In the field of uranium conversion and enrichment, as early as June 1994, there were reports of Chinese nuclear experts assisting in the construction of uranium enrichment plants at Rudan and Shiraz. It was speculated that the town of Fasa, in the Shiraz region, was to be the site of a Chinese-constructed uranium hexaflouride (UF6) plant. The conversion of uranium ore into UF6 gas is a key step in the process of uranium enrichment, and reports of the UF6 plant project, therefore, caused considerable concern.[83] Although enriched uranium had civilian applications, Iran's desire to construct its own UF6 plant was indicative of an intention to use the enriched uranium in a clandestine nuclear weapons programme. Iran could purchase enriched uranium for its civilian reactors on the international market for a fraction what it would cost to develop an indigenous uranium enrichment capability.[84]

Fig 3.5: The Natanz facility, the existence of which was first acknowledged by Iran in February 2003; allegedly overseen by the Atomic Energy Organisation of Iran.

Prior to 1991, China dismissed all reports of nuclear cooperation with Iran as "groundless and preposterous", stating, "China has struck no nuclear deals with Iran."[85] China finally stopped denying reports of Sino-Iranian nuclear cooperation in November 1991, when the Chinese Foreign Ministry admitted that Chinese and Iranian companies had signed contracts for the Chinese sale of the calutron and mini-research reactor in 1989 and 1991, respectively. But the Chinese Foreign Ministry insisted that these items could be used only for peaceful purposes, such as medical diagnosis and physics research, and that the facilities would be under the IAEA safeguards.[86] The Chinese side further argued that the proposed 20 MW research reactor was too small to pose a proliferation threat.[87]

The year 2004 was sensational in the nuclear non-proliferation community with the world discovering that Pakistani scientist Abdul Qadeer Khan had, in fact, provided nuclear weapons-related technology to a number of countries, including North Korea, Iran, and Libya. Far more shocking was the disclosure that, although Khan's activities had been tracked by the US intelligence for more than two decades, little attempt had been made to roll up the network he created. Rather than focussing on this profound long-term strategic danger to national security, the United States had chosen to pursue short-term tactical foreign policy gains with Pakistan.[88]

The spillover effect was all but visible, with other countries too, viewing Pakistan as a source for building nuclear weapons. Khan was involved in selling off surplus centrifuges and components.[89] The spectrum of supplies that could be provided by the AQ Khan network included older and advanced centrifuges, and bomb design (based on the original Chinese design given to Pakistan in 1983).[90] For years, North Korea had been selling missiles to Pakistan. Pakistan had been paying cash for the missiles but ran into a foreign currency reserve crunch around 1996.[91] At that point, it was believed, the North Koreans agreed to a barter transaction involving the provision of centrifuges in exchange for missiles. Nonetheless, the assistance that Iran received from the AQ Khan network, including the advanced (P-2) centrifuge designs, helped in the lead up to Iran's emergence as a relatively near-term nuclear proliferation threat. In buying Khan's wares, Iran took advantage of Article IV of the NPT, which made a just-under-the-threshold nuclear weapons programme feasible and legal for an NPT signatory; and facilitated a demand for nuclear-related components and equipment for such a programme.[92]

These links created the basis for Chinese nuclear transfers as well, particularly in view of Beijing's seemingly cavalier attitude towards nuclear exports. Although China was alleged to have sold Iran components for its sensitive uranium enrichment programme in 1989, such assistance undoubtedly would have been provided for economic, rather than strategic reasons, and would not rule out comparable nuclear assistance for Iran; indeed, China was thought to have supplied arms to both countries during the Gulf War. Through mid-1990, however, no reports that surfaced indicated that such transfers took place.[93]

The Clinton Administration's approach to these developments came in for strong criticism as it opposed application of the commercial and other sanctions against proliferants under US laws and international treaties. The Clinton Administration's role was criticised as one of appeasement. To cite an example, the Administration opposed the demand of Senator Larry Pressler and others to implement the US sanctions required by the 1993 US Defence Authorisation Act (co-sponsored by then Senator Albert Gore) against nations that transfer advanced weapons to Iran. Senator Pressler noted that China's cruise missile deal with Iran violated US law and "is a vital national security matter and demands immediate attention."[94] According to *The Washington Times* of November 21, 1996, a CIA report said that China, in the summer of 1996, delivered almost 400 metric tonnes of chemicals, including carbon sulphide, to Iran, used in the production of nerve agents.[95] The Clinton Administration, in fact, did confirm that China provided assistance for Iran's chemical weapon programme. On April 10, 1997, Deputy Assistant Secretary of State for Non-Proliferation, Robert Einhorn, testified that the Administration was "deeply concerned" by "substantial information" that "various Chinese entities have transferred chemical precursors, chemical production equipment, and production technology to Iran which we expect will use them in its chemical weapons programme." He cited "dual-use chemical-related transfers to Iran's CW program..." In June 1997, the DCI reported that China, during July-December 1996, provided "considerable CW-related assistance" to Iran that consisted of production equipment and technology.[96]

In his testimony to the House International Relations Committee, Under Secretary of State, Lynn E Davis confessed, "We continue to have serious concerns regarding Chinese missile cooperation with Pakistan and Iran, which could contribute to Pakistan and Iran's acquiring delivery systems for WMD; transfers by Chinese entities of dual-use chemicals and equipment that could be used in Iran's chemical weapons programme; and China's transfers of conventional weapons to Iran. We have raised our objections to such activities at the highest levels of the Chinese government. We keep under continuing review the evidence to see whether any of these activities trigger US sanctions. For example, we are now addressing whether the transfer of Chinese built C-802 cruise missiles is sanctionable under the Iran-Iraq Arms Non-Proliferation Act of 1992."[97] The Act provides for the imposition of sanctions when a foreign person or country transfers goods or technology so as to contribute knowingly and materially to the efforts by Iran or Iraq to acquire destabilising numbers and types of (certain) advanced conventional weapons.

Similarly, the US continued to monitor and evaluate reports that cited China's transfer of missiles, missile equipment or related technology to Pakistan or Iran, activities that could trigger sanctions under US law.[98] Furthermore, according to one report, China completed construction of a plant to convert uranium from UF6 gas to metallic form. Such a uranium-conversion facility would be useful in a nuclear-weapons programme. IAEA inspectors reported in early in 1997 that the Isfahan Nuclear Technology Centre, the site of the plant, is "building up at a rate not justified by Iran's declared nuclear activities." In July, Clinton Administration officials denied the plants existence. An ACDA official stated that "[t] hat report is not accurate", and a senior State Department official said, "[t] here is no information–negative–showing such a facility in Iran."[99]

Washington continued to exert pressure on China and other potential suppliers to halt nuclear cooperation programmes with Iran. In

October 1997, China promised to end its nuclear cooperation with Iran, reportedly in part because China recognised that Iranian-sponsored instability in the Gulf could jeopardise China's energy security. At a Press briefing, the US National Security Advisor, Sandy Berger said, "We have received assurances from the Chinese that they will not engage in any new nuclear cooperation with Iran and that the existing cooperation—there are two projects in particular—will end. That is the assurance we have received."[100] China, however, continued to strengthen its ties with Iran. This was partially a function of China's rising energy needs, and expansion of Sino-Iranian relations was a natural and key component of the Chinese strategy in extending its influence to the Central Asian region. China shares a close and budding economic and military relationship with Iran, and Beijing's appetite for oil and its heavy investments in Iran hugely impact upon their relationship. In 2004, China consumed 6.5 million barrels of oil a day and overtook Japan as the world's second largest user of petroleum products. Moreover, China's state-owned oil giant Sinopec signed a $ 70 billion deal with the Iranian government in November 2004 to develop the Yadavaran oil field. According to the US Department of Energy, on completion, this field could eventually produce 300,000 barrels a day, giving China the much required quantum of oil for its energy requirements.

Many analysts viewed that Iran desired to develop a facility capable of manufacturing highly enriched uranium and perhaps planned to ultimately escape from the NPT by invoking Article X. This Article allowed a party's withdrawal without penalty by giving three months notice and declaring, with an explanation, "Extraordinary events, related to the subject matter of the treaty, have jeopardised [its] supreme interests." Although, Iran agreed under pressure to suspend its nuclear enrichment development, it was in violation of its safeguard commitments by not having informed the IAEA of equipment and materials it had either received from Khan or produced indigenously. The IAEA took the position thus far that the violations were technical in nature, not yet calling for referral to the UN Security Council.[101]

Moreover, China also provided Iran with nuclear-capable ballistic missiles, cruise missiles, missile components, and chemicals useful in making nerve gas.[102] According to the CIA, China facilitated Iran in acquiring the capability to manufacture medium-range ballistic missiles. China reportedly "sold Iran 400 tonnes of chemical agents, giving it the largest chemical weapons stockpile of any third world country," and also sold Iran "virtually complete chemical weapon factories including precursor chemicals and glass-lined vessels."[103]

Along with the nuclear assistance, China's most significant contribution to Iran in the area of missile expertise, training and technology had been its assistance in the construction of missile production facilities. Iran's largest missile factory, located near Isfahan, was originally built in cooperation with North Korea, possibly with Chinese assistance in the Eighties.[104] Moreover, by the mid-Nineties, China's missile trade with Iran aroused international concern. Iran's massive defence purchases from China included the sale of C-802 cruise missiles in 1996, questioning Beijing's track record of actually implementing its promises on arms transfers. Beginning March 1988, China pledged that it would not sell Iran more anti-ship cruise missiles. However, after 1990, China began providing Iran with more advanced C-801 and C-802 anti-shipping missiles. Moreover, in the early 1990s, China reportedly helped Iran with indigenous production of the HY-2 Silkworm and may now be helping Iran indigenously produce a medium-range anti-ship missile, the FL-10, which is inherently based on Chinese designs.[105] These latter actions are reflective of a general pattern—after promising to refrain from sales of a particular system, Beijing has instead provided knowhow and technical assistance. Despite stopping sales of the M-9 and M-11 missiles to Iran after US objections, for example, Beijing has provided production equipment, expertise, and technology that have contributed to Iran's indigenous missile development programmes.[106] In the lead-up to the October 1997 US-China Summit, China apparently agreed to stop sales of sensitive items such as the (Silkworm) anti-ship missiles to Iran. A review of China's cruise missile trade with Iran could be divided into three parts: (a) the sale of anti-ship HY-2 (Silkworm) missiles, mostly during the Iran-Iraq War; (b) the sale of C-801 missiles toward the end of the Iran-Iraq

War; and (c) the more recent Iranian acquisitions of advanced C-802 missiles in the Nineties.[107]

In addition, Western diplomats have been quoted as stating that China was assisting Iran in building a plant for manufacturing ballistic missiles possibly with a 500-mile range. In addition, Iran commanded "one of the largest and most capable ballistic missile programmes" in the Middle East. Iran's defence minister publicly acknowledged the development of the Shahab-4 and plans for a progressively longer-range Shahab-5, which could have intermediate-range (3,000-5,500 km) capability. These programmes, undoubtedly, benefited immensely from sustained cooperation with China.[108] China possibly had a larger strategic purpose in mind, particularly with Iran, which its hard-line strategists viewed as a long-term surrogate against US allies and interests in the Middle East, notably in targeting Saudi Arabia. While the primary concern with cruise missiles was their implications for Iran's ability to control oil traffic in the Persian Gulf, or even to threaten foreign naval vessels, the concern about ballistic missiles was based on their possible use in attacks on land-based targets, and particularly their use as delivery systems for weapons of mass destruction.[109]

In recent years, Chinese firms have been sanctioned many times for providing missile-related assistance to Iran in violation of the Iran Non-Proliferation Act of 2000.[110] In January 2002, pursuant to the Iran Non-Proliferation Act, Washington applied sanctions on three Chinese entities for transferring equipment and technology to Tehran that could be used to manufacture chemical and biological weapons. The two-year sanctions were condemned as "unreasonable" by Beijing.[111] Moreover, the sanctioned entities included two of China's largest companies: NORINCO and China Great Wall Industry Corporation. Both were subject to repeated US sanctions since the 1990s and described as part of China's "serial proliferator" problem by senior officials in the Bush Administration.[112] The US State Department on June 26, 2001, announced sanctions under the Iran Non-Proliferation Act on North Korea's Changgwang Sinyong Corporation, for unspecified missile-related transfers to Iran. The announcements represented the second time that sanctions had been imposed under the Act, the first also being on the same corporation on January 2, 2001.[113]

However, vis-à-vis the nuclear facilities, President George W Bush had a different proposal to limit fuel cycle facilities, where he proposed a ban on assistance by members of the NSG for the construction of new enrichment and reprocessing facilities in countries not possessing such plants; however, he did not back this up with a proposal for sanctions against those suppliers who would violate such a ban. In his remarks, Bush also called on nuclear exporters to ensure that states had reliable access at reasonable cost to civilian nuclear fuel if they renounced enrichment and reprocessing.[114] It is unclear if Bush was aware that one version of this proposal had been part of US law for more than twenty-five years. Title I of the Nuclear Non-Proliferation Act (NNPA) of 1978 called on the president to work with other countries to create an International Nuclear Fuel Authority (INFA) to guarantee nuclear enrichment services to non-nuclear weapon states that agreed not to build enrichment and reprocessing plants. Herein lay an irony because it was reported that the president was opposed to the idea of international consortia in this arena.[115] Americans in the international community were of the strong view that in order to curb proliferation of WMD, the nuclear weapon states could take the first steps by a more forceful implementation of their own commitments under the NPT to make good faith efforts toward nuclear disarmament.

In order to check the spread of nuclear proliferation, the 'norm' set in place should bind the signatories, specially the proliferators, with punitive consequences in case finding a diplomatic solution at both bilateral and multilateral levels failed. This would facilitate in checking the spread of sensitive technologies into the hands of unstable regimes and non-state actors. This was the most obvious gap in the non-proliferation system: there was no international consensus on the penalties to which a proliferator ought to be subjected. Pakistan escaped significant penalties despite its horrific proliferation record. An effective regime also required constant review and improvement of export controls. The Khan network made it imperative that export controls be applied to smaller specialised components than had been the case. In a broader context, China's "mixed record" in the multilateral arena underscored the difficulty in ascertaining the degree to which its policy elite and industry managers had imbibed the normative and practical components of export controls and the overreaching non-proliferation "security culture." China's agreement to build additional nuclear reactors in Pakistan while its application to the NSG was pending, and its missile related transfers to Iran while its MTCR application was pending, pointed to a continued bargain-embedded approach toward its non-proliferation obligations.[116]

As for China's role in global proliferation, Assistant Secretary of State for Verification and Compliance Paula D Sutter, stated in July 2003, "At the highest levels, the Chinese government has claimed that it opposes missile proliferation—unfortunately, the reality has been quite different."[117] There is a strong group of analysts who were of the view that the Chinese role in the spread of WMD was an "affordable disengagement strategy," as by almost all measures, strategic proxies were China's most cost-effective method to raise the price of American interventionism and discourage the defence policy of forward engagement, which allowed the United States to form the international security environment far from its own shores. If Beijing's main goal was to prevent Washington from concentrating its forces in East Asia, planting WMD threats throughout the Middle East could spread the US too thin to act decisively at once in multiple theatres.[118] Adding impetus to this line of argument was a statement by Chinese President, Jiang Zemin, on a visit to the Middle East and Europe in 2002, "Beijing envisions a 'multi-polarised' world"—a euphemism for checked US power.[119]

In this backdrop, one wonders how China's role in promoting proliferation could be checked by the US action. In other words, one doubts the veracity of the US logic that nuclear cooperation would encourage China to strengthen its non-proliferation commitments. Most certainly, nuclear cooperation with China would have tremendous backing from the business houses. In fact, US business interests appeared to have begun to lead diplomacy in US-China relations.[120]

Although, the United States made stringent efforts to decrease the risk of the spread of WMD and their delivery capability, successive US Administrations focussed on the IAEA, the NSG, Zangger Committee, the fissile material production ban, as well as strengthening the BWC, CWC, Australia Group, MTCR, Wassenaar Arrangement, START I, II, and III, North Korea Agreed Framework, and bilateral efforts with numerous countries to discourage the spread of weapons technology and its acquisition, deployment, and possible usage. But various constituencies criticised numerous US actions as stimulants for the spread of WMD and their means of delivery, such as the development of a national missile defence; threats to abrogate the Anti-Ballistic Missile (ABM) Treaty; discussions of regional missile defence systems in Asia and the Middle East; the US Senate's refusal to ratify the CTBT; and perceived elevation of economic goals above non-proliferation goals, although proponents strongly defended their actions as in the best national interest. However, it remains questionable whether these US actions actually served the national interests of the United States. The critical challenge in this regard was posed by the proliferation activities of North Korea.

Notes

1. For more details, see Safdar Mahmood, *Pakistan: Political Roots and Development 1947-1999* (Oxford: Oxford University Press, 2000).
2. George Perkovich, *India's Nuclear Bomb* (Berkeley: University of California Press, 1999), p. 176.
3. Gordon Corera, *Shopping for Bombs: Nuclear Proliferation, Global Insecurity and the Rise and Fall of the AQ Khan Network* (London: C. Hurst Publishers Ltd, 2006), p. 44.
4. For more details, see Owen Bennett-Jones, *Pakistan: Eye of the Storm* (London: Yale University Press, 2005) and Rai Muhammad Saleh, "Where Mountains Move—The Story of Chagai," *The Nation*, (Lahore), May 28, 2000.
5. R Jeffery Smith, "US Aides See Troubling Trend in China-Pakistan Nuclear Ties," *The Washington Post*, April 23, 1996.
6. Corera, n. 3, p. 44.
7. Ibid., p. 45.
8. For more details, see Richard L Russell, *Weapons Proliferation in the Greater Middle East* (Oxford: Routeledge, 2005).
9. Corera, n. 3, p. 45.

10. "Pakistan's Atomic Bomb," *Foreign Report*, January 12, 1989.
11. Judith Miller, "US is Holding up Peking Atom Talks," *The New York Times*, September 19, 1982.
12. Corera, n. 3, p. 46.
13. Leonard S Spector, *Nuclear Ambitions: The Spread of Nuclear Weapons, 1989-1990* (Colorado: Westview Press Inc., 1990), p. 61.
14. Ibid., pp. 61-62.
15. Spector, n. 13, p. 62.
16. Leslie H Gelb, "Pakistan Links Peril US-China Nuclear Pact," *The New York Times*, June 22, 1984.
17. Spector, n. 13, p. 43.
18. *Nucleonics Week*, May 23, 1991, p. 1.
19. Mark Hibbs, "China Accord Would Turn up US Heat on Pakistani Reactor," *Nucleonics Week*, August 14, 1997, p. 8.
20. Shahid-ur-Rehman, *The Long Road to Chagai* (Islamabad, 1999), p. 86.
21. Hassan Abbas, *Pakistan's Drift into Extremism* (New York: ME Sharpe, 2004), p. 149.
22. Corera, n. 3, p. 47.
23. John Glenn, "On Proliferation Law, a Disgraceful Failure," *International Herald Tribune*, June 26, 1992.
24. For more details, see Jeffrey T Richelson, *Spying on the Bomb* (New York: WW Norton & Company, 2006), p. 344.
25. Corera, n. 3, p. 48.
26. Gen Aslam Mirza Beg, "Who Will Press the Button?" *Saudi Gazette*, May 8, 1994.
27. "Implementation of the US-China Nuclear Cooperation Agreement: Whose Interests are Served?" Hearing Before the Committee on International Relations; House of Representatives, One Hundred Fifth Congress, First Session, Washington DC, October 7, 1997, p. 68.
28. For a comprehensive coverage of this topic, see the online database of the Centre for Nonproliferation Studies, Monterey Institute of International Studies, at http://www.cns.miis.edu.
29. CRS Report for US Congress, "The 1985 US-China Agreement for Nuclear Cooperation: Moving Towards Implementation?" April 10, 1997, p. 3.
30. Shahid-ur-Rehman Khan, "China Agrees to Supply 300-MW PWR to Pakistan," *Nucleonics Week*, March 1,1990, p. 1.
31. Ibid.
32. Quoted in *Nucleonics Week*, December 12, 1996, p. 10.
33. *Nucleonics Week*, December 12, 1996, p. 10.
34. "Nuclear Negotiations," *Far Eastern Economic Review*, January 19, 1990, p. 6.
35. Corera, n. 3, p. 55.
36. Victor Zaborsky, "Does China Belong in the Missile Technology Control Regime?" *Arms Control Today*, vol. 34, no. 8, October 2004, p. 20.
37. Chintamani Mahapatra, "The US, China and the Ghauri Missile," *Strategic*

Analysis, vol. 22, no. 3, June 1998, p. 364.

38. For more details, see Bates Gill, "Curbing Beijing's Arms Sales," *Orbis,* vol. 36, no. 3, 1992.
39. Zaborsky, n. 36, p. 22.
40. Quoted in CRS Report for Congress, "Possible Missile Technology Transfers from US Satellite Export Policy: Background and Chronology," March 16, 1999, pp. 11-12.
41. Ibid.
42. Zaborsky, n. 36, p. 22.
43. CRS Report for Congress, n. 40, p. 12.
44. For details, see Henry Sokolski, "US Satellites to China," *International Defense Review*, April 1994, pp. 23-26.
45. Cited in Bill Gertz, "CIA Analyst says US Winked at Cheating," *The Washington Times*, June 12, 1998.
46. Corera, n. 3, p. 88.
47. "State and CIA, DIA at Odds Over M-11 Status," *Arms Control Today,* July 1996, p. 30.
48. Chintamani Mahapatra, "Withstanding the Patron's Pressure," *Strategic Analysis,* vol. 16, no. 8, November 1993, p. 1127.
49. Ibid.
50. Peter Roff, "Bhutto Missile Story Raises Hill Hackles," *United Press International*, March 7, 2005.
51. "Pakistan," Foreign Missile Developments and the Ballistic Missile Threat Through 2015, Unclassified Summary of the National Intelligence Estimate, (Washington, DC: US Central Intelligence Agency, December 2001), pp. 24-25.
52. David E Sanger, and James Dao, "US Says Pakistan Gave Technology to North Korea," *The New York Times*, October 17, 2002.
53. Gaurav Kampani, "Second Tier Proliferation: The Case of Pakistan and North Korea," *The Nonproliferation Review*, Fall-Winter 2002, p. 108.
54. Chintamani Mahapatra, *Indo-US Relations: Into the 21st Century* (New Delhi: Knowledge World, 1998), pp. 58-59.
55. Cited in *The Telegraph*, March 21, 1996.
56. Mahapatra, n. 54, p. 59.
57. Ibid., p. 68.
58. Mahapatra, n. 54, pp. 68-69.
59. Ibid., p. 69.
60. CRS Report for Congress, n. 29, pp. 3-4.
61. Ibid.
62. CIA, Unclassified Report to Congress, The Acquisition of Technology Relating to Weapons of Mass Destruction and Advanced Conventional Munitions, 1997, p. 5.
63. Pakistan reportedly has acquired technology for short-range missiles (Hatf-I, Hatf-II,) and (Shaheen) from China and medium-range missiles (Ghauri) from North Korea's range of Nodong missiles, capable of carrying small nuclear warheads. For more details, see CRS Issue Brief for Congress, *Pakistan-US*

Relations, March 10, 2002, p. 8.

64. Quoted in Justin Bernier, "Asia's Shifting Strategic Landscape: China's Strategic Proxies," *Orbis*, vol. 47, no. 4, Fall 2003, p. 631.
65. CIA, Unclassified Report to Congress on the Acquisition of Technology Relating to Weapons of Mass Destruction and Advanced Conventional and Munitions, January-June 2003, at www.cia.gov/cia/reports/721_reports/jan-jun2003.htm
66. Anupam Srivastava, "China's Export Controls: Can Bejing's Actions Match its Words?" *Arms Control Today*, vol. 35, no. 9, November 2005, p. 21.
67. Bates Gill, "Chinese Arms Exports to Iran", *China Report,* vol. 34, no. 3&4, 1998, p. 357.
68. Ibid.
69. Steven Dolley, " China's Record of Proliferation Misbehavior," CRS Issue Brief for Congress, cited at http://www.nci.org/nci/
70. Shirley A Kan, "Chinese Missile and Nuclear Proliferation: Issues for Congress," CRS Report for Congress, August 24, 1992.
71. Ibid.
72. Corera, n. 3, pp. 62-63.
73. Mahmood, n. 1.
74. Farzad Bazoft, "Iran Signs Secret Atom Deal," *The Observer*, June 12, 1998.
75. John Lancaster and Kamran Khan, "Pakistanis say Nuclear Scientists Aided Iran," *The Washington Post*, January 24, 2004.
76. Dalip Singh, "Delhi Dossier on Pakistan Bomb Daddy," *The Telegraph*, February 8, 2004.
77. Spector, n. 13, p. 12; also see, Kenneth Timmerman, *Countdown to Crisis: The Coming Nuclear Showdown with Iran* (New York: Crown Forum, 2005), pp. 38-39.
78. Jeffrey T Richelson, *Spying on the Bomb* (New York: WW Norton & Company, 2006), p. 506.
79. Testimony of CIA Director, James Woolsey before the US Senate Governmental Affairs Committee, "Proliferation Threats of the 1990s," February 24, 1993.
80. Arpit Rajain, *Nuclear Deterrence in South Asia* (New Delhi: Sage Publications, 2005), p. 180.
81. Kenneth Timmerman, "Tehran's A-Bomb Program Shows Startling Progress," *Washington Times,* May 8, 1995.
82. Robert Einhorn, Testimony before the Senate Governmental Affairs Committee, Subcommittee on International Security, April 10, 1997.
83. Gill, n. 67, p. 371.
84. "US Protests Chinese Hex Plant," *Iran Brief*, July 3, 1997, p. 1.
85. Statement of the *Xinhua News Agency* quoted in *China Daily*, December 18, 1991.
86. Ibid.
87. Mark Hibbs, "Sensitive Iran Reactor Deal May Hinge on MFN for China," *Nucleonics Week*, October 1, 1992, pp. 5-6.
88. Leonard Weiss, "Turning a Blind Eye Again? The Khan Network's History and

Lessons for US Policy," *Arms Control Today,* vol. 35, no. 2, March 2005, p. 12.

89. William J Broad, David E Sanger and Raymond Bonner, "A Tale of Nuclear Proliferation: How Pakistani Built His Network," *The New York Times,* February 12, 2004.
90. Ibid.
91. For more details, see CRS Report for Congress, "Weapons of Mass Destruction: Trade Between North Korea and Pakistan," RL31900, May 7, 2003.
92. Weiss, n. 88, p. 16.
93. Spector, n. 13, p. 212.
94. Cited in "Review of the Clinton Administration Nonproliferation Policy," Hearing Before the Committee on International Relations, House of Representatives, One Hundred Fourth Congress, Second Session, June 19, 1996, p. 94.
95. For details, see *Jane's Defense Weekly,* January 8, 1997.
96. CRS Report for Congress, "China's Compliance with International Arms Control Agreements," September 16, 1997, p. 9.
97. Lynn E Davis, "Controlling the Spread of Dangerous Weapons: An Overview of the Clinton Administration's Non-Proliferation Policy," Testimony by the Under Secretary of State for Arms Control and International Security Affairs, for the House International Relations Committee, One Hundred Fourth Congress, Second Session, June 19, 1996, p. 51.
98. Ibid.
99. Cited in "Implementation of the US-China Nuclear Cooperation Agreement: Whose Interests are Served?" 105th Congress, n. 27, p. 65.
100. Briefing by US National Security Adviser, Sandy Berger, Office of the Press Secretary, October 29, 1997.
101. Weiss, n. 88, p. 16.
102. Einhorn, n. 82.
103. Implementation of the US-China Nuclear Cooperation Agreement: Whose Interests are Served? 105th Congress, n. 27, p. 66.
104. Gill, n. 67, p. 365.
105. Bates Gill, "Silkworms and Summitry: Chinese Arms Exports to Iran and US-China Relations," Asia and Pacific Rim Institute of the American Jewish Committee, 1998, p. 9.
106. Ibid., p. 11.
107. Gill, n. 67, p. 359.
108. Quoted in US Department of Defense Briefing, "Proliferation: Threat and Response," January 2001, p. 38.
109. Gill, n. 67, p. 363.
110. The Iran Non-Proliferation Act of 2000 authorises the president to penalise any foreign entity that transfers items to Iran that could aid its pursuit of dangerous weapons.
111. Bernier, n. 64, p. 641.
112. David Sanger, "US is Punishing 8 Chinese Firms for Aiding Iran," *The New York Times,* January 18, 2005.

113. *Fact Sheet,* US Department of State, June 26, 2001, p. 1.
114. Quoted in, http://usinfo.state.gov/regional/ea/uschina/bush0601.htm
115. For details see, Carla A Robbins, "Nuclear Nonproliferation Effort Snags," *The Wall Street Journal,* January 27, 2005.
116. Srivastava, n. 66, p. 24.
117. US-China Economic and Security Review Commission, "China's Proliferation Practices and the North Korean Nuclear Crisis," 108th Congress, First Session, July 24, 2003, p. 7.
118. Bernier, n. 64, p. 636.
119. "Jiang Visits Potsdam, Reiterates National Reunification," *People's Daily,* April 11, 2002.
120. Chintamani Mahapatra, "American Approach to Sino-Pakistan Nuclear and Missile Cooperation," *Strategic Analysis,* vol. 21, no. 10, January 1998, pp. 1415-1416.

4

US, China and the North Korean Nuclear Tangle

There was a period when the relations between the People's Republic of China (PRC) and North Korea [formally known as the Democratic People's Republic of Korea (DPRK)] were, as best described, as close as "lips and teeth." The PRC went to the extent of going to war with the United States (US) in 1950 to ensure North Korea's survival. Somehow, fifty-six years down the road, the situation has changed considerably, with the changed geo-politics witnessed by the world. The relations between North Korea and China experienced their share of ups and downs with the collapse of the Soviet Union, crumpling of the North Korean economy and Beijing's recognition of Seoul in 1992, to name a few factors.

At the turn of the millennium, the DPRK set off a crisis with its October 2002 admission of an active nuclear weapons programme, in violation of the 1994 Agreed Framework with the US. As a matter of fact, the US and North Korea have been technically at war for decades now, since the 1953 armistice was never replaced with a peace treaty. The US was unwilling to discuss even a non-aggression pact, much less a peace treaty or normalisation of ties. The Framework has now become history, and with neither side backing down, the crisis continued unabated for a long spell given the track record of the unpredictable Kim Jong Il regime. During the 1990s—the first decade of the post-Cold War era—the North Korean economy collapsed, with the country's Gross National Product (GNP) more than halved, most of its factories operating at less than 30 percent capacity, and an increasing number of people in the northeastern provinces either falling prey to famines or defecting to China as food refugees.

Pyongyang repeatedly pleaded that it had been a victim of US hostility. Significantly, the US rhetoric toward Pyongyang was far from being conciliatory. The US refused to discuss formulating a non-aggression pact or replacing the 1953 armistice with a peace treaty until the North reassured it that the nuclear programmes had been stopped. Significantly, the US' December 2001 *Nuclear Posture Review* specified North Korea as an "immediate contingency" for which the United States must be prepared to respond with nuclear force.[1] Albeit, North Korea not only existed, but also attracted global prime time coverage with its nuclear and missile brinkmanship diplomacy and the attention of food aid from the US, if not the respect Pyongyang has long craved for.

North Korean Nuclear Background: An Overview

Since the end of the Cold War, the United States has been keen to take advantage of changes in international relations to improve the volatile security situation on the Korean Peninsula. After the establishment of informal US-DPRK diplomatic contacts in the late 1980s, a substantial breakthrough was achieved in 1991 when the George HW Bush Administration announced that the United States would withdraw all tactical nuclear weapons abroad—including those in South Korea. Encouraged by the US initiative, the DPRK regime of Kim Il Sung agreed to a series of North- South meetings that led to the October 1991 Joint Declaration on the Denuclearisation of the Korean Peninsula. Progress was interrupted, however, by growing confrontation in 1992 over North Korea's nuclear programme, especially when there was evidence suggesting that North Korea had reprocessed more plutonium than it had declared to the IAEA.

Though North Korea's nuclear programme started well before 1985, it was only after it joined the NPT in the same year that global attention was focussed on its activities in this field, especially since the country pursued an active programme, in violation of the treaty. These violations centred on a number of facilities at the Yongbyon Nuclear

Research Centre, situated in Yongbyon, a city located about 85 km north of the capital, Pyongyang.

The agreements signed on March 26 and September 7, 1956, between North Korea and the erstwhile Soviet Union on nuclear research and cooperation, led to the establishment of the Yongbyon nuclear research complex. The agreements included the provision for a small number of North Korean personnel being taught nuclear physics within the Soviet Union. This was followed by additional protocols on the peaceful use of nuclear energy that North Korea signed with both the Soviet Union and the PRC. It was during the 1970s that Pyongyang took a decision to pursue both nuclear power and a weapons programme, which resulted in a major expansion of the Yongbyon nuclear research complex and the establishment of facilities throughout the country.[2]

Fig 4.1: Yongbyon 5 MW (e) Reactor

The key facilities at Yongbyon included an operational 5 megawatts electric (MWe) nuclear power reactor, a large-scale reprocessing plant for plutonium extraction which was partially completed, a number of radiochemistry laboratories that could be used for plutonium extraction, a high-explosive testing facility, and a fuel fabrication plant. As has been mentioned above, Pyongyang signed the NPT in 1985, but did not allow the IAEA to carry out inspections, which was required by the provisions of the treaty, until May 1992. This was also the time by when the United States' intelligence agencies were coming close to the conclusion that North Korea had extracted plutonium at the Yongbyon reprocessing plant, and possibly at a number of radiochemistry laboratories, using irradiated fuel rods from the 5 MWe reactor, which was thought to have been partially or fully refuelled in 1989.

However, there was a marked toning down of the anti-US rhetoric that had begun in the spring of 1992, with Pyongyang being especially muted in its response to President's Clinton remarks at the Demilitarised Zone (DMZ) in July that use of nuclear weapons by North Korea would mean the end of their country, as they knew it. It is technically feasible that North Korea could have obtained as much as 12 kg of plutonium, enough to manufacture one or two nuclear weapons. It was assessed by most US intelligence agencies at that time that the amount of plutonium recovered by the country was more than it had declared to the IAEA and that this amount would have been enough to make one or possibly two nuclear weapons.[3]

In May 1992, the IAEA initiated a series of inspections and visits to verify North Korea's initial inventory of nuclear facilities and materials and during the process and course of the year, the agency found discrepancies in the country's declaration of levels of past plutonium production. In an effort to resolve the discrepancies, the IAEA in 1993 called for a "special inspection" of two undeclared sites near the Yongbyon nuclear complex. This arrangement was apparently unacceptable to Pyongyang and in March 1993, it announced that it was withdrawing from the NPT, instead of allowing officials of the IAEA to inspect two nuclear sites in the north of the country. The withdrawal of North Korea from the NPT was to have taken effect on June 12,

1993. The decision to withdraw from the NPT took the international community by surprise and sprung the US Administration into action. It immediately initiated negotiations with North Korea, and by June 1993, had succeeded in persuading the country to suspend its withdrawal. Nevertheless, North Korea refused to have itself considered as a full party to the NPT and, hence, refuted the right of the IAEA to conduct even ad hoc or routine inspections.[4]

The pace of political succession accelerated steadily during 1993 as Kim Jong Il took a greater leadership role. His move up from vice-chairman to his father, Kim Il Sung's post as chairman of the National Defence Commission, raised him a notch higher than his prevailing position of supreme commander of the Korean People's Army (KPA). The new job encompassed broader responsibilities than just the military. The nuclear controversy provided Kim with a chance to prove his mettle and garner maximum benefits for Pyongyang, even as it attracted considerable international attention in 1993. A series of developments that included collapse of the inter-Korean dialogue, the resumption of the US-South Korea Team Spirit military exercise, and unprecedented pressure from the IAEA to open two undeclared sites to special inspections prompted Pyongyang to take the extreme step on March 12, 1993, of giving notice that it intended to withdraw from the NPT. The North Korean government claimed that the two suspect nuclear waste sites were military facilities unrelated to its nuclear programme and that the agency's request was improperly based on "third party intelligence information." Although suggesting a worst-case nuclear "breakout scenario," the withdrawal announcement was couched in conditional language, calling for an end to the US "threat".[5]

Thereafter, two rounds of high-level US-DPRK talks on the nuclear issue were held in 1993 that resulted in a joint statement that laid out the principles underpinning the talks and announced the DPRK's suspension of its withdrawal from the NPT. More specifically, the second round of talks in Geneva in July was noteworthy for Pyongyang's proposal to switch from its graphite-moderated nuclear reactors to light-water reactors that required an external supply of fuel and posed less of a proliferation concern. North Korea in effect agreed to hold discussions with the IAEA on nuclear issues and reengage with the South for improving ties. The two sides also made it clear that Pyongyang had agreed to preserve the continuity of safeguards. Significantly, the North Koreans underscored their interest in having the US involved in the transfer of light-water reactor technology.

A statement by Kang Sok Chu in November 1993 reaffirmed North Korea's commitment to the continuity of safeguards and urged US acceptance of a "package solution"—a theme that became a central feature of the North's public position for the rest of 1993. Kang said the North had gone as far as it could in cooperating with the IAEA in circumstances in which it had only "suspended" its withdrawal from the NPT. The statement warned that the DPRK could still opt to effectuate its withdrawal from the NPT, but noted that a "package solution" could settle all safeguards-related problems. At the year's end, North Korean public characterisation of the state of play in US-DPRK nuclear talks suggested that Pyongyang believed that prospects were improving for a third round of talks.[6] However, by the end of 1993, the director general of the IAEA stated that IAEA safeguards could no longer provide "any meaningful assurances" that nuclear materials were not being diverted for weapons production.[7] In addition to this, Pyongyang's missile programmes, which have been discussed later in the chapter, comprised another cause of concern. Sales of Scud missiles to the Middle East reportedly continued, and North Korea test-fired a Nodong-1 missile into the Sea of Japan at the end of May 1993—the eve of the second round of the US-DPRK talks. The test seemed to be either a warning going into the talks that Pyongyang was not to be taken lightly or an attempt to sour the atmosphere by those in Pyongyang opposed to the negotiations.

By any reckoning, 1994 was a rare year for North Korea, both the best and the worst of times in Pyongyang's checkered international image. The year started with the continuation of nuclear brinkmanship—an endless end game, as it were—but closed with what promised to be a 'grand bargain', if implemented, or the cooperative security of two-plus-four (the two Koreas plus Japan, China, Russia, and the United States).[8]

The North Korean nuclear issue constituted the first major nuclear non-proliferation crisis of the post-Cold War era. The IAEA's demand for "special inspections" of two suspect and undeclared nuclear waste sites at the Yongbyon nuclear complex triggered North Korea's public declaration of withdrawing from the NPT and this, in turn, caused crisis reactions in Seoul, Tokyo, and Washington, since once legally out of the NPT, North Korea would be legally free to proceed with its nuclear weapons programme. There was no great power unanimity in addressing the North Korean nuclear problem. The Chinese threat to veto any punitive sanctions resolution in the United Nations (UN) Security Council against Pyongyang enabled the latter to obtain what it had been seeking from the beginning—direct bilateral confrontation/negotiation with the US.

Pyongyang initially agreed to an IAEA inspection in March 1994, as part of a complicated package deal in which the former agreed to an inspection of its declared facilities but later blocked the agency from taking radioactive samples at the plutonium extraction plant at Yongbyon on the ground that key elements of the deal had not been fulfilled. The crisis grew by mid-May 1994, when the country started to de-fuel the 5 MWe reactor while refusing to implement procedures placed by the IAEA to segregate 300 fuel rods which had been carefully selected from the 8,000-rod core. If an analysis had been made of the radioactive signature of the segregated rods, it could have indicated how long the rods had been in the reactor, which would have permitted the IAEA to determine whether North Korea had the capacity/capability to obtain plutonium for one or two nuclear devices.[9]

North Korea's refusal to comply with IAEA inspection requirements during the de-fuelling of the Yongbyon reactor led the agency to announce on June 10, 1994, that it was cutting off all technical assistance to the country. This, in turn, led Pyongyang to announce on June 13 that it was withdrawing from the agency and that it would develop its own nuclear programme independent of world scrutiny.[10] In an effort to resolve the ongoing impasse, former US President Jimmy Carter decided to accept Kim Il Sung's longstanding invitation and make a peace-making journey to Pyongyang.

Implications of the Agreed Framework

Against this backdrop, the Carter-Kim Summit not only provided a cooling-off period but also a face-saving way for both sides to shift away from confrontation and return to negotiations. This had a fruitful result as on August 12, 1994, after a week of intense discussions in Geneva, the US and North Korea issued a joint statement of principles for settling the dispute via a package deal, and on October 21, 1994, after a month of difficult rounds of discussions, both parties signed a landmark Geneva Accord or what also came to be known as the Agreed Framework and a confidential document as appendix. The accord provided a roadmap to an overall solution of the Korean nuclear issue through a comprehensive quid-pro-quo package deal. According to Samuel S Kim, it is a carefully choreographed "swim or sink together" joint venture of reciprocal steps that both sides would have to take in a nine-year implementation process rotating through five distinct stages, with specific measures to be completed on specified dates.[11]

Each side retained unit veto as the accord gave both sides more or less equal leverage, against reneging. Accordingly, North Korea agreed to (1) freeze, halt, and eventually dismantle its 5 MWe graphite-moderated reactor in operation and the 50 MWe and 200 MWe graphite-moderated reactors under construction, and related facilities; (2) remain a party to the NPT; (3) allow ad hoc and routine inspections by the IAEA; (4) come into full compliance with its safeguards agreement with the IAEA, including taking all steps that may be deemed necessary by the IAEA; (5) take steps to implement the 1992 North-South Joint Declaration on the Denuclearisation of the Korean Peninsula; and (6) engage in North-South dialogue.

In return, Pyongyang too, got a fine deal from Washington—a comprehensive security, political and an economic package. The US agreed to (1) organise under its leadership, an international consortium to finance and supply two light water reactors (LWRs) with a total capacity of 2,000 MW by 2003 (worth around $4 billion); (2) deliver alternative energy in the form of heavy fuel oil shipments to offset the energy forgone due to the freeze at a rate of 500,000 tonnes annually during the transition period; (3) reduce barriers to trade and investment; (4) establish diplomatic relations, starting with a liaison office and gradually elevating to ambassadorial level; and (5) provide formal assurances to the DPRK against the threat or use of nuclear weapons by the US (the no first use pledge).[12]

Immediately after the signing of the accord, North Korea's chief negotiator, Kang Sok Ju, described it as "a very important milestone document of historical significance" that would resolve North Korea's nuclear dispute with the US once and for all. In the wake of the Geneva Accord—and in the first stage of implementation—a remarkable role reversal occurred as the Clinton Administration shifted its policy from mobilising the broadest possible global coalition for sanctions against North Korea to do the exact opposite: help yesterday's foe with free interim energy supplies and the two new light water reactors.

The signing of the Geneva Accord was followed by a flurry of US-DPRK talks in Pyongyang, Beijing and Washington. On November 28, 1994, the IAEA publicly stated that its team visited the nuclear facilities in Yongbyon and Taechon and "confirmed that these facilities were not in operation and that construction work had stopped."[13] The US, South Korea, and Japan agreed on December 16, 1994, to (1) establish "at an early date" a multilateral consortium provisionally named the Korea Energy Development Organisation (KEDO) with headquarters in New York; (2) allow South Korea to play a central role in the financing and construction in North Korea of two 1,000 MW LWRs of a type already used in South Korea; (3) allow Japan to play "an appropriate role" in managing and funding the project; (4) have the US supply heavy fuel oil to North Korea to compensate it for energy lost from its existing reactor, with the first shipment to be made within the month; and (5) mobilise broad international participation in the KEDO.[14] There is widespread belief that once in full operation, the two larger reactors could produce enough spent fuel to reprocess plutonium for at least 20 to 30 bombs per year.

In early December 1994, US and North Korean officials met at the State Department and announced that they had resolved most technical issues required to open liaison offices in their respective capitals and that a US delegation would soon go to Pyongyang to examine potential sites for an office. Thus, the first stage of the Washington-Pyongyang rapprochement began and ended on an upbeat note with most of the issues discussed to mutual satisfaction, only to be threatened again by an incident involving a US Army helicopter that strayed into North Korean air space on December 17, 1994.[15] It would be apt to say here that the Kim Jong Il regime managed to translate nuclear brinkmanship into a diplomatic breakthrough, and in terms of foreign policy, North Korea had a great harvest year. However, the enigma of North Korean politics continued largely unabated in the times ahead, characterised by a lack of policy-making transparency and despite all signs pointing to the need for urgent structural reforms of the economy, a continued hesitancy to do so.

The implementation of the 1994 Agreed Framework on the nuclear issue preoccupied US-North Korean relations for a few years, but by late 1997, Pyongyang began to accuse Washington in increasingly strident terms of failing to abide by the agreement. It cited three concerns: continuing economic sanctions, delayed delivery of heavy fuel oil, and delays in the construction of LWRs by the KEDO. When these pleadings did not elicit the desired responses from Washington, Pyongyang halted work on the canning of spent nuclear fuel and threatened to reopen the reprocessing plant and nuclear reactor at Yongbyon.[16] In Washington, policy-makers expressed concerns about intelligence information indicating that North Korea was constructing a secret underground facility. When the Clinton Administration briefed Congress that North Korea was constructing a secret underground facility, which appeared to be associated with nuclear weapons development, many in Congress voiced their concerns over the very viability of the Agreed Framework. It was becoming increasingly evident that the North Koreans were making progress in developing a threatening nuke capability. Consequently, these nuclear actions by the Kim Jong Il regime were undermining political support for the Agreed Framework in the US, Japan and to an extent in South Korea as well. As the end of 1998 approached, the basis for the Agreed Framework was portentously eroding. President Clinton's visit to Seoul in November 1998 produced the usual statements of alliance solidarity but failed to conceal their very different priorities.

By October 2000, North Korea and the United States held two quasi-summit meetings in Washington and Pyongyang. For over a year, Washington had been negotiating with Pyongyang to send a special envoy, Kang Sok Ju, who negotiated the 1994 US-DPRK Agreed Framework and was known to be Kim Jong Il's close foreign policy adviser.[17] The quasi-summit meeting ended with a US-DPRK Joint Communiqué, in which both sides agreed to take steps to fundamentally improve their bilateral relations, support and encourage international efforts against terrorism, and scheduled Secretary of State Madeleine Albright's visit to the DPRK in the near future to convey the views of President Clinton directly to Chairman Kim Jong Il.[18] All of the above efforts, though, did not succeed in bringing out anything substantial. It was becoming clear that the Agreed Framework was fast corroding.

The Framework was not a formal treaty but rather a set of guidelines designed to help two countries that were deeply mistrustful of each other. But it became evidently clear that both sides began backing out of the Framework well before autumn of 2002. Neither side fulfilled its Framework obligations. The key elements on the US side were a formal statement of non-aggression, providing a light water reactor and making progress toward normalisation of ties. However, the US was four years behind schedule in providing the reactor.[19] Moreover, neither did the US open a liaison office in Pyongyang nor did it provide a formal written assurance against the use of nuclear weapons, and it would be very crucial to mention here that the 2002 US Nuclear Posture Review targeted North Korea with a preemptive strike. The Bush Administration had made it clear from the time it took office how much it disdained the Kim Jong Il regime. President George W Bush clubbed North Korea, Iran and Iraq as the "axis of evil" to give expression to that disdain. The levels of mistrust were extremely high. With the September 2002 National Security Strategy moving the US towards a stated policy of preemptive strikes, the North seemed to be worried that if it agreed to disarm and abandon its deterrent posture, the United States would eventually move and destroy it.

In 2002, Secretary of State Colin Powell added the North's missile programme to the list of conditions necessary for progress on the Agreed Framework. Missiles had originally been excluded from the Framework. Powell said:

> ...First, the North must get out of the proliferation business and eliminate long-range missiles that threaten other countries...the North needs to move toward a less threatening conventional military posture...and living up to its past pledges to implement basic confidence-building measures.[20]

Adding to these remarks, then National Security Adviser Condoleezza Rice stated that North Korea had "aggressively pursued a covert program since 1999," and this referred to the Department of Energy Report indicating that the DPRK tried to buy frequency converters to be used in a gas centrifuge facility to enrich uranium.[21] Furthermore, in October 2002, Assistant Secretary of State for East Asian and Pacific Affairs, James Kelly, set off for two days of talks in Pyongyang with his North Korean counterparts. It is striking to note here that the US had not held any kind of dialogue with North Korea in more than eighteen months. Kelly informed the North Korean delegation that the US had evidence confirming the North's pursuit of a nuclear weapons programme. Initially, the North Koreans denied such allegations but returned the next day with a delegation led by Vice Foreign Minister Kang Sok Ju and asserted that they had the right to pursue such capabilities since the US president had already placed them in the "axis of evil".[22] Acting in accordance with its statements, the North expelled the IAEA inspectors in December 2002 and backed out of the agreement, leading to a nuclear stand-off between the two nations.

The North Koreans went ahead by taking a series of steps at the Yongbyon nuclear site that had been frozen under the 1994 Geneva Accord. They removed the seals at all frozen facilities (experimental reactor, storage building, reprocessing laboratory), dismantled IAEA monitoring cameras, and expelled the three IAEA international inspectors. In defiance of IAEA resolutions demanding that the North Koreans come back into compliance, on January 10, 2003, Pyongyang announced its withdrawal from the NPT.[23] The subsequent North Korean actions included tampering with the stored fuel rods, which were a source of weapons-grade plutonium; announcing plans to restart the experimental reactor; and conducting ballistic missile tests. These developments apparently suggested deliberate and purposeful moves in the direction of producing nuclear weapons.[24]

Acceptance of a North Korean nuclear weapons capability was inconsistent with vital US national security interests. Given North Korea's economic strains, it was conceived that Pyongyang might sell nuclear materials or weapons to other states or terrorists groups, taking the regional threat to a global level. The collapse of the Agreed Framework dealt a serious blow to the security situation in the Korean Peninsula and plunged it into yet another impasse marked by suspicion and mistrust. Along with the threat of selling sensitive nuclear technology, the US, time and again, accused Pyongyang of being involved in the sale of missile systems to nations that have been declared as states of "proliferation concern."

North Korean Missile Programme

Although Pyongyang incessantly claimed that it embarked upon an indigenous missile development programme, in reality, North Korea's missile aspirations started with Soviet and Chinese assistance, the first step in this direction being the production of a Chinese Type 63 (107mm) multiple rocket launcher (MRL).[25] During 1968-69, the DPRK received Soviet S-2 Sopka (SS-C-2b/Samlet) missiles for coastal defence; China assisted in the reorganisation and the expansion of the Samlet maintenance and assembly facilities. China also went on to supply HY-1 naval missiles, which were themselves reverse engineered from the Soviet SS-N-2 Styx missiles.[26] In a few cases, the North Koreans had to assemble the parts of the acquired missiles that were received in knocked down kits; this gave them much needed technical expertise in the field of missiles.

There were assertive assumptions that several hundred North Korean experts had been trained in plutonium separation and other nuclear technologies in China and the Soviet Union since the 1960s.[27] There was widespread belief that China too, could have assisted North Korea's ballistic missile programme. In 1972, a production facility for the indigenous manufacture of the HY-1/SY-1 was set up, that later was upgraded to produce HY-2 missiles, with a significant Chinese content of major components. By 1973, it was reported in the *Military Balance* that the DPRK possessed 24 unguided FROG-5/7 rockets and 6 SS-C-2b missiles.[28] In the mid-1970s, North Korea approached China with a proposal for the joint development of a single stage mobile tactical missile called the DF-61 with a maximum range of 600 km and a cluster/ fuel air explosive payload of one tonne, which was later, scrapped.[29] As a matter of fact, the Scud-C bears similarity to the DF- 61 system and there may, after all, have been a connection between the two programmes. North Korea received rocket engine design technology, production metallurgy and air frames from China to upgrade Scud missiles. The joint North-Korean-Chinese work on the DF-61 missile began but was abandoned later. Yet, it helped North Korea in gaining a breakthrough in some vital technological areas.[30]

Moreover, a Congressional Research Report stated that by reverse engineering Scud-B missiles bought in 1981, North Korea manufactured the Scud-Mod-A with a range of 280-300 km and a payload capacity of 1,000kg by 1984.[31] It was also reported that the Scud-C of North Korea is actually a modified version of the Russian Scud-B, originally supplied to Egypt.[32] Around that time, North Korea started trying to reverse-engineer the FROG-7 rocket, along with reverse-engineering the Scud B missile that Pyongyang received from Egypt coupled with MAZ 543 transported erector-launcher or TEL vehicles during the early 1980s. The Scud-C prototype was tested in 1987 in Hamgyong Namdo and production started in 1990, with a successful test in June 1990.

During 1989, North Korea embarked upon a programme to produce, what is now known as the Nodong-I missile that was capable of striking any part of South Korea. According to Kent E Calder, starting with basic Soviet Scuds, North Korea test-fired the indigenous, mobile Nodong -I in 1993. Since 1997, it has deployed the Nodong -I in substantial numbers. Simple in design, and difficult to preempt due to its mobility, the 1,300-km-range Nodong is viewed as a credible terror weapon against large cities in western Japan. Indeed, Japanese analysts continued to see the No Dong as the principal North Korean missile threat to Japan despite possible problems with its accuracy.[33] The testing of the Taepo Dong range of missiles, which has been discussed in detail later, followed the testing of the Nodong.

It became increasingly clear that the Scud was the keystone of all missiles fielded by Pyongyang. The Scud-B (Hwasong-5) and the Scud-C (Hwasong-6) were the first development programmes; the Nodong-I used a cluster of four Scud engines for increased range and the Taepo Dong presumably uses clusters of Scud engines in two stages to further enhance the range. There were indications that the Taepo Dong-I had a Nodong-I equivalent as its first stage and a Scud-B/C equivalent as the second; on the other hand, in the Taepo Dong II, the first stage was a Chinese CSS-2 equivalent (with the second stage remaining a Scud B/C type.) All the missiles were liquid-fuelled and marked with delayed operational mobility. The US intelligence community was convinced to a large extent that Chinese assistance had been instrumental in North Korea's missile achievements.

Fig 4.2: North Korean Nodong Missile

While estimating North Korean military capabilities is difficult, the economic decline appeared to have led to deterioration in the readiness, training, and equipment of North Korea's conventional forces over the past few years. According to David G Brown, various analysts in Washington believed that the production of most military equipment was at very low levels in 1998, with the exception of favoured sectors, including chemical weapons, missiles, and mini-submarines. With the Asian economic crisis, the contraction of Pyongyang's Gross Domestic Product (GDP) was perceived to be accelerating at an even faster pace. Although, the CIA's National Intelligence Estimate (NIE)-1995 on the missile threat to the US homeland concluded that the threat from the "rogue states" such as North Korea, Iran and Iraq was unlikely in the near future,[34] there were profound concerns within the US and the international community that in a desperate move, the North Koreans could become increasingly dependent on counterfeiting, drugs, and missile exports to various nations in order to raise foreign exchange.

As a matter of fact, the Clinton Administration engaged in missile talks with North Korea since 1996 during which Pyongyang offered to end its ballistic missile programme, i.e., the production, testing and export of medium- and long-range ballistic missiles.[35] During the Clinton years, three assumptions drove the United States policy vis-à-vis Pyongyang's WMD programmes. First, as long as the DPRK nuclear programme remained frozen under the Geneva Accord negotiated in 1994, the US would focus more on the evolving threat from the North Korean missile programme. Second, in contrast to Pyongyang's nuclear weapons programme, the missile issue did not involve DPRK violations of international agreements such as the NPT and the IAEA safeguards regime. Third, North Korea's ballistic missile programme was central to the global proliferation of missile technology.[36]

However, at the initiative of the Republicans in the US Congress who believed that the ballistic missile threat perception to the US could not be ignored or underestimated, a commission was set up under the chairmanship of Secretary of Defence Donald H Rumsfeld by legislation in 1997. The commission had to assess the nature and magnitude of the existing and emerging ballistic missile threat to the US. In preparing the report, the commission examined the ballistic missile threat posed to the fifty states in America. Its assessment included threats posed by ballistic missiles that were deployed on the territory of a potentially hostile country; launched from a surface vessel or submarine operating off the coasts of the US or from an aircraft; deployed by a potentially hostile nation on the territory of a third party to reduce the range required of its ballistic missiles to strike the United States.

The Rumsfeld Commission Report concluded that there were concerted efforts by a number of overtly or potentially hostile nations to acquire ballistic missiles with biological or nuclear payloads that posed a growing threat to the US; its deployed forces and its friends and allies. These newer developing threats in North Korea, Iran, Iraq and Libya were in addition to those still posed by the existing ballistic missiles arsenals of Russia and China, nations which the US now was not in conflict with, but which remained in uncertain transitions. The report went on to say that the "newer ballistic missile-equipped nations" capabilities would not match with those of US systems for accuracy or reliability. However, they would be able to inflict major destruction on America within about five years of a decision to acquire such a capability.[37]

The Rumsfeld Commission's findings, that were put forth in July 1998, appeared to have been vindicated when, within weeks of the report, North Korea, in a surprise move, test-fired a long-range version of its three-stage, solid-fuelled Taepo Dong-I missile on August 31, 1998. US policy-makers opined that while it probably would be several years before Pyongyang or Tehran would be able to deploy operational missiles capable of striking the US mainland, spread of WMD technologies to these countries, which were not particularly friendly to the US and which Washington described as the "world's least responsible states" or "rogue states" was being perceived as threatening to the US and its allies.

The August 31 missile test by North Korea surprised observers, and US sources first portrayed this as the launch of a two-stage Taepo Dong-I missile with a range of 1,200 miles. Pyongyang belatedly announced what it said was the successful launch of its first satellite by a three-stage rocket. Washington subsequently concluded that the test was a failed attempt to launch a small satellite. On the other hand, some analysts leaked estimates that the missile could have delivered a small payload to a distance of 3,000 miles. At a minimum, this first launch of a two-stage missile with a range of well over 1,000 miles represented a major advance for North Korea. If deployed and combined with a nuclear, chemical or biological warhead, this capability would represent a significant new and destabilising threat in Northeast Asia. Although Pyongyang generally tried to soften the impact of the launch by characterising it as a peaceful satellite launch, the military application was apparent.[38]

Fig 4.3: Potential North Korean Long-Range Missile Capabilities

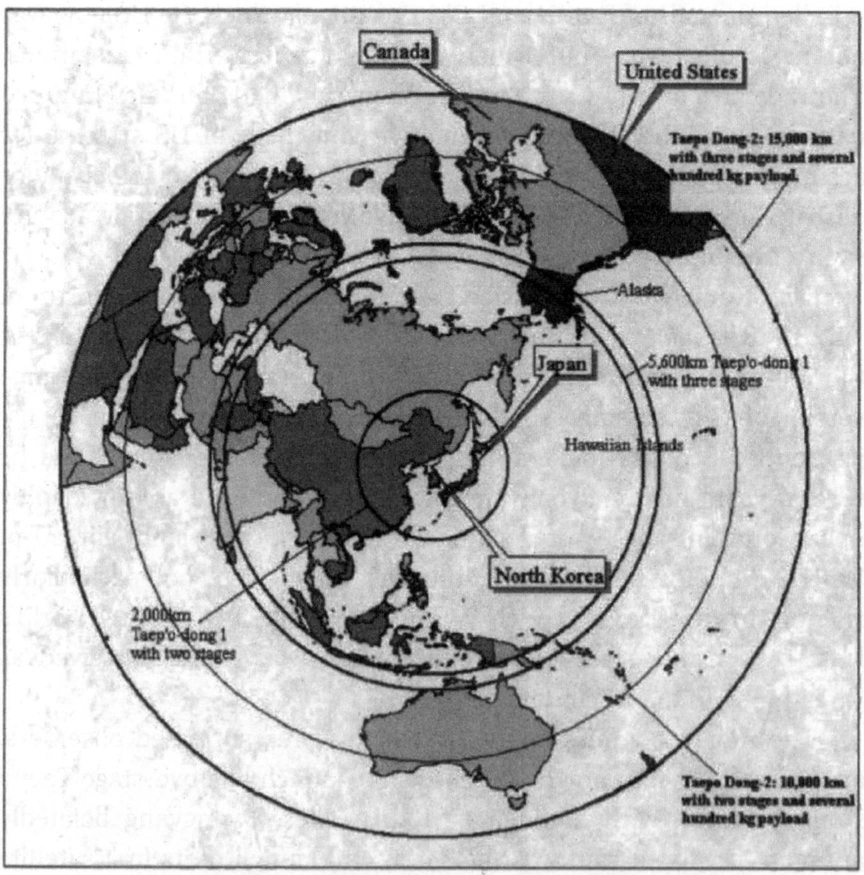

This Congressional Research Service map was updated on September 19, 2006
to reflect comments by the U.S. Intelligence Community.

It became evident that Pyongyang had decided to take on Washington with nuclear and missile brinkmanship in 1998-99, as it had in 1993-94. Although the testing of the Taepo Dong-I missile was a complete surprise to the international community, the Taepo Dong-II missile launch appeared to be the most awaited one. The confrontation was resolved when, in exchange for an on-the-spot inspection of its suspect underground nuclear site in Kumchang-ri in May 1999 and an agreement to suspend the threatened launch of the long-range ballistic missile Taepo Dong -II, capable of reaching parts of the United States with a nuclear weapon-sized payload in September 1999, the US promised Pyongyang substantial food aid and a partial lifting of US sanctions. It is widely believed that during this time-period, North Korea demanded compensation from the US in exchange for stopping the proliferation of missiles.[39] Prior to the demand, a four-member fact finding team of the US House of Representatives International Relations Committee was told during a visit to North Korea that it earned $500 million annually from the sale of ballistic missiles (whereas the US estimate was $1.5 billion).

Reacting to the testing of the Taepo Dong-I, Stanley O Roth, curtly stated, "The United States will not 'buy' compliance with the Agreed Framework." He went on to say that a second long-range missile test would have "serious consequences" and could well "jeopardize KEDO funding and other aspects of our relationship."[40] The Taepo Dong brinkmanship once again brought Pyongyang and Washington to direct bilateral talks in Berlin. The talks ended on September 12, 1999, and the subsequent agreement was termed as the "Berlin Agreement". It was agreed in principle that Washington would lift its sanctions on North Korea in exchange for Pyongyang suspending a Taepo Dong-II firing. In the wake of the Berlin Agreement, Pyongyang declared an official moratorium on Taepo Dong-II test-firing, while, at the same time, it launched no fewer than 43 international diplomatic 'missions' to break out of its self-imposed isolation.[41] In the process, the United States, between January and October 1999, provided food aid worth US $160 million to North Korea via the UN system, accounting for 84.5 percent of global aid to the DPRK amounting to US $190.1 million.[42]

Samuel S Kim considered that the North Korean missile brinkmanship highlighted the trend that when the actualisation of a nation's identity was blocked in one domain, it sought to compensate it in another. He further argued that from Pyongyang's perspective, nuclear and missile development was one of the few areas where it commanded an advantage in the politics of competitive legitimating on the divided Korean Peninsula.

In addition to compensatory deterrence, many strategists are of the view that the North Korean missile threat could be useful as a bargaining chip to extract more economic concessions, as free advertising via global prime time to prospective customers in the Middle East, and as a morale booster for the military at home. Having demonstrated its considerable missile power, Pyongyang may yet decide to trade such weapons for cash.

During August 2000, a CIA Report to the US Congress brought out the North Korea-Pakistan missile nexus. Later on, Kim Jong Il confirmed in front of the South Korean media that Pyongyang had indeed sold missiles to Pakistan, amongst others. Throughout this period, North Korea continued to export significant ballistic missile related equipment, components, materials, and technical expertise to the Middle East, South Asia, and North Africa. Pyongyang attached high priority to the development and sale of ballistic missiles and related technology. Exports of ballistic missiles and related technology were one of the North's major sources of hard currency, which supported ongoing missile development and production.[43] North Korea's behaviour furthered growing scepticism among various analysts in Washington over the validity and efficiency of international non-proliferation agreements such as the CTBT, the BWC, the MTCR, and the NPT itself. Although, in order to provide a legal framework for preventing incidents such as Yemen's 2002 purchase of North Korean Scud missiles, the US Congress threatened sanctions against North Korea with the Missile Threat Reduction Act of 2003. Congress had already stopped funding for fuel oil shipments to the North as part of the Financial Year (FY) 2003 foreign operations appropriations.[44]

In fact, a CIA Report cited that North Korea was not a party to the CWC. During the reporting period, Pyongyang continued to acquire dual-use chemicals that could potentially be used to support Pyongyang's long-standing chemical weapons programme. It went on to state that North Korea's chemical warfare capabilities included the ability to produce bulk quantities of nerve, blister, choking and blood agents, using its sizeable, although ageing, chemical industry. There were worries that North Korea possessed a stockpile of unknown size of these agents and weapons, which could be employed in a variety of delivery means. The CIA Report also gave details of the Biological and Toxin Weapons Convention to which North Korea had acceded, but nonetheless had pursued biological warfare (BW) capabilities since the 1960s. Pyongyang, reportedly, acquired dual-use biotechnical equipment, supplies and reagents that could be used to support North Korea's BW efforts. As of the first half of 2003, North Korea was believed to have possessed a munitions production infrastructure that would have allowed it to weaponise BW agents.[45]

Engagement Strategies: A Debate

The crisis over North Korea's nuclear programme made it evident that the global non-proliferation regime, symbolised by the NPT was inescapably breaking down. This brings us to the fundamental query as to what are the various engagement strategies employed by Washington to deal with the current nuke crisis in North Korea.

An Independent Task Force Report published in 1998, suggested that a bolder approach to North Korea needed to be put forth that was premised on robust deterrence and acknowledgement that the United States did not seek the absorption or destruction of the North and that the policy should move beyond these initial assumptions. The report went on to explain explicitly that following the lead already established by South Korea, the US should expand contacts with the North, including making modest adjustments to US sanctions policy, which could accelerate the forces of positive change. The US should then join with South Korea in offering a larger package of reciprocal moves—beyond those already on the table—that might induce the North to make significant changes in its policies. Finally, the US should be ready to walk away from any expanded assistance to the North (beyond those areas already stipulated in the existing agreements) if Pyongyang rejected the opportunity for reconciliation and threat reduction. The report also stressed on a coordinated approach with Japan and improved consultation with China and Russia in policy toward North Korea.[46]

Against the backdrop of the clear and continuing proliferation threats from Pyongyang, along with a Republican-dominated Congress in Washington, in November 1998, President Clinton established a North Korea Policy Review Team, led by William J Perry, to conduct an extensive review of US policy toward the DPRK. The Perry Report recommended a comprehensive and integrated two-path strategy, having profound implications for the future of US-DPRK relations.[47]

The Perry Report stated that acquisition by North Korea of nuclear weapons or long-range missiles and especially the combination of the two could undermine the relative stability and cause extensive damage, if deterrence failed. Acquisition of such weapons by North Korea could also spark an arms race in the region and would surely do grave damage to the global non-proliferation regimes covering nuclear weapons and ballistic missiles. A continuation of the DPRK's pattern of selling its missiles for hard currency could also spread destabilising effects to other regions, such as the Middle East. The policy review team made key findings that stated that the DPRK's acquisition of nuclear weapons and continued development, testing, deployment and export of long-range missiles would undermine the relative stability of deterrence on the Korean Peninsula, a precondition for ending the Cold War and pursuing a lasting peace in the longer run. These activities by the DPRK could also have serious regional and global consequences adverse to vital US interests. The report went on to say that the US must pursue its objectives with respect to nuclear weapons and ballistic missiles in the DPRK without taking actions that would weaken deterrence or increase the probability of DPRK's miscalculation. Moreover, if stability could be preserved through the cooperative ending of the DPRK's nuclear weapons and long-range missile-related activities, the US should be prepared to establish more normal diplomatic relations with the DPRK and join in the Republic of Korea's policy of engagement and peaceful coexistence. Furthermore, the Perry Report said that unfreezing Yongbyon was North Korea's quickest and surest path to acquisition of nuclear weapons. The Agreed Framework, therefore, should be preserved and implemented by the United States and its allies. With the Agreed Framework, the DPRK's ability to produce plutonium at Yongbyon was verifiably frozen.

Without the Agreed Framework, however, it was estimated that the North could reprocess enough plutonium to produce a significant number of nuclear weapons per year. There was an increasing sense that no US policy toward the DPRK would succeed if South Korea and Japan did not actively support it and cooperate in its implementation. There were hopes that securing such trilateral coordination should be possible, since the interests of the three parties, while not identical, overlapped in significant and definable ways. In its concluding remarks, the report considered the risks inherent in the situation and viewed the isolation, suspicion, and negotiating style of the DPRK. A successful US policy would require steadiness and persistence in the face of provocations. The approach adopted now must be sustained in the future, beyond the term of this Administration.

The Perry Committee recommendations, which went on to become the Clinton Administration's key policy on North Korea, rejected the strategy of "buying objectives." It argued for example, that the DPRK offered to cease its missile exports if the US agreed to compensate it for the foregone earnings from missile exports. The policy review team firmly believed that that such a policy of trading material compensation for security would only encourage the DPRK to further blackmail, and would encourage proliferators worldwide to engage in similar blackmail.

Instead, a two-path strategy combining a comprehensive and integrated approach was recommended. The first path would include the US seeking the complete and verifiable cessation of testing, production and deployment of missiles exceeding the parameters of the Missile Technology Control Regime, and the complete cessation of export sales of such missiles and the equipment and technology associated with them. By negotiating the complete cessation of the DPRK's destabilising nuclear weapons and long-range missile programmes, this path would lead to a stable security situation on the Korean Peninsula. Hopeful that the DPRK would move to eliminate its nuclear and long-range missile threats, the US could consider normalising relations with the DPRK and relax sanctions that have long constrained trade with Pyongyang. The second path of this twin-fold strategy would be to contain the threat that the US has been unable to eliminate through negotiation. Prudence drove this part of the strategy. The report emphasised that the Agreed Framework should remain intact and a direct conflict should be avoided. This, however, was not meant to be, and as has already been discussed above, the Agreed Framework fell apart, leading to a nuclear impasse between Washington and Pyongyang.[48]

The difficulty with this approach was that the key criterion for judging whether or not North Korea was following the path of engagement—Pyongyang's willingness to give up its WMD programmes in a verifiable way—required North Korea to give up its most important piece of negotiating leverage at the beginning of the process.[49] The Agreed Framework attempted to work around this problem by structuring the agreement as a series of reciprocal steps that would eventually produce transparency about North Korea's nuclear history. The Perry recommendations were never fully put into practice.

The Bush Administration inherited from the Clinton Administration a policy that involved a bilateral agreement between Washington and Pyongyang that would have provided certain economic and political benefits for North Korea in return for dismantling its nuclear weapons programme. In coordination with the "sunshine policy" favoured by then South Korean President Kim Dae-jung, the long-term American goal was to promote a so-called "soft landing" in which North Korea would gradually engage in a programme of reform and opening similar to that undertaken by China in the post-Mao years.[50] Significantly, President Bush had been sceptical about North Korea's supposed peaceful intentions. In his state of the union address on January 29, 2002, Bush announced his Administration's tough new approach to, what he termed as the "axis of evil": North Korea, Iran and Iraq. In fact, the Bush Administration's approach towards the Northeast Asian nation was often termed as "hawk engagement", by many analysts. The Bush Administration set up three policy guidelines in dealing with the North Korean nuclear weapons and missile issues: transparency, verification and reciprocity.

Moreover, the Bush team claimed that there were five elements in its policy that were indeed distinct from Clinton's: insistence on improved implementation of the Agreed Framework; verifiable controls on the North's missile production and exports; a way to address the posture of conventional forces; a demand for reciprocal gestures in return for compromises with the North; and close coordination with allies. Moreover, Victor D Cha is of the view that the "hawk engagement" approach acknowledged that diplomacy could be helpful, but saw engagement as the real way to expose the North's true, malevolent intentions—thought to include not just the desire to develop nuclear, biological and chemical weapons, but untimately to expel US forces from the peninsula, overthrow the regime in Seoul, and reunify Korea under Communist rule.[51] Hawk engagement aimed to thwart these goals not only by dealing with Pyongyang in the near term but also by laying the groundwork for punitive actions against it later on. Given below is a tabular presentation of the various approaches to the North Korean nuclear issue that have emerged during the course of the post-Cold War period (Table 4.1).

Table 4.1: Approaches to the North Korean Nuclear Issue

	Views on North Korea	Nuclear Intention	Solutions	Proponents
1. Collapse	Axis of evil; immoral state .	Nuclear arming; threat to peace.	Regime change; military measures; Iraqi model.	US neo-conservatives; first George W Bush Administration.
2. Non-Engagement	Rogue state; problem state.	Nuclear arming for survival.	Sanctions; neglect; Libyan model.	US Republicans during the 1990s.
3. Negotiation	Rational country.	Negotiation card and/or nuclear arming.	Negotiations; reciprocity and verification; Ukrainian model.	Second George W Bush Administration; Roh Moo-hyun government.

4. Sunshine	Fraternal country; divided half to be unified.	Negotiation card.	Security assurances first; no military measure and diplomacy only.	Kim Dae-jung government.

Source: Bong-Geun Jun, *Arms Control Today,* vol.36, no.1, January/February 2006.

The Bush Administration believed that hawk engagement provided a way to convince allies that non-coercive strategies have already been tried—and have failed. The Richard L Armitage Report, tabled in the US House of Representatives in March 1999, titled "A Comprehensive Approach to North Korea" impacted significantly on the materialisation of Bush's North Korean policy goals, that "the failure of enhanced diplomacy should be demonstrably attributable to Pyongyang." The report stated that North Korean missiles had become far more dangerous and that the United States must, in the near future, end Pyongyang's missile testing and exporting. In addition, the report stipulated that the US needed to propose a six-party meeting to deal with the security of Korea. The report continued that if diplomatic negotiation with North Korea failed, the policy options that the US could take would either strengthen deterrence and containment, or preemption.[52] One of the attributes that made hawk engagement different from the other approaches was by being compatible with missile defence. There was a belief that missile defence could actually strengthen the credibility of engagement strategies. After all, engagement was most effective when undergirded by robust defensive capabilities.[53] On this point, the Armitage Report very categorically stated: "One could not expect North Korea to take US diplomacy seriously unless it demonstrated unambiguously that it was, in fact, prepared to bolster its...military posture."[54]

There was growing belief among the supporters of this form of engagement that if missile defence and engagement were pursued simultaneously, Washington could encourage Pyongyang's better behaviour and also neutralise Kim Jong Il's strong card: his ballistic missiles and the threat they posed to the other countries in the region. Another distinct principle of hawk engagement was its insistence on the exchange of tangible compromises. This emphasis was demonstrated by President Bush's inclusion of conventional force reductions on the bilateral agenda with North Korea. However, the revelations made by Pyongyang in October 2002 made the international community ponder on the existing engagement strategies. The US in this backdrop could continue a policy of pressure in the hope that the North would buckle down to the US pressure or collapse ultimately from internal weakness. It had become increasingly clear that North Korea's revived nuclear programme was consistent with its attempts to assure its own security.

Moreover, the Armitage Report also affirmed that there were no signs that the Kim Jong Il regime was contemplating any radical market-oriented reforms. Instead, forced by necessity it seemingly was experimenting at the margins with modest reforms to alleviate food shortages at the local level and gain hard currency, with Chinese aid and a variety of hard currency schemes—missile exports, counterfeiting, narcotics trafficking. The report went on to stress that a new approach to North Korea would necessarily test China's intentions. Beijing was helpful in the process leading to the Agreed Framework and the US publicly cited that cooperation was a major pay-off of its China policy.[55]

According to the admission of Assistant Secretary of State James A Kelly, "Pyongyang's acknowledgement of a covert uranium enrichment programme required us to adjust policy midstream by recognising that in this instance, bilateral diplomacy had failed. We now adhere to the principle that multilateral diplomacy is the best way to ensure that North Korea lives up to its international commitments and obligations."[56] The Bush Administration undertook a more multilateral approach to the North Korean nuke crisis, in which Pyongyang would be subject to concerted pressure from Japan, South Korea, Russia and China along with the US. Moreover, President Bush had been far less willing than his predecessor Clinton to provide North Korea with positive inducements so as to eliminate its capacity to produce weapons of mass destruction.

And, to at least some in the Bush Administration, the collapse of the North Korean regime through a so-called 'hard landing' was preferable to a programme of economic aid or engagement that might increase Pyongyang's political longevity and enhance its national power. However, the Bush Administration had not gone as far as to undertake a preventive war against the North Korean WMD capacity, let alone to attempt regime change by force.[57]

After much diplomatic deliberations, and a significant role played by China, the six-party talks that included North Korea, South Korea, Japan, China, Russia and the United States, hosted by Beijing got underway in 2003 to resolve the ongoing North Korean nuclear impasse. The six-party talks harnessed the diplomatic leverage of the parties most directly affected by the DPRK's proliferation to Washington's effort to dismantle in a permanent, thorough and transparent manner, all of North Korea's nuclear programmes.

China, Japan, Russia and arguably even South Korea would have preferred a muddling North Korea to a nuclear-armed unified state on the Korean Peninsula. China, Russia and Japan might have preferred continuing economic engagement with South Korea and willingness to expand some resources to maintain North Korea as an allied buffer state. It seemed increasingly clear that China had begun to pick up some of the slack left by Russia, North Korea's former patron, though the extent to which Chinese exports of food and other essentials were available on concessional terms remained unclear. Nor was it known what kind of economic or foreign policy conditions were attached to these exports. Beijing's dual goals of continued support for the North and enhanced economic engagement with the South were always considered a delicate diplomatic conundrum.[58]

Whatsoever may be the orientations, whether hawkish or dovish, the US always seemed to want to engage North Korea by elevating the dialogue to the level of a president-appointed special coordinator on the DPRK policy. It appeared that the US policy was treading towards orchestrating international pressure to force North Korea to dismantle its nuclear weapons programme.

Assessing China's Role in the Existing Tangle

Aside from North Korea itself, the key players in the North Korean nuke crisis were the PRC and US. The relationship between China and North Korea was solidified early during the three-year Korean War in the early Fifties. Chinese forces remained on the peninsula for an additional five years until 1958. Finally, an alliance was formalised in July 1961 when Beijing and Pyongyang signed a Treaty of Friendship, Cooperation and Mutual Assistance. The agreement committed one country to aid the other if attacked. Beijing and Pyongyang shared ideological affinity, having weathered the collapse of Communism in Eastern Europe and the Soviet Union. As two of the handful of the world's "Last Leninists," the continued existence of the other was of considerable importance.[59]

China's late paramount leader, Deng Xiaoping, set the tone for much of China's foreign policy in the 1990s when he cautioned Chinese strategists to "keep a low profile and avoid taking the lead."[60] For better or for worse, this saying came to define China's approach to the ominous North Korean nuclear quandary. Although China had significant interest in seeing a peaceful resolution to the ongoing impasse, it found itself severely constrained from taking a more open and proactive role with Pyongyang. China aimed to prevent rapid changes of the political situation in Pyongyang that would lead to less-than-positive outcomes for Chinese strategic interests.[61]

According to David M Lampton, China's principal interest in the Korean Peninsula throughout the 1990s was to avoid three things: a nuclearised peninsula, war that would destabilise the entire region, and a tide of North Korean refugees in Northeast China, fleeing bloodshed, starvation and pestilence. Washington, with 37,000 troops on or near the 38th parallel separating North from South Korea, shared Beijing's aversion to a breakdown on the peninsula.[62] With North Korea on its doorstep, Beijing had to place Pyongyang's nuclear ambitions within a calculus of other, often more important concerns in Northeast Asia and on the Korean Peninsula. All these decisions carried more weight for China than for the United States.

Following Pyongyang's declaration in 2002 of nuclear capability, China recognised that a nuclear-armed North Korea presented a threat to regional stability and China's long-term interests. Rather than seeing a direct threat aimed at China, however, Beijing's concerns focussed primarily on the potential ripple effects throughout Northeast Asia in reaction to a nuclear-armed North Korea. Also, Beijing had a strong interest in avoiding disruptions in its beneficial economic relations with South Korea. In addition, China and South Korea were major trading partners with one another, and South Korea was a significant direct investor in China's manufacturing sector, creating Chinese jobs, adding value to both Chinese and Korean raw materials, and contributing to China's export revenues.[63] More critically, as the provider of 70 percent of North Korea's conventional fuel, China refused to seriously condemn Pyongyang's nuclear weapons programme or exert diplomatic and economic pressure on North Korea, despite repeated appeals to do so from the United States and others.[64] Indeed, in December 2002, shortly after Pyongyang announced its plans to restart the mothballed plutonium-producing reactors, US intelligence officials revealed that a Chinese company sold North Korea 20 tonnes of the chemical tributyl phosphate, which could be used to turn spent nuclear fuel into plutonium for atomic weapons.[65]

Since the end of the Cold War, the Korean Peninsula witnessed the PRC cultivating economic and diplomatic ties with South Korea. At least until the onset of the current ongoing nuke crisis, China's strategy seemed to consist of the following elements: stabilise the North; promote a gradual process of reconciliation and reunification between the North and South in which China itself would play an increasingly central role; cultivate ties with Seoul and move towards an outcome that would leave a unified Korea leaning heavily toward China and increasingly independent of the US. With the Taiwan and Korea issues settled, Japan would stand alone, and the justification for its continuing alliance with the US (except as an open counterweight to Chinese power) would be open to question.[66]

However, in case the world witnessed a nuclear North Korea, it would upset East Asia's entire military balance, causing South Korea, Japan and even Taiwan to consider developing equivalent deterrents.[67] Byung-joon Ahn advocated the case of South Korea and stated that in such a scenario, China, as it "enjoys the best relations with Pyongyang," should be pressed to persuade Kim Jong Il to abandon the nuclear ambitions. The entire Korean Peninsula had been pushed into a period of grave uncertainty.[68]

American and Chinese preferences regarding the North Korean nuclear issue probably did converge, at least to some degree. Both sides were obviously eager to avoid war although, given its proximity and its worries about the implications for its own domestic stability, China was more worried about this prospect than the US. Other things being equal, China appeared to prefer a situation where Kim Jong Il did not openly acquire nuclear weapons, in large part because of its fears about the possible US response. Given its regional commitments and global concerns, Washington was more concerned about this scenario than Beijing. To the extent that the Chinese became convinced that North Korea's actions would lead to further proliferation in Northeast Asia. While the PRC's preferences may be changing, in the light of its own history as an early nuclear "rogue" state, its past assistance to Pakistan, and what could be construed as a record of relative passivity in the face of North Korea's pursuit of nuclear weapons, there are reasons to think that Chinese observers do not regard the prospects of further proliferation with quite the same visceral dread as their American counterparts.[69]

It would be significant to state here that China has never appeared too ardent to stretch the limits by alienating its Communist ally by imposing sanctions. Even though the US intelligence community was long convinced regarding Chinese assistance being instrumental in North Korea's missile achievements, it realised that getting support from Beijing would be crucial to deal with Pyongyang, since China is North Korea's main ally and trading partner. China currently provides tens of millions of dollars' worth of aid to North Korea. Two-way trade with China constitutes about one-third of North Korea's entire trade. Pyongyang's imports from China since 1985 have hung around between approximately $260 million and $600 million annually. Although, estimates of foreign trade statistics suggest that North Korea's foreign trade declined by 55 percent from 1990 to 1997, there have been numerous reports that considerable official and unofficial cross-border trade with China goes unreported, and North Korea's weapons sales too, are not included in most trade estimates.

More critically, the period between 1995-98 saw massive floods devastate an already weakened North Korean economy, with China contributing an estimated $200 million worth of food aid annually. China is also the provider of 70 percent of North Korea's conventional fuel. Chinese President Jiang Zemin visited Pyongyang in September 2000, and agreed to provide grants of 30,000 tonnes of diesel oil and 400,000 tonnes of coal. In addition to this, Pyongyang obtained a promise of receiving 200,000 tonnes of food from Beijing. There have been overriding concerns in Beijing to prevent economic or military crises that would lead to thousands of North Korean refugees fleeing across the 1,400-km border into China. There are already an estimated 300,000 North Koreans illegally residing in China in addition to economic refugees continually crossing the border to seek opportunities in China, placing increased pressure on the Chinese economy.

China always seems to have been apprehensive that isolating North Korea might cause its regime to collapse, which, in turn, could witness harmful strategic consequences. From Beijing's perspective, it is apprehensive that if there comes a moment which leads to the collapse of the Kim Jong Il regime in North Korea, Pyongyang will end up simply being absorbed by the South. This could leave China with a unified neighbour, under the control of a democratic government most likely be allied to the United States, a situation that Beijing in all probability would be absolutely averse to. Beijing would want see the Kim Jong Il regime survive in North Korea, and in addition to this, Beijing envisages itself in a position of having brokered some sort of agreement in Northeast Asia leading to enhancement of its stature as a peace-maker, a regional power and most significantly, a responsible player on the global platform.

From Beijing's perspective, if a sequence of events was set in motion that quickly led to the collapse of the Kim Jong Il regime, North Korea would end up simply being absorbed by the South. This could leave China with a unified neighbour, under the control of a democratic government that would most likely still be allied to the US.[70] China also feared that isolating North Korea would cause its regime to collapse, with the harmful strategic consequences. Various analysts were of the view that unchecked North Korean proliferation could trigger nuclear weapons programmes across Northeast Asia, with damaging implications for Asian peace and security. Significantly, Beijing viewed North Korea as a crucial buffer state when Chinese President Jiang Zemin told his North Korean hosts in September 2001, during a three-day visit to Pyongyang, that because China was "close to the Korean Peninsula, it was concerned about the development of the situation on the peninsula and had consistently worked to maintain peace and stability on the peninsula."

North Korea and the nuclear problem remained front and centre for the US as a critical issue. One could postulate at least three options with respect to an outcome. One of these would be the use of force; the second, a de facto US acceptance of the North Korean nuclear capability; and the third, a negotiated solution. The first two options were difficult to envisage.[71] The option for a negotiated solution seemed to be the only pertinent solution to resolve the North Korean nuke crisis, and the six-party talks have been viewed as a step in the right direction in this regard. In a way, the Chinese diplomatic prestige was tested during the launch of the six-party mechanism, with Foreign Minister Li Zhaoxing asserting time and again, that the six-party process was the only "realistic and viable course," for resolving the nuclear stand-off.

What appeared lucid was that any likely solution would have to fall into the category of a grand bargain. North Korea was expected to re-freeze its plutonium-based programme and dismantle its uranium-based programme with all of the verification and intrusive onsite inspection necessary to ensure that there would be no danger of future violations of any follow-on agreement. On its side, the North clearly wished to receive a written non-aggression commitment from the United States, a repeal of US sanctions against it which North Korea, in a highly unrealistic way, seemed to believe was solely responsible for its economic collapse, and a serious and large provision of economic assistance, with Japan and South Korea helping Washington to provide the bulk of that aid.[72]

Beijing had vital interests on the Korean Peninsula, and many believed that it played a significant role in keeping North Korea afloat, providing over one million tonnes of food to the North in 1997. Earlier, in 1996, the US and the Republic of Korea in a joint communiqué proposed four-party talks to reduce tension on the Korean Peninsula and to achieve permanent peace. China responded affirmatively to the four-party talks proposal, which, however, ended in a stalemate because of North Korea's demands for a huge US food commitment and US troop withdrawal. By virtue of this, it did seem that Beijing was willing to cooperate with the United States at that stage of the diplomacy to avert instability and massive refugee flows across the Yalu, leading to increased influence over events in Korea, and to stabilise the ongoing turmoil.

During the period ranging from 1996-98, Beijing modulated its food and resource shipments to Pyongyang in an attempt to moderate North Korea's behaviour, thereby seeking to stabilise a seriously deteriorating situation in the DPRK.[73] Tensions in the China-North Korea relationship reportedly emerged during this time period over North Korea's unmet demands for Chinese aid or Chinese pressure on North Korea to reform. According to one account, in early 1996, Pyongyang asked for a substantial amount of grain and Beijing responded by offering only its one-tenth. Kim Jong Il was said to have been incensed and threatened to play the "Taiwan card"—that is, develop a relationship with Beijing's nemesis—unless China was forthcoming on an even broader set of demands. Beijing said that it regretted that it was unable to meet all these requests but did offer a more comprehensive aid package, including grain and interest-free loans.[74]

The Bush Administration entered office seemingly committed to the realist proposition that some degree of conflict with a rising China would be inevitable. Where the Clinton Administration had expressed the hope that China could become a "constructive strategic partner" of the United States, the Bush Administration described Beijing as a "strategic competitor", whose growing military power was deemed to be the most important challenge facing America in Asia.[75] With the passage of time, and after weighing all options, China appeared increasingly open to the possibility of multilateral talks. During the first phone conversation between President George W Bush and newly appointed President Hu Jintao on March 18, 2003, the Chinese official media quoted Hu as saying, "The key lies in launching some form of dialogue as soon as possible, especially dialogue between the United States and the DPRK."[76] With the advent of trilateral discussions in Beijing at the end of April, Chinese leaders took their farthest step yet toward becoming fully invested partners in a multilateral approach to this issue. Moreover, in advocating dialogue, Beijing was sending signals on its opposition to applying coercive means such as sanctions or force against North Korea. Even though China appeared to play an instrumental role in bringing Washington and Pyongyang back to the negotiating table, the talks did not bear much fruit and the stand-off persisted.

China appeared to have played an effective role as the mediator as well as the host of the six-party talks in August 2003, which was seen as a stepping-stone to resolve the ongoing impasse. Due to the existent high level of mistrust between the United States and North Korea, China fitted the bill of being the perfect mediator. China's active role in the six-party talks also coincided with its interest in being perceived as a responsible leader in Northeast Asia working toward regional peace and stability and not as a regional hegemon. Although the creation of the six-party negotiating mechanism in 2003 was a positive development, it did not yield tangible results. While the talks did enable the United States to more closely engage China on the issue of North Korea's nuclear future, it remained unclear how far Beijing could or was willing to go in pressuring North Korea to abandon its programme. China appeared averse to the idea of regime collapse in Pyongyang or a war between the United States and North Korea that could result in US troops being placed on the Chinese border.

A high degree of continuity in broad American objectives in the Northeast Asian region was expected, but the priorities assigned to different objectives, and the strategies adopted to achieve them, could continue to change, depending on the geo-political realities and conditions on the ground in Asia, during the second term of the Bush Administration. In conclusion, it seemed that the US was engaged in a long-term struggle for position and preponderance with China in the Northeast Asia region. By maintaining a strong military presence in the region, bolstering its ties to democratic allies and working to promote cooperation among them, the US hoped to be able to counter-balance the PRC's rising power. Discerning China's preferences for the future of North Korea did appear complex. There were fears in Beijing that the process of Pyongyang's collapse would be unmanageable, and the outcome would be a Northeast Asian power configuration not in China's favour.

According to Andrew Scobell, Beijing believes that the status quo was simply not sustainable indefinitely. At the same time, China seemed to be in favour of a gradual change in North Korea and hoped to nurture the emergence of a reform-minded North Korea that would resuscitate its economy, draw down its massive military and initiate threat-reduction and confidence-building measures on the peninsula. There were persistent concerns with China that a continued United States military presence in Northeast Asia would raise a likely alternative—as in resurgence of Japanese military power. In the final analysis, however, any successful medium- and long-term cooperating strategy had to be systemic, consistent and congruent across different areas of policy-making as well as between domestic and foreign policies.[77]

Wrapping up the discussion, it is significant to mention that looking at the chances for a cooperative settlement of the nuclear weapons programme, several critical issues come to mind, the most important being the verification question. If left unresolved, verification might block any future agreement, just as it blocked progress on implementation of the Geneva Agreement in the past. The core problem was that Pyongyang appeared unwilling to open up its nuclear past because if it indeed did, it would have lost its prime bargaining chip with regard to the outside world—something that it was absolutely not prepared to do.

Ramifications of a Nuclear Pyongyang

October 9, 2006, went down in history as the date on which the world community witnessed what had long been suspected, speculated, and to a certain extent feared, when North Korea successfully tested a nuclear device by conducting an underground nuclear test and thereby changed the orientation of the crisis altogether. After having been involved in the six-party negotiations aimed at bringing about a breakthrough to the nuclear impasse for three years, Pyongyang stunned the world by testing a plutonium-based nuclear weapon and becoming the latest entrant to the world's nuclear club. The North Korean Foreign Ministry somewhat grandly claimed that the country had made a great leap forward in the building of a great, prosperous, powerful socialist nation, characterising the test as "a self-defensive counter-measure against the United States' daily increasing nuclear threat and financial sanctions against it."[78]

On the other hand, the US reacted to the nuclear tests by stating that it would continue to strive for implementation of the September 2005 Joint Statement which resulted from the six-party talks, offering North Korea a clear path to a positive future and concrete benefits in return for carrying out its commitment to denuclearise.[79] "We call on all five members of the Six-Party talks and the United Nations Security Council—as stated in United Nations Security Council Resolution 1695—to exert every effort to persuade North Korea that the test of a nuclear weapon would only bring its further isolation and would not be in the interest of the North Korean people."[80] Earlier, sensing the reality of a nuclear North Korea, there were apprehensions that such a situation would upset East Asia's entire military balance, causing South Korea, Japan and even Taiwan to consider developing equivalent deterrents.[81] However, this indeed became a reality and the entire Korean Peninsula was pushed into a period of grave uncertainty.

Since the announcement of the resumption of the six-party talks by Assistant Secretary of State and chief US negotiator Christopher Hill on January 19, 2007, it was expected that Pyongyang would follow through on its disarmament agreement made subsequently on February 13, with Hill expressing hope that Pyongyang would meet the mid-April

2007 deadline set by the deal to halt operations at its Yongbyon nuclear reactor and readmit IAEA inspectors.[82] In return, North Korea would reportedly receive 50,000 tonnes of heavy fuel for energy use initially and eventually receive one million tonnes of heavy fuel or equivalent energy aid if it permanently closed its nuclear facilities and completely disbanded its atomic weapons programme. The US, China, Japan, South Korea and Russia reportedly reached tentative agreements to provide North Korea with $400 million in fuel oil and aid in return for North's starting to dismantle its nuclear facilities and allow inspectors back into country. The North would, for now, hold onto an arsenal that the US believes contains more than six nuclear weapons or fuel. It has to be acknowledged that North Korea has successfully manoeuvred to bring the region back to its former status quo.[83]

In what was widely presumed to be an indication of its intent at bringing the nuclear weapons programme to a standstill, North Korea blew up a 60-foot cooling tower at North Korea's largest nuclear facility at Yongbyon, 60 miles north of Pyongyang on June

Fig 4.4: The cooling tower at the Yongbyon nuclear complex, North Korea, on December 18, 2007 (Xinhua Photo).

27, 2008. The destruction of the tower ended when the towering structure collapsed into a large heap of debris while being witnessed by international and regional television broadcasters. North Korea's handing over the inventory of its nuclear programme paves the way for its removal from the US' terror blacklist and Washington responded to the same after receiving confirmation that North Korea had indeed handed over the details of its nuclear facilities to China. Commenting on the developments, White House spokesperson Dana Perino said, "The United States welcomes the North Korean declaration of its nuclear programme and will respond to North Korea's actions by announcing our intent to rescind North Korea's designation as a state sponsor of terror." Subsequently, this statement was stamped with the final approval by US President George W Bush while he addressed the media at the White House and stated, "North Korean officials submitted a declaration of their nuclear programme to the Chinese government as part of the six-party talks and thereby I am issuing a proclamation that lifts the provisions of the Trading with the Enemy Act with respect to North Korea. Secondly, I am notifying Congress of my intent to rescind North Korea's designation as a state sponsor of terror in 45 days. The next 45 days will be an important period for North Korea to show its seriousness of its cooperation. This can be a moment of opportunity for North Korea. If North Korea continues to make the right choices, it can repair its relationship with the international community—much as Libya has done over the past few years." Just as news of the announcement by Washington trickled in, Pyongyang welcomed its removal from the US' terrorism list and removal of sanctions and the North Korean Foreign Ministry issued a statement through the official Korean Central News Agency stating, "The US measure should lead to a complete and all-out withdrawal of its hostile policy toward [North Korea] so that the denuclearisation process can proceed smoothly."

Obviously, Washington appears wary of North Korea and is approaching the entire process with caution given the endless history of sporadic and fitful deliberations on the North's nuclear programme. And, thus, detailed verification of the disclosures made by Kim Jong

Fig 4.5: The debris after the Democratic People's Republic of Korea destroyed the cooling tower at its nuclear complex in Yongbyon, on June 27, 2008.

Il's regime would be particularly vital in the near future. Even though there is reason to believe that the Kim Jong Il regime now seems ready to go ahead towards disarmament, there are numerous questions that remain unanswered, numerous possibilities that still are under a thick realm of uncertainty. These include the fact that although the sanctions under the provisions of the Trading with the Enemy Act have been lifted, sanctions that North Korea faces for its human rights violations, the conducting of its nuclear test in 2006 and its weapons proliferation will all stay in effect. In addition, all United Nations Security Council sanctions also will be firmly in place. The US and other nations involved in resolving the nuclear stalemate would have to address various significant realities on the ground vis-à-vis Pyongyang's nuclear journey. These include resolving outstanding questions on its highly enriched uranium and proliferation activities as well as relinquishing its already separated stock of plutonium.

As of February 2007, North Korea had a total estimated plutonium stock of between 46 and 64 kg, of which about 28-50 kg are estimated to be in separated form, and usable in nuclear weapons. The vast majority of North Korea's separated plutonium—at least 80 per cent—was produced since North Korea's freeze on production and reprocessing ended in late 2002.[84] Therefore, it would not be prudent to be too optimistic about the sealing and shutdown of the Yongbyon reactor and the destruction of the cooling tower.

Testament to this argument was the North Korean negotiators yet again repeating the pattern of hard bargaining by refusing to participate in the latest round of multilateral negotiations launched in early 2007, saying they were waiting for the transfer of $25 million that had been frozen at a bank in Macau since 2005 due to US accusations of North Korean money laundering and counterfeiting. North Korea has repeatedly said it will not begin implementing the six-nation disarmament accord signed on February 13, 2007, until the money is safely back in its hands. This could well be considered as an erroneous move since giving new incentives and pulling sanctions off would be perceived by Pyongyang and the world as a reward for defying the world and going nuclear. This might just be a triggering point for nations such as Iran that are in the midst of a controversial weapons programme. A steep uphill task is round the corner, with the only difference being that the North Koreans now have actually gained nuclear ability as opposed to the earlier situation of possessing the capability to perhaps go nuclear.[85] A nuclear-armed North Korea has fundamentally altered the geo-political picture in Northeast Asia. A nuclear arms race among Japan, South Korea, and even Taiwan could likely ensue to the detriment of China's own long-term security interests, which would, in turn, weaken the global non-proliferation initiative. Given North Korea's record of selling weaponry and nuclear technology abroad, its proclivities for brinkmanship and the likely domino effect of nuclear proliferation in East Asia, in all it makes the state of affairs even more hazardous.[86] There is increasing belief among some Western analysts that the US and its regional partners, South Korea, Japan, China and Russia should offer Pyongyang carrots but threaten sticks if it remains obstinate.

Indeed, the balance of equations in the Asian context shifted noticeably in the aftermath of North Korea going nuclear with the insecurities of nations such as Japan having risen many notches higher since Pyongyang went nuclear as well as the after the July 2006 missile tests conducted by the Kim Jong Il regime. This sentiment was visibly demonstrated in the statement issued by the Japanese Foreign Ministry when it announced, "In view of the development, deployment and proliferation of ballistic missiles in the region, and the clear and present threats such as the recent missile launches by North Korea in particular, the Government of Japan will continue to do utmost to build up its BMD capabilities in close cooperation with the USG (United States Government) and with a sense of urgency."[87] The Japanese government decided to fund joint technical research on TMD with the US followed by an agreement in August 1999 to launch a five-year research and development programme, focussing on a Navy Theatre-Wide Defence (NTWD) system, which would be deployed on Aegis ships. The Japanese initially were reluctant to participate in the US TMD programme primarily because they had doubts about the technical feasibility and effectiveness of these missile defence components.[88] However, North Korea's missile launch over Japan's main islands in August 1998 proved to be a major catalyst in convincing Japanese policy-makers of the potential danger of a ballistic missile attack.

Going by this argument, a plausible means for the Japanese to maintain and consequently strengthen their existing deterrent against North Korea in the immediate case and against China in the long run would include the acceleration of US-Japan cooperation in the field of BMD. In addition to this, the Japanese Navy held its annual fleet review on October 29, 2006, with rather comprehensible striking capabilities and Japanese Prime Minister Shinzo Abe deftly stating, "Our country's Self-Defense Forces are being called upon to play a more crucial and varied role...I believe this is an excellent opportunity to demonstrate our readiness."[89] Crucially, Abe singled out North Korea as a major threat to Japan, saying its recent ballistic missile test launches and its claim to have exploded a nuclear device on October 9 are "grave and unforgivable."[90]

The pivotal question now is whether the Kim Jong Il regime can survive the political fallout as the world's newest nuclear power in that any shift in policy by China or South Korea would be at least partly based on the anticipated reaction of Japan, the nation that today feels most threatened by North Korea's ballistic missiles. Analysts have assumed that a nuclear-armed North Korea would lead Tokyo to accelerate plans to redraft its pacifist Constitution and rearm itself with a more aggressive military.[91] North Korea may be prepared to restrict some nuclear activities in return for guarantees and commitments from the US and other powers. It would not be prudent, however, to anticipate an early end to Pyongyang's programme or to dangers this programme poses both for security in East Asia and for the future viability of the non-proliferation regime.[92]

These developments have hastened the reactions of the missile defence advocates who feel that the time is ripe to accelerate the process of deployment of the US missile defence systems. In the wake of all these developments, Riki Ellison, president of the Missile Defence Advocacy Alliance (MDAA), made a call to action by the United States based on the lessons learnt of the long-range missile testing of North Korea. "Reflecting on the July 4 incident of the launching of multiple missiles from North Korea against international sanctions, agreements and world opinion last month, a reality that seems to be getting apparent... the people of Hawaii, Washington, Oregon and California are more vulnerable than previously thought and need additional missile defence protection."[93] Clearly, these trepidations have got strengthened since the successful conduct of the nuclear test in addition to Iran's active participation with North Korea, adding ominous ramifications to the international proliferation of ballistic missiles. Therefore, an understanding that seems to be becoming apparent in the backdrop is that there is increasing reason for the United States to expand missile defence bases in other countries so that the US and its allies, with their populations, will have protection against possible ballistic missile attacks stemming from the Middle East and Northeast Asia.

The situation in the post-October 9 scenario raises the stakes many notches higher in that Pyongyang is in possession of both the nuclear weapon and its means of delivery. In addition, North Korea might threaten to sell sensitive nuclear technology to other states that are of considerable proliferation concern or even terrorist organisations in order to fund its regime and revive its collapsing economy. The picture seems bleak and the stakes have never been higher given North Korea's record of selling weaponry and nuclear technology abroad (read Pakistan). Will all these possibilities ultimately plunge the entire Asian continent in general and the East Asian region in particular into an (nuclear) arms race? Apparently this possibility very much exists and cannot be ruled out entirely. The toughest proliferation cases will get tougher in that there are concerns that Iran is taking its cues from the North Korea playbook. Crucially, this might just be a triggering point for nations such as Iran whose nuclear weapons designs have caused much concern across the world. The crisis continues unabated and it appears cogent that any likely solution would have to fall into the category of a grand bargain. A steep uphill task is round the corner with the only difference being that the North Koreans now have actually gained nuclear ability as opposed to the earlier situation of possessing the capability to perhaps go nuclear.

Although the North Koreans have agreed to dismantle nuclear facilities and have destroyed their cooling plant for starters, the regional balance undoubtedly has been upset by the October 9, 2006 nuclear blasts and the dust is not expected to settle any time soon. Pyongyang remains unlikely to give up its nuclear card and would not take the road to complete disarmament and relinquish its nuclear capabilities in totality as is expected by a sizeable section of the world community unless and until it secures massive economic bargains as well as security guarantees for itself from the nations that have been in deliberations with the cloistered Northeast Asian nation. However, what really needs to be watched and judged is how far the US and its allies would be willing to go, so as to completely disarm North Korea. Critically, Pyongyang's going nuclear brings in a new sense of urgency, making it imperative for the concerned parties to strike out a solution to the long-drawn crisis and ensure that strategic stability prevails in the Korean Peninsula as well as in Asia. It appears cogent that any likely solution would fall into the category of a grand barter and, expectedly, Kim Jong Il would repeat the pattern of hard bargaining. Pyongyang's march towards complete disarmament and renouncing its entire nuclear capability palpably entails a heavy price tag.

As for the United States, there were resolute reiterations in the US policy formulation that crucial to any engagement policy was the maintenance of robust defence and deterrence capabilities. The Bush Administration's strategy appeared to be a combination of combating WMD capabilities with a robust, layered missile defence and other counter-proliferation capabilities that could threaten to neutralise "rogue" WMD capabilities, reducing the strategic utility, and thus, attractiveness, of these weapons to would-be aggressors. Accordingly, the Bush Administration adopted the deployment of the missile defence systems to bolster the US deterrent military posture and considered its missile defence systems as a perfect tool to achieve the same. The following chapter deals with the US missile defence programme and its implications on the existing security scenario along with the divergent perspectives that it shares, especially with the People's Republic of China on the said issue.

Notes

1. Department of Defence, "Nuclear Posture Review," Submitted to US Congress, December 31, 2001, p. 16.
2. Joseph S Bermudez Jr., "Exposing North Korea's Secret Nuclear Infrastructure—Part One", *Jane's Intelligence Review,* vol. 7, no. 1, July 1999, p. 41.
3. *"Tracking Nuclear Proliferation, 1998: North Korea,"* available at: http://www.ceip.org/programs/npp/korea.htm
4. Manpreet Sethi, "Post-Cold War Nuclear Proliferation: Patterns and Possibilities," *Asian Strategic Review* 1997-98, p. 196.
5. John Merrill, "North Korea in 1993: In the Eye of the Storm," *Asian Survey,* vol. 34, no. 1, January 1994, p. 10.
6. Merrill, n. 5, p. 11.
7. More details available at, http://www.carnegieendowment.org/files/Tracking_Ch06nkorea.pdf
8. Samuel S Kim, "North Korea in 1994: Brinkmanship, Breakdown and Breakthrough," *Asian Survey,* vol. 35, no. 1, January 1995, p. 13.
9. Kalpana Chittaranjan, "North Korea: Nuclear Issues," *Strategic Analysis,* vol. 23, no. 8, November 1999, p. 1308.
10. Ibid., pp. 1308-09.

11. For details, see Kim, n. 8.
12. For the full text of the Geneva Accord, see News and Negotiations, "US, Pyongyang Reach Accord on North's Nuclear Programme," *Arms Control Today,* vol. 24, no. 9, November 1994.
13. For viewing the entire statement visit http://www.armscontrol.org/factsheets/dprkchron.asp
14. Kim, n. 8, p. 22.
15. Ibid., p. 2.
16. David G Brown, "North Korea in 1998: A Year of Foreboding Developments," *Asian Survey,* vol. 39, no. 1, January/February 1999, p. 130.
17. Samuel S Kim, "North Korea in 2000: Surviving Through High Hopes of Summit Diplomacy," *Asian Survey,* vol. 41, no. 1, January/February 2001, p. 24.
18. Ibid.
19. For more details, see Jay Solomon and Gordon Fairclough, "Troubled Power Project Plays Role in North Korea Showdown," *The Wall Street Journal,* January 30, 2002.
20. Remarks by Colin Powell at the Asia Society, June 2002, cited in the Nautilus Institute Special Report, available at http://nautilus.org/for a/security/0227A_Siga.htm
21. Cited in Brian Knowlton, "North Korea Arms Pact is Now Dead, Powell Says," *International Herald Tribune,* October 21, 2002.
22. For details, see David C Kang, "The Avoidable Crisis in North Korea", *Orbis,* vol. 47, no. 3, Summer 2003, pp. 503-04.
23. Victor Cha, "Mr. Koizumi Goes to Pyongyang," *Comparative Connections,* October 2002, available at http://www.csis.org/pacfor/cc/0203Qjapan_skorea.htm
24. Walter Pincus, "Hints of North Korean Plutonium Output," *The Washington Post,* January 31, 2003.
25. Quoted in Christopher F Foss, available at http://www.cns.miis.edu/nkorea/chrono60-79.htm
26. Cited in article by Joseph S Bermudez Jr., available at http://www.cns.miis.edu/nkorea/chrono60-79.htm
27. Mark Hibbs, "No US Agency Consensus on DPRK Nuclear Progress", *Nucleonics Week,* January 6, 1994, p. 10.
28. *The Military Balance: 1973-74* (London: Chatto & Windus, 1973), p. 53.
29. For more details, see John Wilson Lewis and Hua Di, "Chinese Ballistic Missile Programs", *International Security,* Fall 1992, pp. 5-40.
30. Ibid.
31. CRS Report for Congress, "Ballistic and Cruise Missile Forces of Foreign Countries," October 25, 1996.
32. Ibid.
33. For details, see Kent E Calder, "The New Face of Northeast Asia," *Foreign Affairs,* vol. 80, no. 1, January/February 2001, pp. 106-122.
34. Christopher Marquis, "US Declares 'Rogue Nations' are now 'States of

Concern'," *The New York Times,* June 20, 2000.
35. For details, see Sebastian Harnisch, "US-North Korean Relations Under the Bush Administration: From 'Slow Go' to 'No Go'," *Asian Survey,* vol. 42, no. 6, November/December 2002, pp. 861-62.
36. Gary Samore, "US-DPRK Missile Negotiations," *The Nonproliferation Review,* vol. 9, no. 2, 2002, p. 17.
37. For details, see *Rumsfeld Commission Report,* Findings and Recommendations, July 31, 1998, available at http://www.fas.org/irp/congress/1998_cr/s980731-rumsfeld.htm
38. Brown, n. 16, pp. 129-130.
39. Testimony by Benjamin Gilman, Chairman of the US House of Representatives', International Relations Committee, available at http://www.fas.org/news/dprk/1998/980820-ht.htm
40. Testimony of Stanley O Roth, assistant secretary of state for East Asian and Pacific Affairs, House of International Relations Committee Asia and the Pacific Subcommittee, February 10, 1999.
41. *Frankfurter Rundschau* (Frankfurt/Main), November 15, 1999, at http://www.fr-aktuell.de/
42. Samuel S Kim, "North Korea in 1999: Bringing The Grand Chollima March Back In," *Asian Survey,* vol. 40, no. 1, January/February 2000, p. 155.
43. For details, see CIA's Unclassified Report to Congress, "Acquisition of Technology Relating to Weapons of Mass Destruction and Advanced Conventional Munitions," November13, 2003.
44. Ilsu Kim, "President Bush and North Korea", in Robert M Hathaway and Wilson Lee, eds., *George W Bush and East Asia: A First Term Assessment,* Study by the Asia Program, Woodrow Wilson International Centre for Scholars (Washington, D.C., 2005), p. 164.
45. CIA's Unclassified Report to Congress, n. 43.
46. Morton I Abramowitz and James T Laney, "Managing Change on the Korean Peninsula," Report of an Independent Task Force, Council on Foreign Relations (New York, 1998).
47. For details, see William J Perry, "Review of US Policy toward North Korea: Findings and Recommendations," Unclassified Report, US Department of State, October 12, 1999.
48. Ibid.
49. Philip C Saunders, "Confronting Ambiguity: How to Handle North Korea's Nuclear Program," *Arms Control Today,* vol. 33, no. 2, March 2003, p. 14.
50. Harry Harding, "Change and Continuity in the Bush Administration's Asia Policy," in Hathaway and Lee, eds., n. 44, p. 36.
51. Victor D Cha, "Korea's Place in the Axis," *Foreign Affairs,* vol. 81, no. 3, May/June 2002, pp. 82-83.
52. For details, see Richard L Armitage, *A Comprehensive Approach to North Korea,* Congressional Record, March 4, 1999, available at http://www.kimsoft.com/1997/armitag.htm
53. Cha, n. 51, p. 86.

54. Armitage Report, n. 52.
55. Ibid.
56. James A Kelly, "George W Bush and Asia: An Assessment," in Robert M Hathaway and Lee, eds., n. 44, p. 29.
57. Harding, n. 50, p. 36.
58. Marcus Noland, "Why North Korea Will Muddle Through," *Foreign Affairs,* vol. 76, no. 4, July/August 1997, p. 117.
59. Andrew Scobell, "China and North Korea: The Close but Uncomfortable Relationship," *Current History,* vol. 101, no. 656, September 2002, p. 278.
60. Bates Gill and Andrew Thompson, "A Test for Beijing: China and the North Korean Nuclear Quandary," *Arms Control Today,* vol. 33, no. 4, May 2003, p. 12.
61. Ibid.
62. David M Lampton, *Same Bed Different Dreams: Managing US-China Relations, 1989-2000* (California: University of California Press, 2001), p. 84.
63. Gill and Thompson, n. 60, p. 13.
64. Peter Wonacott, "Korea Tensions Put Beijing in a Tight Spot," *The Wall Street Journal,* January 3, 2003.
65. Bill Gertz, "China Ships North Korea Ingredient for Nuclear Arms," *Washington Times,* December 17, 2002.
66. Aaron L Friedberg, "US Strategy in Northeast Asia: Short and Long-Term Challenges" in US Strategy in the Asia-Pacific Region, A Conference Report, co-sponsored by the US Army's Dwight D Eisenhower National Security Series and The Sorrento Group in partnership with The Asia Program, Woodrow Wilson International Centre for Scholars, Washington, DC, May 5, 2003, p. 22.
67. Byung-joon Ahn, "The Man Who Would Be Kim," *Foreign Affairs,* vol. 73, no. 6, November/December 1994, p. 107.
68. Ibid.
69. Friedberg, n. 66, p. 26.
70. Ibid.
71. Thomas R Pickering, "US Strategy in the Asia-Pacific Region," in *US Strategy in the Asia-Pacific Region*, A Conference Report, co-sponsored by the US Army's Dwight D Eisenhower National Security Series and The Sorrento Group in partnership with The Asia Program, Woodrow Wilson International Centre for Scholars, Washington, DC, May 5, 2003, p. 71.
72. Ibid., p. 73.
73. Samuel S Kim, "The Making of China's Korea Policy in the Era of Reform," in David M. Lampton, ed., *The Making of Chinese Foreign Policy and Security Policy: In the Era of Reform* (California: Stanford University Press, 2001).
74. Ibid.
75. Harry Harding, *A Fragile Relationship: The United States and China Since 1972* (Washington DC: The Brookings Institution, 1992), pp. 36-37.
76. Xinhua News Agency Press Release, March 18, 2003.

77. For details, see Kyung-Ae Park, "Explaining North Korea's Negotiated Cooperation with the US," *Asian Survey,* vol. 37, no. 7, July 1997, pp. 623-636.
78. Official North Korean announcement of the nuclear tests by the Korean Central News Agency, October 9, 2006.
79. The joint statement at the conclusion of the fourth round of Six-Party Talks, released in Beijing on September 19, 2005 by the *Ministry of Foreign Affairs of the People's Republic of China* stated that the Six Parties unanimously reaffirmed that the goal of the Six-Party Talks was the verifiable denuclearisation of the Korean Peninsula in a peaceful manner. The DPRK committed to abandoning all nuclear weapons and existing nuclear programs and returning, at an early date, to the Treaty on the Non-Proliferation of Nuclear Weapons and to IAEA safeguards. The United States affirmed that it has no nuclear weapons on the Korean Peninsula and had no intention to attack or invade the DPRK with nuclear or conventional weapons. The DPRK and the United States undertook to respect each other's sovereignty, exist peacefully together, and take steps to normalise their relations subject to their respective bilateral policies. For more details of the text, visit http://www.state.gov/r/pa/prs/ps/2005/53490.htm
80. Official US Statement on the North Korean Nuclear Test of October 9, 2006, available at http://www.whitehouse.gov/news/releases/2006/10/20061003-10.html
81. Byung-joon Ahn, n. 67, p. 107.
82. For more details, visit http://www.nti.org/d_newswire/issues/2007_3_23.html#A8A72DDF
83. Jim Yardley and David E Sanger, "In Shift, A Deal is Being Weighed by North Korea," *The New York Times*, February 13, 2007.
84. For more details see, David Albright and Paul Brannan, "The North Korean Plutonium Stock till February 2007," Institute for Science and International Security, February 20, 2007.
85. For more details, see Monika Chansoria, "Nuclear North Korea: Shifting Strategic Calculations?" *Asian Defence Review*, Annual Edition 2007 (New Delhi: KW Publishers Pvt Ltd).
86. Michael E O'Hanlon, "Pyongyang: Reform or Abyss," *Financial Times*, October 11, 2006.
87. "Deployment of US PAC-3 to Kadena," Press Release by Japanese Ministry of Foreign Affairs, July 20, 2006, at http://www.mofa.go.jp/announce/announce/2006/7/0720.html
88. Takeshi Yuzawa, *Japan's Security Policy and the ASEAN Regional Forum: The Search for Multilateral Security in the Asia-Pacific*, (New York: Routledge, 2007), p. 138.
89. "Japanese Navy Holds Annual Fleet Review," Associated Press report cited in *Taipei Times*, October 30, 2006.
90. Ibid.
91. Anthony Faiola and Maureen Fan, "North Korea's Political, Economic

Gamble," *The Washington Post*, October 10, 2006, p. A12.

92. Jonathan D Pollack, "North Korea's Nuclear Weapons Program to 2015: Three Scenarios," *Asia Policy*, no. 3, January 2007.
93. For more details, visit http://www.missiledefenseadvocacy.org

5

US Missile Defence Programme: A 'Proportional' Response?

The debate over the long-running politico-military saga concerning the US ballistic missile defence (BMD) systems reflects many factors, including the major underlying theme of BMD's presumed capacity to alter international politics in unknown and unpredictable ways. Given the high stakes involved in the installation of these systems, any wrong decision could lead to possible national military and economic disasters down the road.

The 'Star Wars' Years

BMD, as a distinct technological and political issue, has embarked upon its sixth decade of controversy. The initial idea of a missile defence system dates back to the 1950s when the Pentagon was startled by the successful launch of the Sputnik by the former Soviet Union. Concerned that Moscow would use its space programme for military purposes by manufacturing missiles, strategic thinkers in Washington began to ponder about defending the US homeland against the Soviet missiles even before the American scientists were able to send a spacecraft to outer space. The US, having acquired overkill capability and preponderance in military power, faced challenges to its national security. In order to deal with such threats, the US took counter- measures from time to time that included BMD. Although after the end of the Cold War, the US and other nuclear powers such as Russia were on the move to reduce the existing nuclear capabilities, Washington's attempts to acquire BMD were perceived as a threat to the nuclear deterrent capability of nations, Russia and China in particular.

During the late 1950s, the idea for a national missile defence (NMD) system germinated when US President Dwight Eisenhower, faced with the prospect of Soviet missile fleets, embarked upon a secretive crash programme of anti-missile research that included thoughts for space-based arms and, over a course of time, involved thousands of the country's top scientists. However, designers scaled down their ambitious approach by the mid-1960s by designing ground-based interceptors tipped with nuclear arms. In case a war broke out, these interceptors were to roar out of their underground sites and race upwards to battle incoming waves of enemy warheads, which, in theory, would incinerate them in nuclear fireballs.[1]

The BMD programme received renewed attention under President Ronald Reagan in the form of the Strategic Defence Initiative (SDI), popularly known as the "Star Wars" programme. In the 1980s, the Reagan Administration aimed at strengthening the US strategic forces and continued to pursue the policy of "deterrence by denial." It was believed that a weak US strategic position would provide an incentive to the Soviets to attack America and its allies, and, thus, change the international status quo by converting democratic countries into Communist systems.[2] President Reagan in his famous March 23, 1983 "Star Wars" speech, emphasised the importance of SDI—a device to intercept the Soviet incoming missiles during the boost, post-boost and intermediate phases. In Reagan's opinion, the technological advancement in the field of defence might have offered the US the opportunity to strengthen deterrence by developing an effective defence against ballistic missiles.[3] Reagan's vision of SDI in a world where nuclear weapons were rendered "impotent and obsolete" was the original goal of the initiative. Yet, even before Reagan left office, the initiative began to narrow. As a matter of fact, Phase I of the Strategic Defence System (SDS) was billed as only the initial phase. However, the primary goal of SDS-Phase I was not to protect the American people from a missile onslaught, but to complicate the calculations of military strategists in the Soviet Union, who were suspected of planning a disarming first strike against the US land-based deterrent force. Through successive Administrations, SDI was constricted further to even thinner NMD proposals.[4]

The first phase of the missile defence programme took place during 1987-89, following the "Star Wars" speech in 1983, and led to the creation of the Strategic Defence Initiative Organisation (SDIO) within the Department of Defence. The new SDIO was devoted to developing the technologies needed to create a comprehensive land and space-based strategic defence against ICBMs and similar SLBMs. SDIO devoted virtually all of its initial efforts and budget resources to developing the technologies necessary to deploy a comprehensive ballistic missile defence system. The focus was primarily on three main technology programmes: Surveillance, Acquisition, Tracking, and Kill Assessment (SATKA), Directed Energy Weapons (DEW) Technology and Kinetic Energy Weapons Technology (KEW).[5]

The SDI recommended the setting up of a system of satellites and space platforms that would constantly stay in orbit, equipped with a number of beam weapons capable of destroying Soviet missiles or enemy missiles as soon as they took off and also in all subsequent sections of their trajectory. Such weapons included systems using light beams and lasers operating on fluorinated hydrogen or using beams of nuclear explosions and directed impulses released by nuclear explosions. Nevertheless, Washington did not have to focus on blunting a massive ICBM attack by Moscow in the post-Cold War world scenario. Instead, it focussed on defending against a limited missile strike launched by a "rogue state" or terrorist elements. This meant that the efforts of SDIO towards the theatre missile defence (TMD) could be increased, although attention was maintained towards NMD space-based interceptors.

The SDI programme consumed nearly $ 44 billion between 1983-1993 without producing any deployable systems or technological breakthroughs. Overall, according to a Brookings study, the US has spent more than $ 100 billion on missile defence efforts since the mid-1950s.[6] The second major phase of the NMD programme began during 1989-92, when the Cold War was inching close towards an end, thereby, bringing new emerging strategic calculations to the fore given the fact that a unipolar world was fast emerging. Thus, the focus of the US ballistic missile defence programme changed from comprehensive defence to global protection against limited strikes (GPALS) in 1991.[7] The US long recognised the threat of direct attacks with ballistic missiles, aircraft, cruise missiles and WMD. During the Cold War years, this threat was driven by the strategic forces of the Soviet Union. The US and Soviet competition was seen primarily in terms of mutually assured destruction (MAD) and the threat posed by each to the other's homeland in the context of a global struggle for political influence and power.

All this while, China appeared to pose a secondary challenge given its rivalry with the Soviet Union, and ties to the US then made such a threat seem to have little immediate importance. In fact, the risk of a North Atlantic Treaty Organisation (NATO)-Warsaw Pact conflict escalating to a theatre nuclear exchange and then strategic conflict was perceived as an elevated risk factor. Since the end of the Cold War, however, the missile threat to the US changed from a strategic-driven threat to a mix of current and emerging theatre-driven threats, making Washington believe that its homeland was most likely to be struck as the result of struggles for power in theatres that were remote from US territory.[8] Although Russia and China continued to deploy missiles and nuclear weapons through the course of this period, the risk of war was posed by the ever-escalating possibility of regional conflicts. Tensions and conflicts in regions such as the Middle East, the Persian Gulf, the Taiwan Strait and the Korean Peninsula could have led either to efforts to hit US targets with the threat of missile strikes or to a pattern of escalation that would eventually lead to actual strikes.

Proposed National Missile Defence Architecture

Ballistic missile defence as a concept embodied two distinct but interrelated facets: TMD and NMD. The former envisioned implementing defensive systems capable of protecting US and allied military forces, forward deployed troops, and naval fleets against short range, medium range and intermediate range ballistic missile attacks by immediate adversaries (e.g., battlefield or regional defence). Such systems, therefore, were expected to be mobile, robust and rapidly deployable across a wide range of geographic environments, including deserts, jungles, mountains and the Arctic.

Table 5.1: Classification of Ballistic Missiles by Range

Ballistic Missile Type	Range Parameters
Short-range ballistic missile (SRBM)	Under 1,000 km
Medium range ballistic missile (MRBM)	1,000 to 3,000 km
Intermediate range ballistic missile (IRBM)	3,000 to 5,000 km
Intercontinental range ballistic missile (ICBM)	Over 5,000 km

Source: National Intelligence Council, "Foreign Missile Developments and the Ballistic Missile Threat to the United States Through 2015," Central Intelligence Agency, September 1999.

In contrast to the TMD, national missile defence aims to protect the United States homeland, especially its continental territory, from missile attacks by either SLBMs or ICBMs. Both situations demanded counter- or anti-missile technologies capable of responding to very different threat profiles. The NMD was launched as a fixed, land-based, non-nuclear defence system with a space-based detection system consisting of the following five elements:

- **Ground-Based Interceptor (GBI):** The GBI and its associated components provided the 'weapon' of the NMD system. The mission of the GBI was to strike high-speed ballistic missile warheads in the mid-course or exoatmospheric phase of their trajectories and destroy them by force of impact.
- **Battle Management/Command, Control and Communications (BM/C3) System:** These included BM/C2 and in-flight interceptor communications systems (IFICS); the BM/C3 was the 'brains' of the NMD system. In the event of a launch against the US, the commander-in-chief of the North America Aerospace Defence Command would control and operate the NMD system through the BM/C3 system. The system provides battle management displays and situation awareness information. The IFICS was the BM/C3 communications link to the interceptors during flyout.

- **X-Band Radars (XBRs):** These radars were forward-deployed, ground-based, taskable, multi-function radars. In the NMD role, they performed acquisition, tracking, discrimination, and killed assessment of incoming warheads. XBRs used high frequency and advanced radar signal processing technology to improve target resolution, which permitted the radar to perform more effectively against closely spaced warheads, debris and penetration aids.
- **Upgraded Early-Warning Radars (UEWR):** These radars were large, fixed, phased-array surveillance radars used to detect and track ballistic missiles directed into the United States. Upgrades to America's early-warning radar network would have provided the existing forward-based radars with the capability to support the NMD surveillance function. Prior to the deployment of the satellite/ space-based infrared system (SBIRS) (low) satellites, the UEWRs would be used to detect and track objects during their mid-course phase, primarily to cue the more precise X-band radars.
- **Satellite/Space-Based Infrared System (SBIRS):** This system was developed by the air force as part of the early warning system upgrade that would replace the Defence Support Programme (DSP) satellites with SBIRS (high) and SBIRS (low). In its NMD mission, the SBIRS (low) constellation of sensor satellites would acquire and track ballistic missiles throughout their trajectory. SBIRS had an estimated system cost of roughly $20 billion and was intended to provide new and improved warning and sensing capabilities well into the century, allowing the accomplishment of a greater number of missions from space.[9]

The central feature of the proposed system would be an "exoatmospheric kill vehicle" (EKV) that was designed to be carried atop a rocket, which would then guide itself to a collision with an incoming warhead. The EKV weighs 130 pounds, is 54 inches long and was made by Raytheon at a plant in Tucson, Arizona. The weapon was required to find and ram an incoming warhead at about 7,000 miles per hour. While in space, its function is to guide itself towards the target, as its tiny computer analyses sensor readings and fires thrusters. Travelling at about two miles a second, the EKV was expected to slam into the nuclear warhead in space and demolish it by the force of the impact.[10]

Proposed Theatre Missile Defence Architecture

The emerging interest in TMD was partially motivated during the Gulf War in 1991 when Israel and Saudi Arabia faced Iraqi Scud missile attacks. The Patriot air defence system, which was then designed more to shoot down aircraft than missiles, was deployed to defend against the Iraqi Scuds.[11] In fact, the duel in the desert in 1991 during the Gulf War saw the Patriot anti-missile defensive efforts complicated by the physical break-up of the incoming Scuds; their very obsolescence enhanced their survivability against US efforts at mounting an effective counter-attack. Fortunately for the US, that situation likewise prevented the Iraqis from achieving any real accuracy in warhead delivery. Even more futuristic scenarios envisioned the employment of lasers and particle beams to shoot down attacking missiles.[12] A facet about the TMD systems is the fact that they are expected to be less costly and less technologically complex and able enough to protect against considerably larger attacks of shorter-range missiles. The TMD systems are generally divided into two categories: the lower-tier and upper-tier systems with an interception altitude of 40 km marking the threshold boundary between them. A complete TMD system would combine both upper-tier and lower-tier elements, intended to intercept and destroy short and medium-range ballistic missiles with ranges up to 3,500 km.[13]

The lower-tier defence systems were designed for a smaller defended area (footprint), roughly within a radius of 50-60 km of where the interceptor missiles such as the Patriot Advanced Capability Level-3 (PAC-3) are deployed. Another lower-tier option under development was the Navy Area Defence (NAD) system.[14] The PAC-3 is a tactical system designed to defend overseas US and allied troops in a relatively small area against short-range missile threats (such as Scuds), enemy aircraft and cruise missiles. Developmentally, it is the most advanced US missile defence system, and a small number has been made available for deployment although testing has not yet been completed.

Fig 5.1: Patriot Advanced Capability Level-3

PAC–3-flight testing began in 1997. From 1997 to 2002, 11 developmental flight tests were conducted, including four flight intercept tests with two or three targets being attempted at once. As an improved version of PAC-2, the PAC-3 is equipped with a new extended-range interceptor technology (Erint) hit-to-kill interceptor designed to hit targets at around 30 km in altitude. However, the PAC-3 was not designed to counter long-range threats and no flight intercept tests have been conducted to demonstrate how it might be incorporated in a terminal defence layer. A version of PAC-3 that would be effective in national missile defence was foreseen as probably a decade away then.[15]

The NAD was the sea-based equivalent of the PAC- 3. The NAD system was being designed to defend forward-deployed navy ships against relatively short-range threats. NAD systems relied on Aegis cruisers and destroyers with vertical launch systems. The effectiveness of Aegis cruisers in defence and coverage of defended areas was subject to incoming missile speed, ship location and the support of detection and sensor equipment. But in December 2001, the programme was cancelled because its cost and schedule overruns exceeded the limits defined by law. The NAD system was poorly defined to allow speculation about when it would accomplish such a demanding mission.[16]

Upper-tier defence systems, designed to cover larger defended areas, included the ship-based navy theatre wide defence (NTWD), land-based theatre high altitude area defence (THAAD) systems and other boost-phase intercepting systems like the airborne laser (ABL) systems.[17] The NTWD programme was originally intended to defend an area larger than that to be covered by the NAD system—that is, aircraft carrier battle groups and nearby territory and civilian populations against medium-range missiles during their mid-course phase. In this sense, NTWD was the sea-based equivalent of THAAD. In January 2002, the NTWD programme conducted its first successful flight intercept test, but a dozen or more developmental flight tests would be required before it could be used for realistic operational testing.[18] The THAAD user operational evaluation systems (UOES) was a rapidly deployable, air transportable prototype that consisted of four launchers, two ground-based radars and two battle management suites. It was slated to intercept ballistic missile outside and inside the atmosphere and was designed to be capable of taking two shots at attacking ballistic missiles. This capability would also enable systems like the Hawk and Patriot to have this shoot-look-shoot capability. The THAAD missile was a hit-to-kill missile and was expected to neutralise some or all of the destructive effects of WMD missiles warheads. THAAD FUE, the first unit equipped (FUE) and improved version of the UOES would militarise the UOES design and upgrade certain components, such as the infrared seeker, radar and BMC3.[19]

From 1995 to 1999, 11 developmental flight tests were performed, including eight in which an intercept was attempted. After the first six of these flights intercept tests failed, the programme was threatened with cancellation. Finally, in 1999, THAAD had two successful flight intercept tests. Although THAAD was to defend a larger area against longer-range threats than the PAC-3, it was not designed to protect the US from incoming ICBMs. Finally, in the TMD upper-tier systems came the ABL programme. It was to develop a high-power chemical laser that would fit inside a Boeing 747 aircraft and is touted as the most technically challenging programme of any of the theatre missile defence programmes. Furthermore, it involves toxic materials, advanced optics and the coordination of three additional lasers on board for tracking, targeting and beam correction. The first objective of the programme is being able to shoot down short-range enemy missiles. Subsequently, it is hoped the ABL programme would be able to play a role in NMD by destroying strategic missiles in their boost phase. The full rate production, probably slated not before 2010 costs, over $ 1 billion per aircraft.

Debates on Missile Defence Systems

There were strong ongoing debates within the US vis-à-vis NMD over the potential consequences of a possible deployment of a missile defence shield. The first, promoted most actively by conservative Republicans in the US Congress, called for near-term deployment of a robust NMD system that would include land-, sea-, and space- based elements. It would build space-based assets [placing space-based infra-red sensors (SBIRS) in high and low orbit] and a larger nation-wide ground component than the Clinton plan envisioned, while discarding the "now defunct" ABM Treaty.[20] The problem with this approach is that even a fully tested and operational NMD system, with multiple layers, would either be wholly or partially ineffective against certain missile threats (such as cruise missiles or depressed trajectory sea-launched missiles).

Moreover, it would also do nothing to combat threats stemming from terrorist strikes, suitcase bombs, or chemical and biological weapons not delivered by a missile, which may be the more likely threats facing the US homeland. Given the expenditures that would be required to construct a full-scale NMD system, these trade-offs surely need to be addressed. Beyond these concerns, a full scale NMD system is likely to create a range of regime problems with respect to the ABM Treaty, the MTCR, the proposed Fissile Material Cut-off Treaty (FMCT) and the Outer Space Treaty, among others.[21]

Another approach that received extensive consideration and enhancement under the Clinton Administration aimed at development of a limited NMD system that would eventually consist of some 100 interceptors and be designed to defend against launches of up to 20-30 missiles. It would have an optional upgrade after deployment to as many as 250 interceptors (total) at two sites. The third approach was suggested by a wide range of critics in the arms control community, who pointed out a range of purported flaws in the plans of the first two groups. Their arguments also challenged the seriousness of the threat facing the US, noting the lack of long-range missile capability in any of the main states purported to threaten the American homeland (Iran, Iraq, and North Korea).[22]

It became amply clear from the above arguments that there were various ways of looking at missile defence. Analysts argue that NMD might have some deterrent value in the future against a violence-prone regime or possibly would offer some protection against an accidental launch. On the other hand, there were proponents who favoured the system with the declared purpose of managing a threat from the 'rogues' of the world, though they envisage it as the first step towards a system really designed to neutralise China's strategic arsenal. As opposed to this line of argument, there was another lobby in the US foreign policy arena that was absolutely not in favour of the missile defence systems since they regard NMD as a system that could potentially threaten the future viability of the entire concept of deterrence as well as the arms control structure. It is also likely to create major difficulties with America's allies and agitate its competitors, especially Russia and

China. Less committed opponents opined that Washington should not rule out all forms of missile defence and should rather focus on building smaller, theatre missile defence systems. However, they stress that the most effective way of coping with a threat of a missile attack was to deter it with awesome strategic power.

Despite these four different arguments on NMD, there were clear areas of majority agreement within the US Congress and policy-making community: (1) missile proliferation posed an increasing threat to US and allied security; (2) NMD was defensive and did not threaten anyone; (3) NMD might have provided a means to render offensive missiles increasingly irrelevant; and (4) US leadership in the new area of technology was a valuable hedge, preventing the US and the rest of the world from being held hostage at some future point.[23] Given these numerous perspectives, it is not surprising that both Moscow and Beijing view unilateral US efforts to build a BMD as a threat to their security as well as towards the regimes and norms in which they have invested considerable resources. In addition, there are widespread apprehensions that the American determination to operationalise an NMD system to protect itself from errant incoming missiles launched from states of "proliferation concern", as also a TMD system for its "friends and allies" in Europe and Asia, threatens to throw the traditional concept of nuclear deterrence out of gear.[24]

Hiccups During the Clinton Years

The third phase of the NMD programme, or the "technology readiness" phase, took place during 1993-95 with an aim to reduce the deployment time for a ground-based system. The scope of the NMD effort was further narrowed and more emphasis was placed on theatre missile defence, which led to another reorganisation of the management of the US missile defence effort in 1993. As a result, SDIO was rechristened the Ballistic Missile Defence Office (BMDO). This reorganisation led to a further major restructuring of the programme that broadly outlines three areas of activity and objectives. The first is the TMD and supporting the deployment of a robust TMD capability as soon as possible. This primarily involves development and flight-testing of the THAAD, PAC-3 and NAD systems. The second phase is the NMD that positions the readiness of the US so as to defend the homeland against a limited ballistic missile threat. The third was the advanced technology effort, which supported both TMD and NMD in an attempt to continue to advance US capabilities to counter future and possibly more complex threats. This activity had a total cost of roughly $9.2 billion during 1993-95. Significantly, by the first quarter of 1996, the Department of Defence altered the purpose of the NMD programme from being a technology readiness programme to a deployment readiness programme and designated it as a major defence acquisition programme while seeking mature technologies for possible use in NMD systems. This fourth 'deployment readiness' phase lasted from 1996-99 and had a total cost of about $14.2 billion. Although it continued to put the bulk of its resources into TMD, the focus remained on NMD as a major defence acquisition and deployment readiness programme. This programme, also termed as the "3+3," seeks to develop an NMD system capable of being deployed after a deployment decision at a Deployment Readiness Review (DRR) in 2000.

The missile defence debate actually gained substantial attention in the decade of the Nineties when there was increasing consensus that NMD was aimed at ensuring that regional aggressors, made newly powerful and ambitious by their acquisition of WMD (and especially nuclear weapons), were not able to achieve a relationship with the US analogous to the relationship of mutual assured destruction that prevailed between the US and Soviet Union.[25] The CIA's National Intelligence Estimate (NIE)–1995 on the missile threat to the US had concluded that the threat from "so-called rogue states" such as North Korea, Iran and Iraq was unlikely in the near future.[26] However, at the initiative of the Republican members in the US Congress who believe that this threat perception underestimates the actual ballistic missile threat to the US, the Rumsfeld Commission, named after its chairman, former US Secretary of Defence Donald H Rumsfeld, was set up to assess the emanating threat from ballistic missiles in 1997. In preparing the report, the commission examined the detailed ballistic missile threat posed to all the 50 American states. Its assessment included threats posed by ballistic missiles that were deployed on the territory of a potentially hostile country; launched from a surface vessel or submarine operating off the coasts of the US or from an aircraft; deployed by a potentially hostile nation on the territory of a third party to reduce the range required of its ballistic missiles to strike the United States.

The report tabled by the Rumsfeld Commission concluded that concerted efforts by a number of overtly or potentially hostile nations to acquire ballistic missiles with biological or nuclear payloads posed a growing threat to the US; its deployed forces and its friends and allies. These newer developing threats in North Korea, Iran, Iraq and Libya were in addition to those still posed by the existing ballistic missiles arsenals of Russia and China, nations which the US was not in conflict with at that given point, but which remained in uncertain transition. The newer ballistic missile equipped nations' capabilities would not be able to match the US systems for accuracy or reliability. However, they would be able to inflict major destruction on America within around five years of a decision to acquire such a capability.[27]

The Rumsfeld Commission's findings that were put out in July 1998 appeared to have been vindicated when, within weeks of the report, North Korea, in a surprise move, test-fired a long-range version of its Taepo Dong I missile on August 31, 1998. While it might be several years before Pyongyang or Tehran or Baghdad, would be able to deploy operational missiles capable of striking the US mainland, the spread of WMD technologies to these countries which Washington described as the "world's least responsible states" or "rogue states" was widely perceived as threatening to the United States and its allies.[28] Earlier, on March 21, 1996, the Senate Majority Leader Robert Dole and House Speaker Newt Gingrich, introduced the Defend America Act, mandating deployment of a nationwide system of satellites, radars and missile interceptors by 2003. Dole called it "one of the key defining pieces of legislation the Congress will consider this year," adding that, "national missile defence must be America's top defence priority." Furthermore, Gingrich promised it would be "the most important national defence debate since Churchill argued for building the radar." Conservative activists pressed Republican politicians for a resurrected "Star Wars" programme.[29]

The domestic divisions within the US government became visible when the Joint Chiefs of Staff (JCS) firmly opposed a crash programme for the deployment of an NMD. In January 1996, the JCS wrote that with "Russia and China as the only countries able to field a threat against the US homeland, the funding level for (NMD) should be no more than $ 500 million per year and (TMD) should be no more than $ 2.3 billion per year." Such funding levels would allow a "balanced and proportional" programme that could meet war-fighting needs and ensure that no critical funds were diverted to a programme that promised little real defence against a threat that might not develop for decades.[30] The Clinton Administration, based on the Joint Chiefs' advice, had its own "3 plus 3" plan to develop an NMD system within three years and, if necessary, to then deploy the system within the next three years. Most of the funds in this almost $ 3 billion per year effort were formulated to be devoted towards developing defences against the near-term threat posed by Scud-type missiles and the development of the THAAD systems and other medium-range interceptors.[31] The initial goal of the NMD 3+3 programme was to develop and demonstrate, by FY 2000, an initial, limited capability system that could be deployed by FY 2003. In a briefing on January 20, 1999, US Secretary of Defence William Cohen, along with Army General Henry Shelton, chairman of the Joint Chiefs of Staff, spelt out the proposed deployment of an NMD system. Regarding budgeting of funds for the NMD programme, the allocation of additional funds to the missile programme was approved by the Clinton Administration totalling to $ 6.6 billion over five years to field such a system. This amount was in addition to $ 4 billion already allotted for research and development. Cohen affirmed that there was a growing threat that he expected would pose danger to US troops both at home and abroad. There must be a threat to warrant the deployment of an NMD and at the same time, America's NMD development, must have proceeded sufficiently so that the US was technologically able to proceed.[32]

The fundamental document of the National Missile Defence Act which was passed by the US Congress in 1999 called for the US to deploy, "as soon as technically feasible, an NMD system capable of defending US territory against ballistic missile attacks." The new schedule had the BMDO give its recommendation to US Secretary of Defence William Cohen by the end of July 2000.

Although President Clinton effectively deferred a deployment decision to the successor Administration, it would still be relevant to consider how the Administration described its NMD efforts as it exit the White House. Secretary of Defence Cohen issued the *Annual Report* to the president and Congress for FY 2001 where he stated that the Department of Defence (DOD) had made significant progress on the NMD programme in recent years, "including the completion of environmental impact statements for possible interceptor sites in Alaska and Grand Forks, North Dakota." The DOD also conducted three intercept tests (in October 1999 and January and July 2000).[33] Subsequently, President Bill Clinton signed a legislation calling for a deployment of a BMD system as and when it was technically feasible and simultaneously made it clear that the decision was based on four criteria: whether the system was technically mature; the threat required it; the cost acceptability in terms of other priority; and, finally, the implications of the decisions for the overall security of the US, including the future of arms control. Since 1997, the ground-based mid-course programme had conducted eight major flight tests known as IFTs of which the first two, named IFT-1A and IFT-2 were fly-by tests designed simply to collect target information, following which were the next six tests, IFT-3 through IFT-8, all flight intercepts tests.[34] In what was described as a serious setback to plans for a missile defence system to protect the US, the Pentagon announced in January 2000 that a missile fielded from the Marshall Islands in the Pacific failed to hit a mock warhead fired earlier from a California air base.[35]

This apparently was considered an extremely crucial test, as President Clinton was scheduled to arrive at a decision within a few months on whether to proceed with the programme to shield the US from limited missile attacks from "rogue states" and other potential adversaries. Moreover, it was also the first time the Pentagon had tested a fully integrated system of radars coupled with sensors intended to guide the missile as it sped into space searching for the target. The failure of this test further fuelled the already deep divide between politicians and NMD opponents over the prospect of building the $ 12.5 billion shield. If built, it would be the most complicated weapon system ever designed. Over the last four decades, the Pentagon has spent nearly $ 100 billion on missile defence systems with not many successes to count on.

Resultantly, Clinton decided in September 2000 not to bring about deployment of ground-based mid-course components such as the new X-band radar on Shemya Island in Alaska. The pace of successful testing has, thus, become one of the primary determinants of how quickly the US would be able to operationally field an NMD. While giving a speech at the Georgetown University on September 1, 2000, President Clinton acknowledged that the technology was not yet ready for an effective national missile defence system and passed the decision of future deployment of NMD to his successor. Clinton stressed, "We have made progress, but we should not move forward until we have absolute confidence the system will work. An NMD, if deployed, should be part of a larger strategy to preserve and enhance the peace, strength and security we now enjoy, and to build an even safer world."[36] Later, in an interview to the CNN in November 2000, Clinton reiterated that he had postponed decision-making on an NMD deployment because he was unable to justify violating the terms of the ABM Treaty, given that the US did not really possess the necessary technological capabilities for building an effective anti-missile shield at that given point.[37]

The ABM Treaty

Following an accommodative approach vis-à-vis scrapping the ABM Treaty, the Clinton Administration sought for the ABM Treaty to be 'amended' so as to permit it to build and deploy the NMD and TMD systems. US Defence Secretary William Cohen admitted that NMD deployment could require modifications to the treaty, restating that the Clinton Administration was working on determining the nature and scope of those modifications.[38] Subsequently, the Clinton-Putin June 2000 Summit witnessed the meeting of the two leaders in Moscow wherein Russian Foreign Minister, Igor S Ivanov firmly believed that the ABM Treaty should "remain a cornerstone of strategic stability." While responding, US Secretary of State Madeleine Albright stated that the US Administration, too, wanted to preserve the treaty but also wanted to adapt it to "21st century needs," a reference to the missile threats that intelligence experts had warned were fast approaching.[39] However, in contrast, President George W Bush bluntly described the ABM Treaty as obsolete and virtually declared it dead soon after assuming office.

The fall 2001 meeting between President Bush and Russian President Vladimir Putin in Crawford, Texas, was under immense limelight owing to speculations regarding striking of a deal on modifying the ABM Treaty. In spite of efforts to arrive at an understanding, President Bush announced on December 13, 2001, that the US had decided to invoke a six-month withdrawal clause in the 1972 ABM Treaty ostensibly because the treaty was restricting testing of mobile missile defences against ICBMs. Bush said that he had given Russia notice on the US withdrawal, stating, "I have concluded that the ABM Treaty hinders our government's ability to develop ways to protect our people from future terrorist or rogue-state missile attacks."[40] Bush's relentless stress was on the proliferation of sensitive technologies pertinent to WMD to "unstable regions such as Asia and the Middle East" while arguing that the plan looked for explicitly recognising that Russia was no longer an adversary and that the system "did not" target China. Thus, as of mid-June 2002, the United States stood free to develop, test and deploy missile defences in any manner it desired.

In response to an operationally deployed NMD, the Russians could well overwhelm the former with a rush of new warheads (MIRVs) fastened onto new missiles. The alarm of just such expensive spirals of anti-missile action and reaction had, in fact, prompted the US and former USSR to sign the "Treaty Between the United States of America and the Union of Soviet Socialist Republics on the Limitation of Anti-Ballistic Missile Systems." The treaty was signed in May 1972, ratified by the Senate in August, and it entered into force in October. The ABM Treaty was part of the Strategic Arms Limitation Treaty (SALT) along with the Interim Agreement on Limitation of Strategic Offensive Arms, SALT-I, and was signed on May 26, 1972, by the United States and the former Soviet Union. Under its provisions, the parties undertook not to deploy ABM systems for the defence of the territory of their countries or to provide the base thereof and not to deploy ABM systems for regional defence except as specifically provided. Sea-, air-, space- and mobile land-based components were prohibited; this was essentially because mobility was inconsistent with the basic prohibition of other than limited regional defence. The ABM Treaty banned the deployment of strategic capable defence with nationwide coverage, with an exception of one limited regional system for each country. Such a deployment area could not hold more than 100 ABM launchers and 100 interceptors.[41]

Under the treaty, the Parties undertook not to give non-ABM missile launchers and radars the capabilities to counter strategic ballistic missile or their elements and agreed not to test such equipment "in an ABM mode." Thus, air defences or any kind of defences could not be tested against strategic missiles.[42] A 1974 amendment subsequently reduced the permitted number of ABM systems to one site in each country. The ABM Treaty, therefore, signified recognition by both sides that current and further technology could not provide an adequate and effective defence against nuclear attacks. Based on this logic, the ABM Treaty was viewed as an arms control mechanism obviating the need on both sides to carry on adding more and more weapons to their arsenals. The US going ahead with its NMD deployment by breaking away from the obligations of the ABM Treaty would surely heighten tensions among the US, Russia and China, the ripples of which would be felt elsewhere across the globe as well.

Furthermore, the deployment of the contemplated US NMD programme presented two critical near-term problems in terms of a violation of the ABM Treaty. The first being that the very phrase "national missile defence" system made it apparent that the system was intended to be national and not limited to the kind of area defence permitted under the treaty. Secondly, the US plans to deploy the first site in Alaska intended to maximise coverage against potential missile strikes from North Korea and Iran, thus, implying deployment in a prohibited area.[43] President Bush, on December 18, 2001, served formal notice to Russia that Washington was withdrawing from the ABM Treaty in order to deploy a national missile defence, in accordance with the treaty, which had been kept in place for 30 years through the doctrine of mutually assured destruction. In an address at the White House, Bush stated, "I have concluded that the ABM Treaty hinders our government's ability to develop ways to protect our people from future terrorist or rogue state missile attacks."[44]

The Russian reaction to the US missile defence deployment and the withdrawal from the ABM Treaty was evident from the emanating tensions between Moscow and Washington in early 2002 over offensive nuclear forces.[45] While the offensive arms race continued through qualitative changes, neither the US nor the Soviet Union appeared willing to negotiate a limit on its offensive forces until the ABM Treaty put a cap on the defences those forces would face. Even though both sides agreed in late 2001 to reduce their long-range nuclear arsenals substantially—to between 1,700 and 2,200 operational warheads on the US side and down to 1,500 warheads in Russia—they disagreed over whether to make the cuts irreversible.[46] MIRVing of missiles and improvements of accuracy that gave counter-force capability had been conducted under the numerical limits imposed by SALT II and I. Even though the latter had expired and the US Senate never ratified the former, both sides kept their missile forces within the limitations of those agreements. The reason for restraint was that greater numbers of missiles were not necessary to assure a devastating retaliatory capability in the absence of large-scale defences.[47]

Ballistic Missile Defence: George W Bush Administration

During the 2000 presidential election campaign, George W Bush and his campaign strategists were lucidly coherent on robustly operationalising the missile defence programme. Missile defence undoubtedly was touted to become the centrepiece of the national security policy, even if all or most of the world's other major capitals saw national missile defence, especially the US approach to it, as irrelevant or unresponsive to plausible threats and a potential danger to global security and stability. During his campaign for presidency as the Republican nominee, Texas Governor George W Bush emphatically stated, "America must build an effective missile defence designed to protect all 50 states and our friends and allies and deployed forces overseas from missile attacks by 'rogue nations' or accidental launches."[48] After assuming office, President George W Bush stressed that he had, all along, backed a more extensive system based on land, at sea and possibly in space that would protect the US and its allies in Europe, the Middle East and Asia. Bush backed "robust missile defences" and was vocally critical of the Clinton White House for becoming "hopelessly entangled in its commitment to an obsolete treaty signed in 1972."[49] The Bush Administration repeatedly conveyed the notion that constructing a US missile defence was a "foregone conclusion."

Bush's commitment towards the intention to deploy the "son of Star Wars" i.e., an NMD that was clearly prohibited by the terms of the ABM Treaty, came across loud and clear during his famous speech at the National Defence University on May 1, 2001. President Bush stated, "We need a new framework that allows us to build missile defences to counter the different threats of today's world,"[50] thereby declaring NMD as the cornerstone of future US security strategy. According to Secretary of Defence Donald Rumsfeld, the goal for US NMD deployment "is to explore a variety of ways that missile defence can conceivably evolve without pre-judging exactly which ones will be the most fruitful. And there is no question but that the use of land and sea and air and space are all things that need to be considered, if one is looking at the best way to provide the kind of security from ballistic missiles that is desirable for the US and for our friends and allies."[51] Official statements, as well as excerpts from the classified Nuclear Posture Review stated that the Pentagon undertook at Congress' direction, and formally completed in January 2002, suggested that in the coming years the Administration hoped to deploy what it called "a rudimentary ground-based mid-course system."[52] The system used the technology that the Clinton Administration was developing and consisted of a few interceptor missiles based in Alaska. To make rapid deployment feasible, the Bush Administration had forgone the dedicated high-resolution X-band radar that the Clinton Administration had planned for Shemya Island and instead simply relied on the existing radar systems.[53]

The Bush Administration made missile defence one of its top priorities, giving it prominence in policy, funding and organisation. In the Nuclear Posture Review, the Bush White House outlined the specific elements of an NMD that it wanted to have ready between 2003–2008: an air-based laser to shoot down missiles of all ranges during their boost phases; a rudimentary ground-based mid-course system, a sea-based system with rudimentary mid-course capability against short-and medium-range threats; terminal defences against long-range ICBMs capable of reaching the US; and a system of satellites to track enemy missiles and distinguish reentry vehicles from decoys.[54] During the first defence budget, the Administration requested a 57 percent increase in funding for missile defence—from $ 5.3 billion to $ 8.3 billion, of which it received $ 7.8 billion. It was decided that the $ 5.1 billion that the US would spend on missile defence in FY 2001 would be equally divided between TMD and NMD, according to the Centre for Strategic and Budgetary Assessments in Washington.[55] Subsequently, Secretary Donald Rumsfeld reorganised the Ballistic Missile Defence Organisation (BMDO) into the new Missile Defence Agency (MDA) and changed the programme's goal from being able to field a complete system against specific targets to simply being able to field various missile defence capabilities as and when they become available.

To NMD advocates, the threat of a ballistic missile attack did not change significantly during 2001. More so, given the National Intelligence Council release of an unclassified version of the National Intelligence Estimate (NIE), summarising the official views of the US intelligence community on the nature of the ballistic missile threat.[56] The report's conclusions about the threat from long-range ballistic missiles largely tracked the previous NIE, released in September

1999. Significantly, both NIE reports noted that North Korea could probably test a multiple Taepo Dong-II missile theoretically capable of reaching parts of the United States with a payload of several hundred kilograms within short order if North Korea made the political decision to do so.

The July 2006 series of missile tests conducted by North Korea from its east coast in July 2006, crucially including the long-range version of the North Korean Taepo Dong-II missile in the tests, stirred enormous concern in the United States courtesy a possibility that if successfully launched, this missile would be capable of reaching Alaska and possibly striking the West Coast of the United States homeland. These developments have hastened the reactions of the missile defence advocates who feel that the time is ripe to accelerate the process of deployment of the US missile defence systems. In the wake of these developments, Riki Ellison, president of the Missile Defence Advocacy Alliance (MDAA), made a call to action by the United States based on the lessons learned of the long-range missile testing of North Korea. "Reflecting on the July 4 incident of the launching of multiple missiles from North Korea against international sanctions, agreements and world opinion last month, a reality that seems to be getting apparent—the people of Hawaii, Washington, Oregon and California are more vulnerable than previously thought and need additional missile defence protection." Ellison added that Iran's active participation with North Korea adds ominous ramifications to the international proliferation of ballistic missiles.

Another gripping claim of the NIE was that Iran was not likely to test its first ICBM until the last half of the decade, if then. However, it would also be significant to mention that in November 2006 and January 2007, Tehran conducted several short- and medium-range ballistic missile and rocket launches in what could be described as an overt demonstration of its offensive capabilities to the world.[57] Iranian pursuit of newer and longer-range missile systems and advanced warhead designs, including an extended-range version of the Shahab-3 that could possibly strike US allies in the Middle East and Europe as well as its deployed forces, is a source of concern. Tehran is also said to have been building a new Ashura medium-range ballistic missile capable of reaching Israel as well as US bases in Eastern Europe.[58] Moreover, according to the August 3, 2006 Reuters report, North Korea has been working closely with Iran to develop its long-range ballistic missiles, possibly using Chinese technology. Iran's development of a space launch vehicle using technologies and designs from its ballistic missiles means Iran could have an ICBM capable of reaching the United States by 2015.[59] Apparently the MDA's request of about $1.7 billion for FY 2009 to expand the defence of the United States is also specially catered to include the limited Iranian long-range threats.[60]

When in January 2002, the secretary of defence directed the MDA to restructure the missile defence programme to deal with the urgency, enormity and complexity of developing, testing and building a missile defence system, the agency redirected its efforts towards developing and testing the elements of a BMDS capable of engaging all classes of ballistic missile threats. The programme integrates command, control, battle management and communications (C2BMC) elements into layered defence segments to engage threat targets in all phases of flights.

Fig 5.2: Capability-Based Block Structure

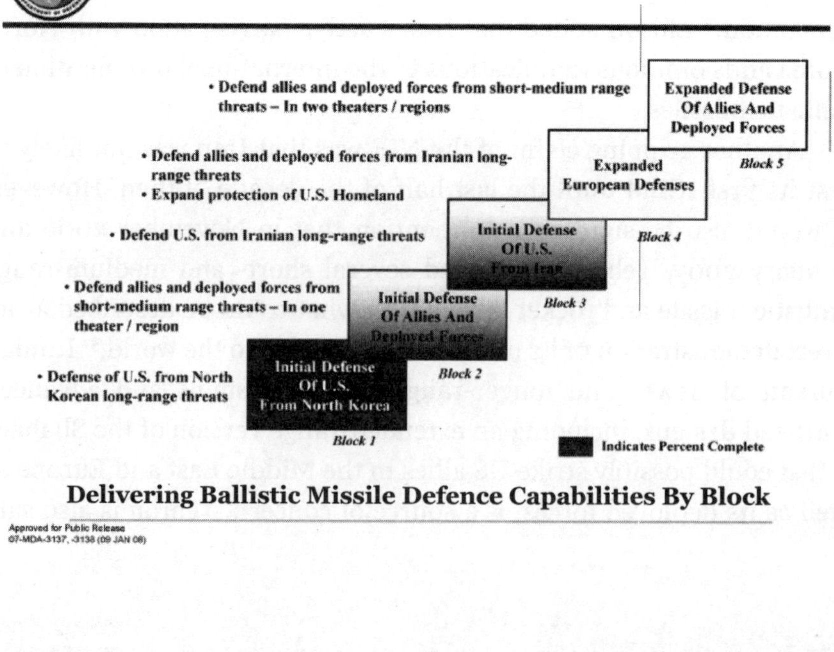

Continuing their endeavours, the MDA and the army went ahead and conducted a missile defence test over the Pacific on May 30, 2002, in which one advanced Patriot Advanced Capability (PAC-3) missile intercepted its target, although the second Patriot failed at the launch stage. The point of the test was to launch two Lockheed Martin PAC-3s in rapid succession against a two-stage modified Minuteman missile designed to demonstrate the Patriot's ability to classify the high-velocity, low-radar signature target as a tactical ballistic missile, discriminate between the reentry vehicle and accompanying debris, and destroy the target off Kwajelein Atoll. In fact, this was the fourth operational test for the PAC-3 system, which was slated for full-scale development in the fall of 2002.[61] Having successfully transitioned the PAC-3 to the US Army in March 2003, the US continues to maintain configuration control and work with that Service to improve and upgrade PAC-3 and Medium Extended Air Defence System (MEADS) performance. Today, PAC-3 fire units are being integrated into the forces of US allies, many of whom face immediate short- and medium-range threats.[62] Moreover, the PAC–3 achieved seven hit-to-kill intercepts of ballistic missile targets in eight attempts in 2006. The MEADS capability is designed to counter theatre ballistic missile threats in their terminal phase in addition to cruise missiles and other air-breathing threats. Combining these systems with the THAAD system capability being developed by MDA, with a planned fielding in FY2009, aims to bring an unprecedented level of protection against missile attacks directed at deployed US forces and allies well into the future.[63] In fact, flight-testing involving the redesigned THAAD interceptor continued in July 2006, with successful engagement of a unitary target high in the atmosphere. THAAD is expected to provide transportable terminal protection for the American troops and areas along the US coasts or on the territories of US allies. In his testimony to the Senate Armed Services Committee, Henry A Obering stated that the first unit was expected to be fielded in 2009, with subsequent units fielded by 2012, for which the MDA requested $858 million in FY 2008 for THAAD development and fielding.[64] The Bush Administration's commitment in installing the THAAD from November 2005 through January 2007, was for four successful flights of the production interceptor. Two of these test flights involved intercept of targets, and both of those intercept flight tests were successful hits.[65] The MDA is also working closely with the army to begin developing and fielding by 2009 two THAAD fire units, with the plan to deliver them by 2010 and 2011.

Moreover, in 2006, the US deployed the first forward-based X-band radar to Japan, accelerating its deployment and supporting C2BMC equipment to its operational location in Shariki Air Base, Japan, thereby achieving partial mission capability in October 2006. Also, since 2004, the Aegis ships have been periodically put on station in the Sea of Japan to provide long-range surveillance and tracking data to the US battle management system. The Standard Missile-3 interceptors began to be fielded in 2004, evolving to a more capable interceptor; and a growing inventory of Standard Missile-3 interceptors on Aegis ships, could, in fact, provide a flexible sea-mobile capability to defeat short- to intermediate-range ballistic missiles in their mid-course phase.[66] The transition of the transportable forward-based X-band radar at Shariki Air Base, Japan, from the interim site to a permanent location came about in 2007, which provides precise early detection and tracking to increase the probability to destroy any lethal target launched by North Korea. The sea-based X-band radar (SBX) completed crew training and testing off the coast of Hawaii and transited to the North Pacific to conduct a cold weather shakedown off Adak, Alaska, where it will be home-ported in 2009. Significantly, by 2009, the US also plans to install additional planning and situational awareness capabilities to facilitate executive decision-making in the European Command.

Since 2006, the Missile Defence Agency conducted more than 35 major tests and met primary test objectives in 14 out of 15 flight tests. In fact, during a 90-day period in summer 2006, successful hit-to-kill intercepts in the lower atmosphere with the PAC-3 were achieved, in the upper reaches of the atmosphere with the THAAD element and in space with the Aegis Standard Missile-3 and the ground-based mid-course defence elements. Therefore, since 2001, a ratio of 26 successful hit-to-kill engagements in 34 attempts has been recorded.[67]

Missile defence continues to receive more funding than any other weapons programme in the annual Pentagon budget. Full-scale spending on missile defence became a stark reality that was further assured by the Pentagon's FY 2003 budget proposal, which requested a $ 7.8 billion for overall missile defence; the same level of spending Congress had appropriated a year earlier. Moreover, the Bush Administration requested an enhanced $10.4 billion for missile defence in FY 2007, up roughly $2.6 billion from the $7.8 billion received in 2003. The Bush Administration did propose shifting the spending allocation somewhat among various categories under the missile defence umbrella such as for shorter-range (or theatre) systems and long-range (national) missile defence systems.

In its February 3, 2006, Quadrennial Defence Review, the Pentagon listed the deployment of missile defences as one of its accomplishments since 2001. It stated that this action provided a "nascent defensive capability." President George W Bush's FY 2007 budget request reaffirmed his Administration's commitment to deploying an array of anti-missile systems, including to Europe, despite continuing uncertainty about whether they work. The Administration has requested $8.9 billion for the MDA in FY'2009, up roughly $350 million from the current $8.6 billion. The request includes $720 million for the third missile defence site in Europe ($96 million for development, $382.6 million for fielding, and $241.2 million for military construction). Furthermore, test plans for 2008 and 2009 will continue to use more complex and realistic scenarios for system-level flight tests and demonstrate interceptor capabilities against more stressing targets.

Table 5.2: FY'09 REQUEST FOR BALLISTIC MISSILE DEFENCE (Budget Authority in Millions of Dollars)

	FY'08 Total	FY'09 Request
Terminal Defence (MDA)	1,045.3	1,019.1
Boost Defence (MDA)	510.2	421.2
Mid-course Defence (MDA)	2,243.2	2,076.7
AEGIS BMD (MDA)	1,126.3	1,157.8
BMD Sensors (MDA)	586.1	1,077.0

Space Tracking & Surveillance (MDA)	231.5	242.4
BMD Technologies (MDA)	108.4	118.7
Advanced Concepts (MDA)	196.9	288.3
BMD System Interceptors (MDA)	340.1	386.8
Multiple Kill Vehicle	229.9	354.5
Other Programmes (MDA)	1,934.0	1,748.3
Joint Theatre Air Missile Defence Org. (Joint Staff)	53.7	55.3
Total Ballistic Missile Defence	**8,605.6**	**8,946.1**
MEADS/Patriot CAP (Army)	370.0	462.3
Patriot/PAC-3	480.5	523.3
Space Based Infra-Red System-High (SBIRS-High) (Air Force)	982.6	2,328.2
GRAND TOTAL Ballistic Missile Defence	**10,438.7**	**12,259.9**

Source: DOD FY 2009 Budget Request Summary Justification, *Major Weapons Systems*, February 2008.

It is evident that the preeminence accorded to missile defence in US defence budget allotments, and the ongoing progress vis-à-vis operational deployment along with a breakout from the ABM Treaty have, in fact, altered all existing security calculations and the strategic shift is going to have an impact on Russia and in particular on China so as to inundate the American BMD.

Washington-Beijing Spat over BMD

The People's Republic of China has responded to the US missile defence systems as an offensive move and has always maintained a critical overtone on the issue, expressed primarily in terms of cross-Strait relations between Taiwan and itself. Deeply conscious of its vulnerability, Beijing believed a BMD system would likely neutralise and, consequently, threaten the survivability of its strategic force. Beijing has always maintained as well as categorically stated on numerous occasions that US missile defence was directed against Chinese forces. In all certainty, Beijing would hedge against the prospect by expanding its strategic forces beyond the upgrades now underway in accordance with its rapidly progressing military modernisation programme. China could equip itself with multiple warheads, a step that missile defence has made more attractive as a potential responding measure. Since the early 1990s, concerns that NMD had as much to do with US intentions as with capabilities have loomed large among Chinese policy-makers and strategists. As Shen Dingli of Fudan University argues, "China remains strongly suspicious of the US intentions in terms of NMD development."[68] Moreover, Chinese foreign policy experts posed two key questions: does Washington intend to use NMD to harm China's interests? Could China count on balance-of-power politics to help check whatever intentions US might have had? Following the collapse of the Soviet Union, the United States emerged as China's most important military planning problem, given the unresolved dispute over Taiwan. Adding to the quandary, a *China Daily* article argued, "The envisaged NMD cannot stop an all-out Russian nuclear attack... Therefore, Beijing can only view the US NMD as being designed to most effectively neutralise China's strategic deterrent... Even interceptors deployed in one single site are enough to knock out all China's full-range ICBM force (CSS-4)."[69]

Just as the US TMD programme had the potential to cause instabilities in the nuclear balance in Asia, so did the US lead in the revolution in military affairs (RMA) technologies that could have led to military competition, raising the level of tensions. China and other Asian powers with the technological base to improve their own RMA would be encouraged to further undertake the hi-tech leap. An arms race in Asia, particularly among China, India, and Pakistan as well as the US classified "rogue states" namely Iraq, Iran and North Korea would not be difficult to envision given that all these nations would strive to keep their deterrent edge alive in order to remain in the loop with, and against, each other.

As a matter of fact, Beijing itself made no bones about the fact that it considers missile defence as a threat to its national security. Tang Jiaxuan, former Chinese foreign minister, had stated in this regard in 1999, "The development and research of NMD exerts a negative impact on the global and regional strategic balance and stability."[70] Besides, the Chinese Foreign Ministry also came critical of the US

NMD programme and identified a number of reasons behind China's opposition to this:

> ...Once the US deploys the NMD and regardless of the fact whether it is effective or not, the fact that it exists will promote the tendency to use force in international affairs...The NMD programme will also undermine the process of the international military control and disarmament and could even spark the war...the places, scale and capability of the NMD deployment will directly infringe upon China's strategic security interests...China...will thus adopt necessary measures according to the changing conditions of the global and regional security situation in order to guarantee nuclear counterattack capability, because it cannot brook the threat of nuclear blackmail once more.[71]

As a potential negative consequence of NMD, it was possible that the US and China would get into a defence/offence arms race or what was referred to as the "action-reaction cycle." China appeared to be wary that Washington was inching towards militarisation of space—of missile defence—and was in the process of turning space into an arena of competition. If Washington chose to try to cap China's growing arsenal, however large it got, such an arms race appeared likely—today, in Beijing it is intolerable to accept the loss of face associated with the loss of credibility of its deterrent, especially at a time of such deep concern about America maintaining its unipolar moment.

Expectedly, China could well respond to a defence/offence race with actions outside the realm of nuclear forces and their disposition. In many respects, US missile defence deployments were viewed to be more important to Beijing than to Moscow. However, both nations agreed on the notion that Washington's NMD design was a quest for unilateral advantage by a power, already in possession of the relevant strategic advantages. And both Russia and China deplored the Bush Administration's apparent disregard of the arms control process.[72] China, with less than two-dozen long-range missiles, stands far more vulnerable to a US missile defence than Russia and are also more prone to a conflict with the United States based on divergent strategic realities. This possibility presented a potential problem for Washington because Beijing had the wherewithal to make the United States pay a substantial strategic price for building missile defences that China perceived as threatening. All these developments could goad Beijing to upgrade its nuclear missile force, frustrate US efforts to stem nuclear and ballistic missile proliferation, and obstruct US policy in other areas. Although, the Bush Administration's proposal to open a dialogue with China on strategic stability may have lessened the chances of a rift, Beijing would clearly be watching not just what Washington said but also what it actually did.

Expressing reservations regarding the US missile defence programme, Chinese Disarmament Ambassador Sha Zukang, stated, "If the US is genuinely concerned, as it claims, about the threat to its security caused by proliferation of WMD and their means of delivery, the right thing to do would be to abandon its hegemonic mentality and behavior, respect the legitimate security interests of other countries, strengthen international cooperation and dialogue, and shore up—and where possible build on—the international arms control and non proliferation regimes. The development and deployment of TMD and NMD systems may be able to psychologically and temporarily satisfy some people's anxiety for absolute security, but it will do little to reduce the threat of WMD and their means of delivery. Furthermore, disrupting the global strategic balance and stability would put up front certain grave concerns vis-à-vis the future of arms control and non-proliferation, and in the end adversely affect the security interests of all countries, including the US."[73]

In fact, China's strategy in regard of NMD/TMD encompassed three main elements: enhancement of its nuclear deterrence capabilities through military modernisation; alignment with like-minded countries; and increase in its bargaining power by holding out threats of proliferation of WMD technologies to countries perceived as "states of concern" by the US. As of now, China's nuclear deterrent comprises about 20-odd, slow-reaction, liquid-fuelled missile systems of dubious reliability; their warheads and fuels have been stored separately. In this regard, China's upgrade was most likely to create a force that was more than a deterrent—one that might have actually threatened America.

With a limited ICBM force, China looks upon the American missile defence deployment as having the potential to severely constrain its ability to deter the US. Therefore, a BMD that threatened to curtail Chinese manoeuvrability by virtually disarming it, would most likely be met by an increase in the number, sophistication and survivability of missiles in order to saturate US defences. A People's Liberation Army (PLA) security expert, Luo Yuan stressed, "Such growing power politics is poisoning the trend towards multi-polarity, undermining the conditions necessary for establishing new political and economic orders and breeding the potential danger of a new arms race."[74]

In the event of a fully operational missile defence deployment, a US National Intelligence Estimate (NIE) of the year 2000 studied its impact and warned that it could "prompt China to expand its nuclear arsenal tenfold."[75] There was a growing perception that the limited number of Chinese ICBMs would not be able to pose a credible enough threat to Washington, thus, compelling it to increase its missile arsenal and perhaps, graduate to MIRVs in order to saturate the American defences by increasing the number of targets within the US. It is not difficult then to fathom the cascading impact this would have on the entire region. The NIE also stated that Russia could place multiple warheads on ballistic missiles that now carry only one.[76] Adding to this possibility, Russian President Vladimir Putin stated, "It will cost almost nothing" to put "new warheads...on existing missiles such as Topol-M ICBM." This statement in a way reflected the Russian mindset that an extensive missile defence system, together with the US decision to withdraw from the ABM Treaty, was a signal of an emergent US bias towards reliance on offensive defence and away from deterrence. Significantly, on the issue of BMD, Russia and China found themselves on the same side of the fence, having decried the US move. Russian arms sales to China have increased and so has the bilateral trade. All these developments could be perceived towards strengthening Beijing's hand, economically, politically and diplomatically.

Following these developments, a report published in the *New York Times* elaborated on China's R&D that was speculated to be graduating to a new generation of solid fuelled, multiple warhead and road-mobile missiles, viewed apparently as a move to augment its missile arsenal. The first of these new missiles, the Dong Feng (DF)-31, was tested in July 1999 and the US NIE revealed in August 2000 that China could decide to deploy up to 200 ICBMs by 2015. Beijing is also believed to be using the global positioning system (GPS) to make significant improvement in the accuracy of its missiles in that it reached an agreement to share the Russian space-based global navigation satellite system.[77] The urge to uphold a credible survivability factor is evident as China modernises and enhances its delivery system with its new series of DF-31, along with its submarine-launched versions Julang (JL)-20 and DF-41. According to reports appearing in the Hong Kong Press, the PLA Navy submarine units and the Second Artillery troops conducted a series of tests in August 2001 to improve the submarine launch capability such as the JL-2 series.[78]

Another significant aspect potentially leading to escalating tension in the Asian continent in particular is the US-Japan cooperation on TMD systems. On August 16, 1999, the US and Japan formalised an agreement to conduct joint technology research on TMD. The US-Japan agreement, which came in the form of a memorandum of understanding (MoU), called for the US Department of Defence and Japan's Defence Agency to formally begin studies on an upper-tier navy theatre wide system, a mobile, sea-based configuration capable of being carried on Aegis-equipped ships.[79] As discussed earlier, the close US-Japan TMD cooperation is progressing thereby in anticipation making Chinese experts argue that the deployment of an upper-tier, space-based TMD system in Northeast Asia could well be intended to nullify China's strategic leverage. They go on to assert that the US would develop NMD technology in the name of TMD and a Japanese TMD system would, therefore, be at the 'forefront' of the US NMD. Earlier, China cited five reasons for its opposition to a Japanese-US TMD network: (1) concerns over possible Taiwanese involvement in TMD; (2) the possibility that China's deterrence capability might be undermined; (3) the threat of Japan's remilitarisation; (4) the further strengthening of the US-Japan alliance; and (5) the negative impact it would have on the global arms control process.[80]

As far as the US is concerned, the participation of Japan in TMD offers the potential to enhance bilateral security cooperation, in addition to providing technology, and funding for this complex and expensive programme. TMD could be spotted as setting both Japan and the US on a collision course with Beijing.[81] Thus, China could be seen as escalating vertically from a strategy of minimum deterrence to a more threatening one of limited deterrence. China has constantly expressed concern about a militarily independent and strong Japan and the timed increase in the numbers of deployed short-range ballistic missiles like DF-11 and DF-15 effectively displays this concern.

Fig 5.3: US Missile Shield

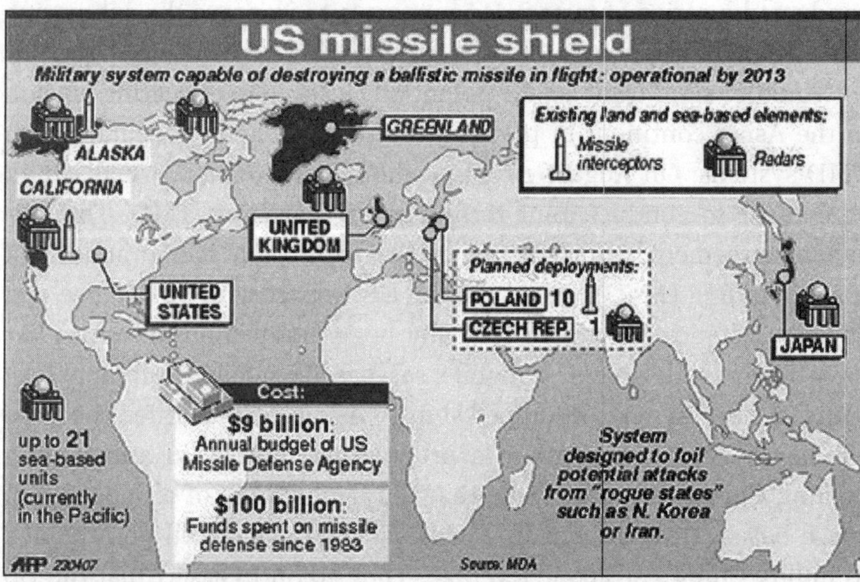

Source: Missile Defence Agency

China and the United States might not appear to be engaged in a strategic weapons arms race. Nonetheless, their modernisation and sizing decisions increasingly are framed with the other in mind. Nuclear weapons are at the core of this interlocking pattern of development. In particular, China is the only permanent member of the UN Security Council that is expanding its arsenal; it is also enhancing its arsenal. The basic facts of Chinese strategic modernisation are well known, even if the details remain frustratingly opaque. Beijing is deploying road-mobile, solid-fuelled missiles, giving it a heighted degree of security in its second-strike capability. It is beginning to deploy ballistic missile submarines (SSBNs) and furthermore is researching a wide range of warhead and delivery systems technologies that will lead to increased accuracy and, more pointedly, increased penetration against ballistic missile defences. The size of China's deliverable arsenal against the United States will undoubtedly increase beyond the few dozen that it possessed recently.[82] The final endpoint remains mired in opacity and uncertainty, although several score of deliverable warheads seems likely for the near term. These developments on the strategic side are coupled with elements of conventional modernisation that impinge on the strategic balance.

Space and missile defence is increasingly intertwined with traditional nuclear issues. US missile defence certainly complicates the calculus of potential adversaries, as also the traditional approaches to reducing the dangers of strategic weapons. International relations theory has trouble putting nuclear weapons and missile defence systems into an "offensive-defensive" dichotomy because most theorising about nuclear weapons took place in the era of mutually assured destruction when the utility of nuclear weapons for anything other than retaliation made little sense. The space realm is clear in that area. Anti-satellite weapons are clearly offence dominant today: first-strike attacks against satellites confer great advantages, and defences are costly and not currently deployed.[83] Even a moderate-scale missile defence system—the Pentagon is planning on 50 interceptors by 2012—provides important capabilities against any surviving Chinese missiles. In this, President Barack Obama and his Administration could take certain confidence building measures, which were quite simply off the table under the Bush Administration—the Russians have received extensive briefings on US missile defence systems and were offered the right to observe control rooms in Eastern European missile defence facilities. As for China, in the area of space policy, numerous small steps can be taken in terms of codes of conduct, launch notifications, noninterference pledges, and other issues.[84] Chinese proposals on "Prevention of an Arms Race in Outer Space" require much further development before they can be adequately evaluated. Several issues are critical from the US perspective: the status of various missile defence technologies under that proposal, dual-use technologies, and the nature of verification in general. Still, more active US diplomacy on this issue, whether at the Conference on Disarmament or in other fora, would be beneficial. An Administration less wedded to complete freedom of action on missile defence technologies and scale should be willing at least to begin these discussions.[85]

China's opposition to US deployment of missile defence systems and related cooperation with Japan or Taiwan and its threat to significantly increase its nuclear missile force while displaying concern that missile defence would spur an arms race, negate its deterrence capabilities, forge closer US-Taiwan military cooperation and violate the MTCR. During Defence Secretary William Cohen's visit to China in July 2000, the PRC reportedly warned that it would continue missile proliferation activities if the United States provides missile defence to Taiwan.[86] A US decision to proceed with NMD—together with a decision to bring about TMD in cooperation with US friends and allies in East Asia—could have a profoundly disturbing effect on Beijing's policy towards Taiwan. Beijing might consider attempting a military solution to the Taiwan issue before US missile defences become fully operational, thereby bringing military confrontation between the two powers under the nuclear shadow. Further, Taiwan's entry under the TMD umbrella would have serious implications on China's Taiwan policy.

TMD's potential application to Taiwan reduces the belief that Beijing's threat to use force deters an overt declaration of independence by Taiwan. Though many analysts doubt that China could successfully invade Taiwan to suppress independence, Taiwan is clearly vulnerable to China's short-range missile force. Deployment of TMD in or near Taiwan would reduce China's ability to use missile threats to politically intimidate the Taiwanese leadership. Moreover, any US role in such deployment would signal (to both Taipei and Beijing) a greater likelihood of US military support to Taiwan in the event of an overt conflict. Thus, China worries that TMD deployment would bolster Taiwanese independence sentiments. Because of Beijing's concern over its domestic legitimacy, there would be a real danger that China would use force regardless of the level of support it expects the US to provide to Taiwan. Crucially, US deployment of a TMD system applicable to Taiwan would dramatically heighten the risks of a war in the Taiwan Strait and would likely embroil China and the United States in direct conflict.[87]

China has periodically tried to link the issues of missile proliferation and US conventional arms sales for Taiwan's defence. After President George H W Bush approved the sale of 150 F-16A/B fighters to Taiwan in September 1992, the PRC ended its participation in the "Arms Control in the Middle East" talks. During the 1998 summit in Beijing, the Clinton White House reportedly considered a PRC request for a US pledge to deny missile defence sales to Taiwan, if China promised to stop missile sales to Iran; but no agreement was reached.[88] On February 26, 2002, before the Director General in charge of arms control at the PRC Foreign Ministry, Liu Jieyi, attended meetings in Washington on March 4-6, an unnamed PRC Foreign Ministry official told the Associated Press that the United States "can't just accuse us of violating our commitments and at the same time, sell large amounts of arms to Taiwan," since such arms sales are "also a kind of proliferation."[89]

In this context, another major development took place when President George W Bush, during the waning days of his presidency, notified Congress on October 3, 2008, regarding his approval for selling defensive weapon systems worth a staggering $6.9 billion to Taiwan. This came as a surprise to many since there was intense speculation that the Bush Administration would leave the decision to the new occupant of the White House (read the Obama Administration). The Pentagon's Defence Security Cooperation Agency, however, notified the Congress on the proposed arms sales and gave it 30 days to raise objections to the plan, if any. The package of weapon systems includes $3.1 billion PAC-3 guided missile systems, $2.5 billion worth of Apache Longbow attack helicopters, $250 million in equipment for upgrading Taiwan's E-2T Hawkeye surveillance aircraft and $200 million in Harpoon anti-ship missiles. The proposal also includes more than $300 million in spare parts for Taiwanese aircraft, including F-5 and F-16 fighter jets. In addition to these, $47 million in Javelin guided missiles and command systems, radars and control systems designed to defend against missiles and aircraft, anti-missile systems sold by Raytheon and helicopters from Boeing are also a part of the package. A US State Department statement described the arms package as "a significant and tangible demonstration of the commitment of this Administration to provide Taiwan the defensive arms its needs to be strong."

In a swift response, the Taiwan government expressed admiration at the move and stressed that the leadership in Taipei wanted to maintain a strong defence while striving to improve relations with China. According to a Taiwanese spokesperson, "President Ma Ying-jeou would like to express gratitude to the US for the arms package. A strong defence and peace in the Taiwan Strait are necessary for Taiwan's prosperity." As a matter of fact, this latest deal stands at nearly half the package of $12 billion that was envisioned initially. Moreover, it does not include advanced F-16 C/D Falcon jet fighters, without which, Taiwan claims, it would find it hard to maintain a balance in air defence in the Taiwan Strait, especially given the rapid modernisation programme of the PLA Air Force. Expectedly, the announcement of the sale of these systems has Beijing red in the face, with China decrying the move and simultaneously issuing a warning that the weapons deal would cause further deterioration in ties. Chinese Vice Foreign Minister He Yafei called for a meeting with the US chargé d'affaires in Beijing to protest the sale. Furthermore, Chinese Foreign Ministry spokesman Liu Jianchao said the arms sale would interfere in China's internal affairs and national security and that the Chinese government and people strongly opposed the sale, since it would harm relations between China and the United States.

This newest weapons package was proposed way back in 2001 during the first term of the Bush Administration. It, however, got delayed owing to budget fallouts within Taiwan and political concerns in Washington regarding future ties with Mainland China. Defending its move, State Department spokesman Karl Duckworth said, "The sale is consistent with US policy and all foreign military sales are discussed and approved through long-established procedures. We appreciate

President Ma Ying-jeou's administration's efforts to reduce tensions in the Taiwan Strait and to build on the already excellent ties between the people of Taiwan and the US." Nonetheless, this latest arms deal would be viewed as yet another spoiler, given the recent warming of ties between China and Taiwan in the few months since the landslide victory in the Taiwanese presidential poll in 2008, of Kuomintang (KMT) Party candidate Ma Ying-jeou, who has rejected the push for independence of Taiwan, although he opposes unification with China.

Having said this, the divergent approaches of Washington and Beijing towards the BMD systems come along expected lines. US-China economic convergence is deftly matched by a seemingly ceaseless trend of strategic divergences. A growing concern over the future behaviour of an economically powerful and militarily robust China has often come to haunt American strategists and policy-makers. America watchers in China factored diverse American opinions into their calculations while examining American military plans, particularly the debate on the BMD systems. Besides, the events of September 11, 2001, provided the world with a warning that the unthinkable could happen. Although, ballistic missile technology may not be spreading rapidly, the threat of non-state actors laying their hands on sensitive technologies cannot be entirely negated. In the possibility of a terrorist organisation or a non-state actor finding refuge on the territory of a state possessing long-range ballistic missiles and warheads outfitted with WMD, the US and its allies could face severe convolution in pursuing or further countering the group or overthrow the regime of the country that harboured them in the first place.

In a broader sense, however, September 11 dramatically changed the perception of the ballistic missile threat. Some analysts argued that the terrorist attacks on the US were proof enough that the country's adversaries were prepared to do the unthinkable and it was just a matter of time before they laid their hands on actual missiles. This heightened perception of the threat helped them in putting forth their case of the missile defence debate. On December 11, 2002, President Bush issued his National Strategy to Combat WMD, resting on the three pillars of counter-proliferation, non-proliferation and response. The first pillar, counter-proliferation, included interdiction, deterrence, and defence (including preemptive measures and missile defences). Analysts argue that missile defence plays a critical role in the strategy to counter the proliferation threat. However, there was also the other side of the prevailing argument that the terrorist strikes of September 11 demonstrated, that ballistic missiles were not necessarily the tools of terrorist networks or non-state actors. Hence, whenever the missile defence debate resumes, there must be a renewed appreciation that in addition to all the thinking and money spent on ballistic missiles technologies, there should be equal if not more energy spent on the most likely threat named terrorism.

The stakes are high in the sense that erroneous decisions could lead to possible national military and economic disasters down the road. By its very nature, a BMD, especially in the nuclear age, holds grave consequences. A failed defensive system could conceivably lead to a devastated society due to excessive uncertainty concerning the technology's effectiveness measured empirically by missile defence's capacity to reliably and repeatedly intercept incoming warheads, including WMD. This has yet to be achieved by Washington. However, there has been significant progress in many aspects of the programme, although much still needs to be built upon. At the same time, changes in strategic objectives and constant programme perturbation have also led to a great deal of discontinuity in the execution of the BMD programme, which would be seen as a stumbling block in the long run. The irony lies within. A credible BMD—one that could overcome the simpler and cheaper gadgets designed to spoof it—might in the end just be out of reach. Nevertheless, requisite obligatory efforts in resources, time and energy would not have been much ado about nothing and above all, the political damage would have been done.

In conclusion, the United States finds itself on the horns of a dilemma. One option is to increase its own security along with that of its allies through largely unilateral action, although at the risk of a harsh international response. An arms race and crisis instability, unleashed by highly capable defences deployed in the absence of a revised ABM Treaty, threaten to undermine America's strategic position over the long term. On the flip side, Washington finds it difficult to avoid defence deployments, given the proliferation of ballistic missile threats and other WMD technologies coupled with domestic demands for protection, especially in the post-9/11 scenario. Despite this missile defence dilemma, the time surely has arrived for Washington to undertake realistic and pragmatic choices keeping in mind long-range US strategic interests within Asia and beyond.

Notes

1. Kalpana Chittaranjan, "US NMD: An Issue that Just Won't Go," *Strategic Analysis,* vol. 24, no. 10, January 2001, p. 1928.
2. Nirmal Jindal, *War as a Political Weapon in the Nuclear Age: A Study with Special Reference to the US Concept of Limited Nuclear War* (New Delhi: Intellectual Publishing House, 1987), p. 146.
3. Ibid., p. 156.
4. Erik K Pratt, "Missile Defense Sponsors: Shifting Political Support for Strategic Defense after Reagan," *Asian Perspective,* vol. 25, no. 1, 2001, p. 14.
5. Based primarily on "Ballistic Missile Defense Organization Budgetary History," BMDO Fact Sheet, April 1999.
6. Joseph Cirincione, "Why the Right Lost the Missile Defense Debate," *Foreign Policy,* no. 106, Spring 1997, p. 50.
7. BMDO Fact Sheet, n. 5.
8. Anthony H Cordesman, *Strategic Threats and National Missile Defenses: Defending the US Homeland* (Westport, CT: Praeger Publishers, 2002), p. 1.
9. For more details, see *Jane's Defense Weekly,* December 8, 1999, p. 8.
10. William J Broad, "A Missile Defense with Limits: The ABC's of the Clinton Plan," *The New York Times,* June 30, 2000.
11. Wei-Chin Lee, "Thunder in the Air: Taiwan and Theater Missile Defense," *The Nonproliferation Review,* vol. 8, no. 3, Fall-Winter 2001, p. 110.
12. Roger Handberg, *Ballistic Missile Defense and the Future of American Security: Agendas, Perceptions, Technology and Policy* (Westport, CT: Praeger Publishers, 2002), p. 6.
13. Ibid.
14. James Clay Moltz, "Missile Proliferation in East Asia: Arms Control Vs TMD Responses," *The Nonproliferation Review,* no. 4, Spring-Summer 1997, p. 66.
15. Philip Coyle, "Rhetoric or Reality? Missile Defense under Bush," *Arms Control Today,* vol. 32, no. 4, May 2002, pp. 3-4.
16. Ibid., p. 5.

17. Moltz, n. 14, p. 66.
18. Coyle, n. 15, p. 5.
19. Tara Kartha, "Ballistic Missile Defences: The Debate in the US," *Strategic Analysis*, vol. 24, no. 1, April 2000, p. 91.
20. The Clinton plan called for the deployment of a BMD system only when it was technically feasible and emphasised that the decision to deploy the system should be based on four criteria: whether the system was technically mature; the threat required it; the cost acceptability in terms of other priority; and finally, the implications of the decision for the overall security of the US, including the future of arms control.
21. James Clay Moltz, "The Impact of NMD on Nonproliferation Regimes", *The Nonproliferation Review*, vol. 7, no. 3, Fall-Winter 2000, pp. 63-64.
22. Ibid. (Moreover, in the 90s, North Korea did not have a credible missile capability to challenge US interests).
23. Ibid.
24. Mark Bromley, "European Missile Defense: New Emphasis, New Roles," *BASIC Paper*, no. 36, May 2001.
25. Brad Roberts, "Ballistic Missile Defences," in Jasjit Singh, ed., *Reshaping Asian Security* (New Delhi: Knowledge World, 2001), p. 233.
26. Christopher Marquis, "US Declares 'Rogue Nations' are now 'States of Concern'," *The New York Times*, June 20, 2000.
27. For details see, Donald H Rumsfeld Commission Report, Findings and Recommendations, July 31, 1998, at http://www.fas.org/irp/congress/1998-cr/s980731-rumsfeld.htm
28. Manpreet Sethi, "Ballistic Missile Defences: Implications for India," *Strategic Analysis*, vol. 25, no. 6, September 2001, pp. 739-740.
29. Cirincione, n. 6, p. 39.
30. Ibid., pp. 47-48.
31. Ibid.
32. US Department of Defence, News Briefing (Backgrounder), January 1999.
33. For details, see Secretary of Defence William Cohen, Annual Report to the US Congress for FY 2001, Department of Defence, Washington DC, January 2001.
34. Coyle, n. 15, p. 6.
35. Elizabeth Becker, "Missile Deployment Uncertain–Setback for Scaled-Down 'Star Wars' Plan", *The New York Times*, January 19, 2000, p. A1.
36. Excerpts from President Clinton's Speech, "A Call for Realism and Prudence," cited in *The New York Times*, September 2, 2000.
37. Eric Schmitt, "President Decides to Put off work on Missile Shield," *The New York Times*, September 2, 2000.
38. US Department of Defence (DOD), News Briefing (Backgrounder), January 20, 1999.
39. Cordesman, n. 8, p. 78.
40. *The Washington Post*, December 18, 2001.
41. Kalpana Chittaranjan, "A Russian Perspective of the START Process and

NMD," *Strategic Analysis*, vol. 25, no. 5, August 2001, p. 678.

42. Ibid.
43. Cordesman, n. 8, p. 53.
44. White House Transcript, December 18, 2001.
45. For details, see Ivo H Daalder and James M Lindsay, "A New Agenda for Nuclear Weapons," *Brookings Policy Brief*, no. 94, February 2002, available at www.brook.edu/dybdocroot/comm/policybriefs/pb94.htm
46. Ibid.
47. Robert M Bowman, *Star Wars: A Defense Insider's Case Against the Strategic Defense Initiative* (New York: St. Martin's Press, 1986), pp. 31-32.
48. Alison Mitchell, "Bush says US Should Reduce Nuclear Arms," *The New York Times*, May 24, 2000.
49. Marc Lacey, "Missile Defense Issue Lands in the Middle of the Gore-Bush Campaign," *The New York Times*, September 2, 2000.
50. Speech by President George W Bush, National Defence University, Washington, May 1, 2001; White House transcript, available at www.whitehouse.gov/news/releases/2001/05/20010501-10.htm
51. Steve Lee Myers and James Glanz, "Taking a Look at the Workings of a Missile Shield," *The New York Times*, May 3, 2001.
52. US Department of Defence, *Nuclear Posture Review*, available at www.globalsecurity.org/wmd/library/policy/dod/npr.htm
53. James M Lindsay and Michael E O'Hanlon, "Missile Defense after the ABM Treaty," *The Washington Quarterly*, vol. 25, no. 3, Summer 2002, p. 168.
54. Coyle, n. 15, p. 3.
55. James Glanz, "Other Systems Might Provide a US Missile Shield," *The New York Times*, September 4, 2000, p. A8.
56. National Intelligence Council, "Foreign Missile Developments and the Ballistic Missile Threat Through 2015," December 2001, at www.cia.gov/nic/pubs/index.htm
57. Unclassified Statement of Director, Missile Defence Agency, Henry A Obering, on the Missile Defence Programme and Fiscal Year 2008 Budget, before the Senate Armed Services Committee, Strategic Forces Subcommittee, April 11, 2007, p. 4.
58. For more details, see Statement of Lt Gen Michael D Maples, February 5, 2008, Washington DC.
59. Estimated by the "Current and Projected National Security Threats to the United States," Vice Admiral Lowell E Jacoby, US Navy Director, Senate Armed Services Committee, March 17, 2005, available at http://www.dia.mil/publicaffairs/Testimonies/statement17.html
60. According to the testimony of Henry A Obering, Director, Missile Defence Agency, Fiscal Year 2009 Budget, before the Senate Armed Services Committee, Subcommittee on Strategic Forces, April 1, 2008.
61. "Missile Defense Test Results," *Backgrounder*, US Department of Defence Report, May 31, 2002.
62. Statement by Henry A Obering, n. 57, p. 8.

63. Ibid.
64. Statement by Henry A Obering, n. 57, p. 21.
65. Testimony of Charles E McQueary, before the US Senate Armed Services Subcommittee on Strategic Forces, Office of the Secretary of Defence, April 11, 2007.
66. Statement by Henry A Obering, n. 57, p. 8.
67. Ibid., p. 14.
68. Shen Dingli, "Ballistic Missile Defense and China's National Security," *Jane's Special Report,* April 17, 2000.
69. For details, see Shao Zongwei, "US Nuke Action Concerns China," *China Daily,* April 14, 2000.
70. George Seigle, "Russia and China Worried Over US Plans for NMD System," *Jane's Defense Weekly,* March 24, 1999.
71. Sha Zukang, "The Global Strategic Balance and Stability Brook no Disruption," *Beijing Review*, August 2000, pp. 8-10.
72. John Newhouse, "The Missile Defence Debate," *Foreign Affairs,* vol. 80, no. 4, July/August 2001, p. 100.
73. Sha Zukang, "US Missile Defence Plan: China's View," *Disarmament Diplomacy*, no. 43, January/February 2000, pp. 4-6.
74. *Asian News Digest*, January 29-February 4, 2001, p. 898.
75. US National Intelligence Estimate (NIE) 2000 available at, http://en.wikipedia.org/wiki/Commission_to_Assess_the_Ballistic_Missile_Threat_to_the_United_States
76. Ibid.
77. *A New York Times* report, cited by Charles D Ferguson and John E Pike, October, 2000.
78. Quoted in, MV Rappai, "China's Nuclear Arsenal and Missile Defence," *Strategic Analysis*, vol. 26, no. 1, January- March 2002, pp. 70-71.
79. Kori J Urayama, "Chinese Perspectives on TMD," *Asian Survey,* vol. 40, no. 4, July/August 2000, p. 599.
80. Associated Press Report, "China Condemns US Missile Plans," November 25, 1999.
81. Michael J Green and Patrick M Cronin, eds., *The US-Japan Alliance: Past, Present and Future,* (New York: Council on Foreign Relations Press, 1999), p. 175.
82. For a comprehensive discussion of what is known about the Chinese nuclear arsenal in open-source literature, see Robert S Norris and Hans M Kristensen, "US Nuclear Forces, 2008," *Bulletin of the Atomic Scientists*, vol. 64, no. 1, March/April 2008, pp. 50-53.
83. Christopher P Twomey, "Chinese-US Strategic Affairs: Dangerous Dynamism," *Arms Control Today*, vol. 39, January/February 2009.
84. For details, see James Clay Moltz, *The Politics of Space Security: Strategic Restraint and the Pursuit of National Interests* (Palo Alto, CA: Stanford University Press, 2008).
85. Twomey, n. 83.

86. Cited in *The Washington Post*, July 12, 2000.
87. For more details, see Wade L Huntley and Robert Brown, "Missile Defense & China," *Foreign Policy in Focus*, Nautilus Institute, vol. 6, no. 3, January 2001.
88. As reported in the *Far Eastern Economic Review*, July 16, 1998.
89. CRS Report for US Congress, "China and Proliferation of Weapons of Mass Destruction and Missiles: Policy Issues," February 26, 2003, p. 19.

6

Conclusion

Throughout the period of the Cold War, the context of an international system was defined by fierce competition between the two superpowers, the United States and the erstwhile USSR, for global hegemony. Although significantly weaker than either of the superpowers, the PRC was adept at extending its own influence in international politics beyond the limits of its tangible power by playing upon American and Soviet hopes and fears. At that time, US nuclear strategy and arms control experts showed little concern over the Chinese nuclear capability, as it did not feature as a major factor in the US nuclear calculus, which in any case remained centred on the Soviet nuclear arsenal.

However, since the end of the Cold War, China managed to increase its regional influence and sought to expand its sphere of influence even beyond its immediate region through various ways. During the said time period, the Sino-American relationship could best be described as a complex interplay of conditions. While the United States and China had enormous interests at stake in their bilateral relationship, neither was particularly deft in dealing with the other. David M Lampton appositely portrayed these inherent conditions and titled his book, *Same Bed, Different Dreams* that best describes Sino-US ties. Inspired by an ancient Chinese expression, it captures the essence of a relationship between two people whose lives are intimately intertwined but who do not fundamentally communicate with each other. Sino-US relations appear fittingly descriptive of the above expression.

The post-Cold War setting provided for a crucial phase in the evolution of US-China relations given that these years constituted the formative years of an era marked by the presence of the sole remaining superpower of the globe and the absence of the Cold War climate. Consequently, China lost its traditional strategic significance to the US, but went on to become a progressively more attractive place for American investment. These years also witnessed China's emergence as a major military and economic power in Asia, capable of projecting air, land and naval forces well matched by the engine of its economic growth. Gradually, it emerged that such capabilities emboldened Beijing to resort to coercive diplomacy or threat of direct military action in an attempt to resolve in its favour, various outstanding territorial claims or to press other vital issues affecting the future economic and security environment of the region. In retrospect, the distinct sense of acute awareness of the Cold War's pervasive nuclear threats kept the issue of US nuclear policy at the forefront of the national consciousness for decades, which, however, with the fall of the Soviet Union appeared beginning to fade. The doctrine on which the massive US nuclear arsenal was based became less relevant as the attention turned to arms control and ways to cope with other states' emerging nuclear capabilities.

The dramatic threats posed by terrorism and the proliferation of WMD determined the subsequent role and missions of the US approach to nuclear weapons. The Clinton Administration, thus, adopted a policy of 'constructive engagement' to derive as much benefit as possible from China. Nevertheless, a contradiction soon surfaced because the Clinton White House simultaneously chanted the non-proliferation *mantra* and, thus, came afloat the entire debate on Beijing's role in the proliferation of WMD especially in the Asian continent where the People's Republic of China was found at the centre of empowering an age of nuclear proliferation in Asia through Pakistan, North Korea and Iran.

In would be apposite to state that Sino-American relations perpetually seem to be in a state of flux vis-à-vis the issue of WMD proliferation. Subsequent US Administrations have tried very hard to abide by the principles of non-proliferation, expressed their concerns at the Chinese behaviour intermittently, and imposed modest sanctions on China occasionally, thereby not coming down rigidly against Beijing. This could be amidst the backdrop that as one of the largest international arms merchants, as well as a nuclear weapon state, China's cooperation is apparently essential if there has to be a more effective international regime to control the spread of highly lethal weapon systems. And, thus, it is a trial not just for Washington but also for the international community since China figures prominently as one of the major concerns on account of proliferation of sensitive WMD technology to countries such as Pakistan, North Korea and Iran.

In order to understand the dangers and opportunities that would define America's strategy in the new era, US analysts argue that it must see the post-Cold War world in much the similar fashion that George Marshall saw Europe after World War II and returned to 'prevention' by means of his strategy of preventive defence. Preventive Defence as a concept of defence strategy for the US in the post-Cold War era stresses upon the need to anticipate security dangers that, if mismanaged, have the potential to recreate Cold War-scale threats to US interests and survival. The foci of Preventive Defence are: proliferation of weapons of mass destruction, terrorism, 'loose nukes' and other military technology, significantly coupled with the peaceful rise of China.[1] Thus, according to the advocates of this apparatus, the content of engagement should be a preventive defence strategy—a focussed, pro-active programme to shape the US-China security relationship, of which a significant strand is that of encouraging greater participation by China in counter-proliferation and other international security efforts. Indeed, a clear difference between a policy of preventive defence and one of containment is that the former encourages while the latter discourages Chinese participation and influence.[2]

A veracity uppermost in the mind of the Americans since the first term of the Clinton Administration has been the economic opportunities offered by the Chinese government in China. Moreover, at that point, the PRC's international status rested heavily on its rapidly growing economy and its increasing integration with the world economy. The economic imperatives bound the US to Asia and it appeared that economic considerations took precedence over political imperatives while providing a new-found foundation for a wider range of cooperation. Increasingly, the development of the Chinese economy depended on American capital, technologies, markets and information and injected additional vitality into Sino-US relations. If, on the one hand, the days of the Soviet challenge witnessed Washington forging strategic ties with China, the post-Soviet era observed American economic stakes in China exercising a more determining influence on US-China relations, on the other. In the scenario wherein the gains China reaps from deeper integration into the world economy are only a source of power and not of constraint on future behaviour, then the engagement policy may come back to haunt US policy-makers. But if deeper integration empowers vested interests with a strong stake in that integration and supports the leadership's economic goals, then Chinese decision-makers will be less inclined to pursue conflictual and expansionist political-military policies.[3]

As a result, the non-proliferation measures adopted against Chinese policies did not have teeth in the true sense of the term. After Clinton's exit from the White House, the incoming George W Bush Administration did not have any intention to carry on the Clinton strategy of constructive engagement and openly characterised China as a strategic competitor. President Bush's speech to the National Defence University on May 1, 2001, on national missile defence was clearly a blunt message to China. During the early years of his Administration, President Bush began to confront a serious challenge to non-proliferation from North Korea and Iran. Understandably, there was little option for Washington except to coopt China to address such challenges. Moreover, the terrorist attacks on the US on September 11, 2001, changed the global scenario, which included a shift in the Bush Administration's approach to China.

In the absence of a peer competitor of the Soviet Union's magnitude, regional players gained prominence in the US strategic environment. The "rogue states" or "states of proliferation concern" characterised as sponsors of terrorism, WMD proliferators, and regional competitors were viewed by the United States as upcoming security threats. This threat particularly played out dramatically in Iran and North Korea, among others. As the US focussed its attention on nuclear proliferation, the issue of nuclear and missile technology transfer by China became one of the most prominent stumbling blocks leading to a divergence of Chinese and American security interests. Beijing showed a darker side in its dealings in the realms of proliferation and technology transfer of which the greatest concern to Washington was the documented Chinese behaviour contributing to the spread of technology relating to WMD along with their means of delivery to states located in regions that have always been a cause of concern to the United States, especially Iran and North Korea. The US Congress has long been concerned about whether US policy was effective in reducing the role of the PRC in the proliferation of WMD and missiles.

As the Director of Central Intelligence (DCI) reported, China remained a "key supplier" of weapons technology—particularly missile or nuclear technology, with persisting concerns about the PRC's assistance to Pakistan's nuclear facilities. As reported in 1992, China began to build a nuclear power plant at Chasma and was suspected in 1994 of helping Pakistan to build an unsafeguarded, plutonium-producing reactor at Khushab. The Arms Control and Disarmament Agency's *Annual Report on Arms Control* for 1998 stated, "There continued to be some contacts between Chinese entities and Pakistan's unsafeguarded and nuclear weapons programme." In early 1996, several Congressmen called for sanctions after reports disclosed that China sold unsafeguarded ring magnets to Pakistan, apparently in violation of the NPT and in contradiction of US laws, including the Arms Export Control Act and Export-Import Bank Act, as amended by the Nuclear Proliferation Prevention Act of 1994. *The Washington Times* first disclosed intelligence reports that the China National Nuclear Corporation, a state-owned corporation, transferred 5,000 ring magnets to the AQ Khan Research Laboratory in Kahuta, Pakistan, which could be used in gas centrifuges to enrich uranium. In addition, the US State Department confirmed that "between late 1994 and mid-1995, a Chinese entity transferred a large number of ring magnets to Pakistan for use in its uranium enrichment programme."[4] The Clinton Administration's decision-making was further complicated by considerations of US corporations doing business in China. Moreover, in 2000, according to numerous reports, former US non-proliferation and intelligence officials suspected that China provided equipment for Pakistan's secret heavy water production plant at Khushab where an unsafeguarded reactor allegedly generated weapons-grade plutonium.

Furthermore, the DCI reported in January 2003 that the PRC previously provided "extensive support" to Pakistan's nuclear weapons programmes and that, in the second half of 2001, "continued contacts" between PRC entities and Pakistani nuclear weapons entities could not be ruled out despite the 1996 Chinese promise not to assist unsafeguarded nuclear facilities. The policy-making circles in Washington have held that the nuclear proliferation ring among China, Pakistan, Iran and North Korea needs to be addressed in the starkest form of reality if the ever-growing peril of proliferation of WMD and their respective means of delivery is to be checked. However, since the US adopted a policy of strategic engagement of Pakistan, it did not seem overtly concerned about Sino-Pak nuclear and missile cooperation. Though Washington raised a hue and cry about the Chinese hand in the possible nuclear capabilities of nations in the Middle East and Northeast Asia, it was conspicuously soft on the same issue vis-à-vis Pakistan and the nuclear black market web woven by disgraced Pakistani nuclear scientist AQ Khan. These developments compel us to ponder on a mounting notion: can a few countries can be trusted with WMD and their means of delivery, while others cannot? And this trust would ultimately depend on, and consequently shift, as American attitudes, interests and policies changed.

This misguided policy approach appears to be continuing till date as even the George W Bush Administration remained unsuccessful in fully breaking apart the Abdul Qadeer Khan network, and tied to the short-term goal of building a relationship with Pakistan's President, Pervez Musharraf in order to wage its war on terror in Asia (read Afghanistan—thereafter percolating into the borders with Pakistan).

China's vital assistance to Pakistan's nuclear and missile programme has intensified and complicated the regional security dynamic, implicating China more fully in it than many international officials recognise. The 2009 release of AQ Khan from house arrest has indeed caused panic not just within South Asia (read India and elsewhere) but also across the globe. While condemning AQ Khan's release, Chairman of the House Foreign Affairs Committee, Howard L Berman stated, "It is very alarming that AQ Khan, the worst proliferator of nuclear weapons technology in history, has been freed... It is unclear whether the illicit smuggling network he created was fully dismantled even after he was placed under nominal 'house' arrest... By releasing him, the Pakistani government may in effect be giving him license to resume, perhaps directly, his past actions to aid, abet and profit from the spread of nuclear weapons."[5] Berman further noted, "US officials have been prevented from interviewing Khan to try to determine the extent of the damage he has done... Congress will take this into account as we review and create legislation on US-Pakistan relations and the circumstances under which US assistance is provided to Islamabad."[6]

Given the rising influence of the Afghan Taliban coupled with the reemergence and reestablishment of the Al Qaeda in the Pashtun areas of Northwest Pakistan, AQ Khan's release could not have come at a worse time, with his past record of illegal nuclear trade. Besides, the February 2009 acceptance by Pakistan's government of a peace deal with the tribal militants in Pakistan (read hand-in-glove with the Taliban) in addition to other extremist and radical militant outfits on either side of the Durand Line is proof enough that the writ of the Pakistani governance is fast corroding. These developments further indicate that Pakistan is incapable of negotiating from a position of strength and that this deal would be the official platform for the creation of a safe haven for militants. This situation is exceedingly precarious, especially for India, given Pakistan's history and the fact that it is nuclear-armed.

Paradoxically, the long-term future of Pakistan depends especially on the army voluntarily nurturing independent civilian institutions and leaders to displace it from many positions it now occupies. Perhaps the greatest challenge, for the army leadership, as well as civilians, will be to impose control from top to bottom over the ubiquitous intelligence services, some of whose personnel operate autonomously. Reform of the intelligence services is undermined by the Central Intelligence Agency's dependence on these services in combating the Taliban, Al

Qaeda and other terrorist actors and sponsors. Ultimately, though, such reform is the key to an effective non-proliferation strategy as well as to stability in South Asia.[7]

Therefore, US policy must turn its attention to the regional policies and strategic imperatives behind China's proliferation behaviour. Policy debates concerning the PRC's technology transfers have often centred on questions of whether to impose unilateral sanctions under US laws, to enact new legislation to tighten mandates for sanctions or reports, or to integrate the multiple laws. Also, there have been the issues of whether to target the PRC government or PRC 'entities' (usually state owned defence industrial organisations like CPMIEC or NORINCO). This related claim that China's central government has only a limited ability to control arms transfers is inaccurate given that China's weapons export system is, in fact, quite centralised, with the most sensitive transfers of complete systems requiring the approval of the Central Military Commission.[8] It is assumable that decisions on sanctions impact US credibility and leverage on the non-proliferation issue. While certain PRC transfers may not violate any international treaties, sanctions may be required under some US laws that Congress has passed and these need to be implemented so as to set US non-proliferation policy and shore up non-proliferation treaties and standards. These laws, as amended, include:

- Export-Import Bank Act (PL 79-173)
- Arms Export Control Act (AECA) (PL 90-629)
- Export Administration Act (EAA) (PL 96-72)
- Nuclear Proliferation Prevention Act (Title VIII of PL 103-236)
- Iran-Iraq Arms Nonproliferation Act (PL 102-484)
- Iran Nonproliferation Act (PL 106-178)
- Executive Order 12938, as amended by Executive Order 13094
- Executive Order 13382.[9]

The Democrat Administration in the immediate years after the end of the Cold War pursued a policy of "engagement" with Beijing which, in a way, was more of a cooperative approach aimed towards entangling the Dragon. Critics of the "engagement" policy argued that the US needed a tougher approach to counter Chinese activities that potentially would undermine US security interests. They noted that PRC weapons proliferation activities have continued and repeated PRC assurances have proved to be unreliable. In fact, according to them, US security interests are better served with a stronger approach to stigmatise sensitive transfers, which would include some sanctions. However, sanctions are counter-productive and are too broad. Rather, they assert that China needs to recognise non-proliferation for its own national interests and develop stronger export controls, perhaps with US assistance.

Significantly, sanctions tend to be seen in China as mere reflections of American domestic politics, not policy. The current honeycomb of uncoordinated sanctions laws is ineffective and a burden on policy-making. While the US needs to rationalise its sanctions policy, it should also continue to maintain control of transfer of munitions to China. Careful review of controls on dual-use exports is warranted in order to give appropriate balance to national security and economic objectives.[10] As the most portentous geo-strategic development in America's westward vista, the emergence of China is a development that calls for a preventive defence strategy. 'Containing' China is not a viable option. Such a strategy could eventually produce precisely the adversarial kind of China that Washington would like to avoid and both the American public and its allies in the region are unlikely to support the kind of expense involved. The US should aim at using its influence towards building a solid foundation for US-China relations and to shape that relationship to both countries' present and future mutual benefit.[11] Several Chinese analysts have noted that the coming generation of Chinese leadership could well be less inclined to view international relations in 'zero-sum' terms[12] and be less hostile toward US dominance. However, the Taiwan factor has always been, and shall continue to be, a potential flashpoint between Washington and Beijing.

It should be highlighted that China sought to use weapons sales and technology transfers to Pakistan not just solely to undermine its rival India, but also to induce Washington to reduce weapons sales to

Taiwan. During the waning days of his presidency, on October 3, 2008, US President George W Bush notified the Congress his approval for selling defensive weapon systems worth a staggering $6.9 billion to Taiwan. The package of weapon systems includes the $3.1 billion worth PAC-3 guided missile systems, $2.5 billion worth of Apache Longbow attack helicopters, $250 million in equipment for upgrading Taiwan's E-2T Hawkeye surveillance aircraft, $200 million in Harpoon anti-ship missiles and $47 million in Javelin guided missiles and command systems, radars and control systems designed to defend against missiles among others. A US State Department statement described the arms package as "a significant and tangible demonstration of the commitment of this Administration to provide Taiwan the defensive arms its needs to be strong."

Expectedly, the announcement of the sale of these systems had Beijing red in the face, with China decrying the move and simultaneously issuing a warning that the weapons deal would cause further deterioration in ties. Chinese Vice Foreign Minister He Yafei called for a meeting with the US chargé d'affaires in Beijing to protest the sale. Furthermore, Chinese Foreign Ministry spokesman Liu Jianchao said the arms sale would interfere in China's internal affairs and national security and that the Chinese government and people strongly opposed the sale, since it would harm relations between China and the United States. The sentiment has precisely been referred to in the 2008 White Paper on *China's National Defence* in which Beijing indirectly points at the United States as its "major" adversary and protests against continuing US arms sales to Taipei. The White Paper states Beijing's claim that it has "succeeded in thwarting Taiwan independence."[13]

Taiwanese President Ma Ying-jeou of the Kuomintang Party (KMT) has rejected the push for independence by Taiwan since his days of campaign for the presidency and seeks closer ties to Mainland China, although he opposes unification with the Mainland. However, enduring US arms sales among others fuel concerns on whether the KMT would find comprehensive power to push Taiwan towards a new era in cross-strait relations, given that Taiwan has incessantly featured as a sticking point in Sino-US relations in particular, and the Asian-Pacific security apparatus in general. The latest arms deal and Taiwan's constant dependence on US weapons sales to keep pace with China's massive arms build-up will surely be a major hiccup in the current situation and cause turbulence in the Asia-Pacific security situation. Beijing always has used and will continue to use every bit of leverage it has to halt weapons sales to Taipei. Hawks within Washington's policy-making circles remain sceptical that China views non-proliferation in its national interest, since Beijing has made progress in non-proliferation commitments as part of improving relations with Washington and simultaneously tried to use its sales as a form of leverage against Washington, especially on the issue of US arms sales to Taiwan. From Beijing's perspective, it remains evident that it has tactically also used its intermittent weapons sales and technology transfers as a means to solidify relations with significant countries. For instance, China sold IRBMs to Saudi Arabia—a transaction that not only raked in money for Beijing, but also helped induce Riyadh to recognise the PRC and sever official ties with Taiwan in 1990.

The concerns in China regarding the possible deployment of TMD on Taiwan are paramount. China's missile deployments along the Fujian Coast facing Taiwan serve as an effective deterrent against any future move for Taiwanese independence. Deployment of advanced missile defence systems required an integrated command and control system, which, in China's view, would equal a *de facto* military alliance. These developments would probably prod Beijing to a rapid build-up of both conventional and nuclear weapon arsenals on the Mainland. Beijing consistently argues that the US' pursuit of the missile defence programme will undermine the global strategic stability by making other nations insecure. These concerns have played out in the PRC's naval build-up, for instance. The discovery of the new naval base in Sanya on Hainan Island is vital since it is capable of housing a large fleet of surface warships and serving as an underground base for submarines. In fact, the Hainan Base would allow China larger influence in the South China Sea; greater access to the critical Strait of Malacca; and superior naval presence closer to important sea lanes.

With a successful ballistic missile defence programme, the United States could well become the first nuclear state to be able to protect itself from retaliation in kind—at least from the smaller nuclear states. Several Chinese analysts have argued that this would give the United States greater freedom of action that could encourage it to mount preemptive attacks. Nations might be forced to enhance their particular nuclear and missile arsenals to counter the proposed US shield, which, in turn, would spark an Asian arms race and complicate future arms control initiatives.

One scenario likely to provoke a large-scale military response by China thereby jeopardising its economic ties with Washington would be Taiwan's nudge towards legal independence. Economic convergence would likely take a back seat to the more serious problem that declaration of independence by the island would raise for Beijing. Yet, as Thomas Christensen notes, a military response by China to Taiwanese steps toward independence would not be an indication of an expansionist foreign policy in Beijing. "If Taiwan declared independence and was then attacked by the mainland," he notes, "one could not draw conclusions about Beijing's expansionist designs any more than one could draw conclusions about American expansionism from the Northern states' reaction to the South's secession."[14] Because large segments of the Chinese electorate benefit from integration into the world economy and key elements of the Chinese leadership have made a strong commitment to internationalist economic policies, one could conclude that China is unlikely to pursue aggressive and highly conflictual foreign policies. Thus, by integrating China's economy more closely into world markets, maintenance of the policy of engagement will make Chinese belligerence even less likely.[15]

But it is evident that deeper integration into the international fora has not exactly goaded the Chinese leadership into comprehending the dangers of the proliferation of nuclear, biological and chemical weapons coupled with the spread of ballistic missiles and transfers of certain types of conventional weapons to unstable regions or regimes. Along with Pakistan, China has been under the US scanner vis-à-vis its missile and nuclear activities in North Korea. The *National Security*

Agency (NSA) Report of March 1999 suggested that China sold specialty steel for use in North Korea's missile programme. Moreover, in June 1999, US intelligence reportedly found that PRC entities transferred accelerometers, gyroscopes and precision grinding machinery to North Korea, as was reported by *The Washington Times* of July 20, 1999. Another *Classified Report* dated October 20, 1999, said China's Changda Corp sought to buy Russian gyroscopes that were more of the same that China supplied to the North Korean missile programme earlier that year, according to the November 19, 1999 *Washington Times*. In December 1999, the NSA discovered an alleged PRC deal to supply unspecified PRC-made missile-related items to North Korea through a Hong Kong company. PRC technology transfers had further implications for secondary, or retransferred proliferation, since North Korea reportedly supplied technology to Iran, Syria, Pakistan, Egypt, Libya, and Yemen. A serious case involved North Korea's secret programme to enrich uranium to develop nuclear weapons, a programme surprisingly acknowledged by North Korea during talks on October 4, 2002.

At this given point, it would be pertinent to stress that China's nuclear technology indirectly contributed to North Korea's nuclear weapons programme via Pakistan, since China was the 'principal supplier' to Pakistan's nuclear weapons programme. In fact, there potentially would not have been a Pakistani nuclear weapons programme sans Chinese aid and assistance, although questions do persist regarding China's past or present knowledge about the Pakistani-North Korean trade and whether Beijing is indeed sharing that information. According to Henry Sokolski, at the Nonproliferation Policy Education Centre, "One might call on Pakistan, Russia and China to detail what nuclear technology and hardware they allowed North Korea to import." Since the October 2002 disclosure about North Korea's ongoing nuclear weapon programmes, the Bush Administration sought China's cooperation in a multilateral effort in bringing about a halt to it.

The North Korean nuclear and missile quandary has gripped the Korean Peninsula and beyond for decades now. After having agreed to arrive at a solution towards resolving the nuclear impasse, starting with the destruction of the cooling tower at its nuclear complex in Yongbyon on June 27, 2008, speculation is rife that Pyongyang's regime is contemplating a possible test launch of North Korea's longest-range missile–the Taepo Dong-II, capable of striking the US homeland. Furthermore, North Korea has successfully deployed 3,000 km range short- and intermediate-range ballistic missiles. In this backdrop, the new Obama Administration appears to be reviewing its Pyongyang policies. In fact, the entire region is experiencing a whirlpool effect and the direct outcome is accelerated efforts towards deployment of ballistic missile defence systems by US allies in Asia. According to the Japanese Kyodo news agency on March 3, 2009, Tokyo is likely to deploy both its ballistic missile interceptor warships to the Sea of Japan and further Tokyo would send two naval destroyers with high-tech Aegis radar systems and Standard Missile-3 (SM-3) interceptors to the Sea of Japan, between Japan and the Korean Peninsula.[16] Apart from SM-3s, which are designed to shoot missiles down in the mid-phase of flight, Japan's second layer of defence in the form of land-based PAC-3 interceptors are positioned at military bases mostly close to Tokyo. Besides, Washington has also stationed anti-ballistic missile ships in Japan and is now urging the Republic of Korea (South Korea) to join the US missile defence umbrella in Asia. While emphasising the need for deeper cooperation, Chief of the ROK-US Combined Forces Command (CFC) and the United Nations Command (UNC), Gen Walter Sharp stressed the need for South Korea to develop a multi-layered missile defence system interoperable with the US high-altitude ballistic missile defence shield for defence against a possible North Korean missile attack. "The Republic of Korea does not have a robust missile defence capability in place and this would likely be one of the bridging capabilities the US would provide until the ROK improves this."[17] These developments within Northeast Asia are surely being observed very closely by Beijing since it has been one of the most vocal critics of the BMD programme. Any move by Washington to alter the strategic situation in the region is likely to be met by a stern response from China.

Indeed, it is ironical that Washington requires Chinese support to deal with the nuclear and missile proliferation activities of nations such as North Korea and Iran, that sought and received crucial Chinese assistance to develop their nuclear and missile capabilities along with its means of delivery. Beijing may prefer keeping the North Korean issue—a threat to US interests—alive as a counterweight to US interests in Taiwan—an overriding Chinese concern.[18] Washington believed that leaving China out of the process would lead to increased instability in the East Asian region. Although lucidly, China refused to seriously condemn Pyongyang's nuclear weapon and missile programmes, or exert diplomatic and economic pressure on North Korea, despite repeated appeals to do so from the US and other nations. Specifically, China has a strong interest in avoiding political disruption in North Korea and has incessantly argued in favour of seeking a negotiated solution to the North Korean crisis. The improvement of Sino-US ties, however, did not prevent observers within Washington's policy-making circles from censuring the Bush White House for failing to forcefully press China's leadership on weapons non-proliferation as a priority issue, even while imposing numerous US sanctions. This was visible, for instance, when former Assistant Secretary of State for Non-Proliferation in the Clinton Administration, Robert Einhorn, criticised the Bush Administration, stating in April 2003, "Sanctions are used, but they are usually simply imposed rather than used as a vehicle for trying to leverage better behavior... There seems to be no real strategy today to try to promote continued improvement in China's nonproliferation record."[19] China might just be more cooperative if it helped to draw up the 'rules', but there are concerns that China's participation would risk its obstruction of tighter export controls, possible derailing of arms control efforts and crucial linkage of non-proliferation to the interminable Taiwan issue.

In addition to North Korea, the Islamic Republic of Iran has been under international scrutiny for its nuclear quagmire. After President Clinton signed certifications in January 1998 to implement the 1985 Sino-US nuclear cooperation agreement, as promised at the 1997 summit, *The Washington Post* on March 13, 1998 reported that at a closed hearing of the Senate Foreign Relations Committee on March 12, 1998, Clinton Administration officials disclosed negotiations in January 1998 between the China Nuclear Energy Industry Corporation and Iran's Isfahan Nuclear Research Centre to provide "a lifelong supply" of hundreds of tons of anhydrous hydrogen fluoride (AHF), or hydrofluoric acid, under falsified documents about end-users. Beijing did stop the sale owing to protests lodged by Washington. Besides, in his testimony before the Senate Governmental Affairs Subcommittee on International Security, Proliferation and Federal Services on June 6, 2002, Assistant Secretary of State John Wolf stated concerns about possible PRC-Iranian interactions "despite China's 1997 pledge to end its nuclear cooperation with Iran." Furthermore, the DCI reported in January 2003 that "some interactions," in the second half of 2001, between the PRC and Iranian entities "may run counter" to Beijing's 1997 commitment and noted that the two projects were not yet completed. In testimony to Congress on February 11, 2003, DCI George Tenet pointed to China's 'firms' (rather than the government) and warned that they "may be backing away from Beijing's 1997 bilateral commitment to forego any new nuclear cooperation with Iran." The real question here is whether these 'firms' can actually go around doing sensitive nuclear technology transfers with nations without the knowledge and prior approval of the government.

The PRC technicians assisted Iran in order to build a calutron, or electromagnetic isotope separation system for enriching uranium at the Karaj nuclear research facility, according to "confidential reports" submitted to Iranian President Rafsanjani by his senior aides, according to the *Sunday Telegraph,* as reported in the September 25, 1995 *Washington Times*. The US confirmed in May 2002 that sanctions under the Iran Nonproliferation Act of 2000 (PL 106-178) were imposed on three PRC entities for conventional transfers to Iran related to unspecified missiles. It was also noted that the Administration did not impose new missile proliferation sanctions (under the AECA and EAA) between November 2001 and May 2002.[20] All these statements are cursors to the prevalent and known Chinese behaviour of going back and forth on its commitments towards sensitive nuclear and missile technology transfer and to the arduous futuristic approach regarding China's undertaking punitive measures against nations like North Korea and Iran. It should be mentioned that time and again, China's pledges to restrain its activities on the nuclear and missile proliferation front have been blemished. For instance, China signed the Biological Weapons Convention (BWC) in 1984 and the Chemical Weapons Convention (CWC) in 1993 but continued to export equipment and materials to Iran. In palpable terms, China has consistently and in a pointed fashion refused to engage in truly viable arms control at the international level and has incessantly devised nifty channels to proliferate without technically flouting international agreements.

Regarding the Iranian missile programme, *The Washington Times* on September 10, 1997, cited Israeli and US intelligence sources as saying that China Great Wall Industry Corp. (which markets satellite launches) was providing telemetry equipment used in flight-tests to Iran for its development of the Shahab-3 and Shahab-4 MRBMs (with ranges, respectively, of about 800 and 1,250 miles respectively). Citing a May 27, 1998 intelligence report, China discussed selling telemetry equipment (for testing missiles) to Iran. In the late 1990s, Iran began to import and possibly assemble imported components of the Nodong missile, improvements for which had reportedly been made with possible Chinese assistance, resulting in the Shahab-3.[21] Subsequently, the Pentagon confirmed that the July 1998 tested Iranian mobile Shahab-3 missile was actually based on the North Korean Nodong MRBM. The Shahab-3 is now the mainstay of Iran's missile forces and the foundation for its nascent space programme, which test-launched two sub-orbital missiles in 2008 as well as launching the home-made Omid satellite in February 2009. The November 2008 test launch of Iran's new Sajjil missile indicates a significant shift in Tehran's missile development programme.[22] The immediate strategic impact will be limited, since neither the range nor the payload capacity of the Sajjil is greater than that of the existing Iranian Shahab-3. However, the transition from the liquid-propelled Shahab to production of the multi-stage, solid-fuelled Sajjil would be important if shown by further tests to be sustainable.

Although China has reportedly agreed not to make further transfers of anti-shipping missiles to Iran, it remains to be seen whether it accepts as a general principle that it should not sell certain types of conventional weapons to countries like Iran.[23] As a matter of fact, China's transfers of conventional weapons are likely to continue at the reduced levels they have sustained.[24] According to a study by the Carnegie Endowment for International Peace, "Diplomacy would be augmented by the realistic possibility of economic sanctions on investment in Iran imposed by all countries.... China's unwillingness to support economic sanctions to enforce international rules is intensified by its growing dependence on Iranian oil."[25] The claim that China's arms transfers are motivated primarily by the desire to generate export earnings is inaccurate. In fact, virtually all of China's arms transfers are partly driven by foreign policy considerations.[26]

China increasingly nurtures closer energy and economic ties with Iran and envisions it as a major source of its ever-growing energy needs. From 1998 to 2003, crude oil from the Middle East accounted for 50.9 percent of China's total energy imports of which Iran accounted for 13.6 percent of China's oil imports, second only to that of Saudi Arabia's 16.7 percent, signalling that Iran is indispensable to China's energy security. China imported 130 million tonnes of crude oil from Iran in 2004, accounting for 15 percent of its total imports of crude oil. On October 28, 2004, China signed a Memorandum of Understanding (MoU) with Iran that awarded Sinopec, China's second-largest oil giant, the rights to participate in developing Yadavaren, an Iranian oil field, in exchange for an agreement to purchase 10 million tonnes of liquefied natural gas (LNG) over 25 years. One of the world's largest undeveloped oil fields, Yadavaren is estimated to have a total production capacity of around 300,000 barrels per day, according to the US Department of Energy, half of which would eventually be exported to China. It is understood that this deal, also covering the LNG construction on-site, could be as large as $70 billion.

The proliferation of WMD weapons undoubtedly would be a continuing and mounting quandary in the coming future. As relations among powers shift, in perhaps unpredictable ways, more countries may perceive it to be in their interests to have WMD weapons as a sort of security blanket against the unexpected. In what is more crucial, as the number of actors possessing nuclear arms and other weapons of mass destruction increases, seemingly, does the perilous likelihood of their falling into the hands of individual or group non-state actors who may see them as usable instruments. There appears an expansive consensus within the US that the greatest danger it confronts is the nexus between WMD and terrorism, for which the contribution of China's proliferation of WMD and related technologies would always be tainted.

In what could prospectively be a whiff of things to come, Chinese influence over the contentious nuclear quagmire involving Iran and North Korea has driven Washington policy-makers to the crossroads regarding the options by which they could possibly checkmate the 'China factor'. With the end of the global threat, the US has in place a regional defence strategy incorporating an understanding of US vital national security interests in West Asia as well as Northeast Asia. The significance of West Asia may be attributed to the West's ever-increasing dependence on Persian Gulf oil. As demonstrated during Gulf War I as well as its present status vis-à-vis Iraq, the US is willing to go to war to prevent hostile regional hegemony. Long-standing US ties to Israel also contributed to the region's critical importance. In the possibility of certain states in West Asia in possession of WMD along with long-range missiles, there is trepidation that these states might then be able to threaten Western Europe and beyond. Thus, recent events of nuclear and missile proliferation by Iran and North Korea are considered primary drivers for Washington to move faster on fronts like increasing counter-proliferation capabilities in several areas, including ballistic missile defence among others. In order to be effective in counter-proliferation, the US advocates the need of increased defence capability for both active and passive defence against ballistic as well as cruise missiles. This particularly holds importance for securing cooperation from regional allies in confronting a regional adversary armed with nuclear or biological weapons and missiles capable of reaching their territory.

Although historically terrorists have not used WMD, this might change in the coming future. There has been growing perception that the terrorist attacks on the US are proof enough that the country's adversaries are prepared to do the unthinkable and it's just a matter of time before they lay their hands on actual operational missiles through the channels of unstable nations and regimes. To hedge against this possible danger, subsequent US Administrations, including the present Obama Administration, appear unswerving towards focus on an increased capability for detecting and outlasting these threats. The ongoing US led operations in Afghanistan and Pakistan could be one such endeavour viewed in this light.

However, the US actions to shore up its 'defensive capabilities' brings centre-stage the very crucial offensive-defensive equation that is central to deterrence as a concept. The US missile defence systems will, in fact, pose a direct threat to the survivability of Chinese deterrent capabilities and in all likelihood, present China with both an operational military challenge and a long-term politico-security threat. Concerns about the effectiveness of its deterrent forces and about a possible conflict with the US over Taiwan could be interpreted as a few of the major drivers of the modernisation programme launched by China. The launch of the US missile defence systems could trigger an Asian missile race and complicate future arms control initiatives. In addition, development of US theatre missile defence in Asia would drive Beijing to expand its missile arsenals and, consequently, Beijing might no longer feel constrained from offensive missile exports to countries that the US perceives as "states of proliferation concern" or "rogue states"—a step by which the US' objective of bringing China completely into the fold of the non-proliferation regime stands to be washed out.

Beijing has not completely accepted the norms embodied in some arms control regimes and, thus, often reverts to excessive legalism when interpreting its obligations, using any loophole in an opportunistic fashion to continue transfers.[27] The effectiveness of policy tools such as restricting access to key technologies is, thus, limited and further comes under a spell of uncertainty. Thus, a future envisaging China not only abiding strictly by its undertakings on Pakistan and Iran, but beginning to move from an adherent of global non-proliferation norms to co-designer and enforcer of such norms and regimes is still far-fetched. The decision to participate in international arms control regimes apparently reflects a judgment by the Chinese leadership that the costs of openly refusing to adhere to international non-proliferation norms exceed the costs of accepting them. Nonetheless, in spite of issuing denials in response to accusations of violations, Beijing's ambivalence toward restrictions on arms transfers would suggest that China's adherence to these regimes is imperfect. Nevertheless, there is a positive upward trend in Beijing's increasing adherence to global non-proliferation norms, but precarious circumstantial developments on flashpoints such as Taiwan might just revert all the developments and put a sudden halt to cooperation provided by China on the issue. Given the current inertia of the disarmament process, part of China's recent improvement in its proliferation behaviour stems from its reluctance to be isolated. Perhaps the greatest point of leverage is that China wishes to portray itself as a responsible player on the global podium and distinguishes that open violations of non-proliferation agreements would be detrimental when it comes to fulfillment of this image.

There has been no systematic enunciation of America's longer-term stakes in the Asia-Pacific region; the underpinnings and expectations of a larger strategy; and how the United States proposes to achieve its long-term objectives. Ensuring regional stability, maintaining America's military advantage and enhancing various political, economic and security partnerships seem largely self-evident goals.[28] At this stage, it should be emphasised that it is highly desirable for the United States to avoid confrontation with China, since the cost of such a hostile relationship would be enormous. Treating China as a potential military adversary would require far larger deployments in the western Pacific than the United States envisioned in the post-Cold War world. Even a diplomatic confrontation with China would complicate the ability of the United States to manage the strategic, economic and environmental issues, where Beijing could play an important role. A hostile policy toward China, moreover, would throw the broader Asia policy into disarray.

The major thrust for the US policy-makers should be to track and analyse the key drivers behind China's proliferation conduct. Going by the cases of Pakistan and Iran in particular, American strategists and policy-makers have to comprehend and accept the fact that China has been a major player in the proliferation web across Asia. Having directly aided the nuclear programme of Pakistan and the North Korean missile programme, Beijing indirectly backed Pakistan's missile programme as well, given that Islamabad's missile arsenal has benefitted substantially with assistance from North Korea, in addition to all the assistance Beijing provided Iran vis-à-vis WMD—thereby stressing the need to provide external leadership by outside actors to facilitate and complement direct negotiations of confidence-building and arms control measures by regional actors.

Although using its influence to shape up a relationship with China in order to seek benefits would surely be in American interest, the key question is 'at what cost'? While subsequent US Administrations have been pressing for a hard non-proliferation policy, Chinese trends in this regard during the past have not been encouraging. Notwithstanding the fact that President George W Bush characterised Iran and North Korea as the "axis of evil" way back in 2001, the "China factor" remains common and Washington has not really addressed this reality in the starkest possible manner. The nuclear and missile crises in Iran and North Korea in addition to the delicate and dangerous political reality of a nuclear Pakistan, surely comprise a litmus test for both Washington and Beijing in which thoughtful analysis of current trends and careful projection of the politico-military climate of the future would be the call of the day in order to take on these pressing challenges of the 21st century.

Notes

1. As per the views of William J Perry and Ashton B Carter, "The Content of US Engagement with China," *Special Report of the Preventive Defense Project*, (A Research Collaboration of Stanford University and Harvard University), vol. 1, no. 2, July 1998, p. 9.
2. Ibid., p. 21.
3. Paul A Papayoanou and Scott L Kastner, "Assessing the Policy of Engagement with China," Institute on Global Conflict and Cooperation, *Policy Paper*, no. 40 (University of California), 1998, p. 13.
4. US Department of State Report, *Nonproliferation Efforts in South Asia*, January 21, 1997.

5. For the entire text, see Statement by Howard L Berman, chairman, House Foreign Affairs Committee, February 6, 2009, Washington D.C.
6. Ibid.
7. George Perkovich, Jessica T Mathews, Joseph Cirincione, Rose Gottemoeller and Jon B Wolfsthal, *Universal Compliance: A Strategy for Nuclear Security*, Carnegie Endowment for International Peace (Washington, DC, March 2005), pp. 165-166.
8. Daniel Byman and Roger Cliff, "China's Arms Sales: Motivations and Implications," RAND's Project AIR FORCE (RAND Corporation, 2003), p. 45.
9. CRS Report for Congress, "China and Proliferation of Weapons of Mass Destruction and Missiles: Policy Issues," December 13, 2007, pp. 43-44.
10. Perry and Carter, n. 1, p. 23.
11. Ibid., p. 26.
12. Byman and Cliff, n. 8, p. 40.
13. For more details, see *China's National Defence 2008*, Information Office of the State Council of the People's Republic of China, January 2009, Beijing.
14. For more details, see Thomas J Christensen, "Chinese Realpolitik," *Foreign Affairs*, vol. 75, no. 5, 1996, pp. 37-52.
15. Papayoanou and Kastner, n. 3, p. 19.
16. *Kyodo News Agency Report*, "Japan May Deploy Missile Defence Ships," March 3, 2009, Tokyo.
17. For the complete interview, see "USFK Chief Urges Seoul to Join US BMD," *The Korea Times*, February 25, 2009.
18. *Universal Compliance: A Strategy for Nuclear Security*, n. 7, p. 187.
19. CRS Report for Congress, n. 9, p. 39.
20. The Iran Nonproliferation Act authorises sanctions on a foreign person based on "credible information" of a transfer to Iran (not necessarily a weapons programme) of technology controlled by multilateral non-proliferation regimes.
21. "Iran's Missile Develeopment," Strategic Comments by the International Institute of Strategic Studies (IISS), vol. 15, no. 1, February 2009.
22. Ibid.
23. Byman and Cliff, n. 8, p. 46.
24. For more details, see Stockholm International Peace Research Institute, *SIPRI Yearbook*, 1995.
25. *Universal Compliance: A Strategy for Nuclear Security*, n. 7, p. 173.
26. Byman and Cliff, n. 8, p. 45.
27. Ibid, p. 46.
28. For more details, see Jonathan D Pollack, "The Bush Administration and East Asia: Does the United States Need a New Regional Strategy?" in Robert M Hathaway and Wilson Lee, eds., *George W. Bush and East Asia: A First Term Assessment*, Study by the Asia Program, Woodrow Wilson International Centre for Scholars (Washington DC, 2005), p. 99.

Select Bibliography

Primary Sources

BMDO Fact Sheet, Ballistic Missile Defense Organization Budgetary History, April 1999.

Boese, Wade and Miles A Pomper, "Defending Missile Defense: An Interview with Missile Defense Agency Director, Henry Obering," *Arms Control Today,* vol. 35, no. 9, November 2005.

China's National Defence 2008, Information Office of the State Council of the People's Republic of China, January 2009.

China's National Defence 2002, Information Office of the State Council of the People's Republic of China, December 2002.

"*China, Nuclear Weapons, and Arms Control: A Preliminary Assessment*", Chairman's Report of a Roundtable Jointly Sponsored by the Council on Foreign Relations, National Defense University and the Institute for Defense Analyses, 2000.

CIA, Unclassified Report to Congress on the *Acquisition of Technology Relating to Weapons of Mass Destruction and Advanced Conventional and Munitions,* January-June 2003.

Cox Committee Report; House Select Committee on *U.S. National Security and Military Concerns with the People's Republic of China,* May 25, 1999.

Congressional Research Service Issue Brief for Congress, *Chemical Weapons Proliferation: Issues for Congress,* (Washington D.C., March 11, 1994).

__________________, *Pakistan-U.S. Relations,* (Washington D.C., March 10, 2002).

Congressional Research Service (hereafter CRS) Report for Congress, *Asian-Pacific Security Arrangements: The US-Japanese Alliance and China's Strategic View* (Washington D.C., March 1997).

__________________, *China and Proliferation of Weapons of Mass Destruction and Missiles: Policy Issues* (Washington DC, February 26, 2003).

__________________, *China: Ballistic and Cruise Missiles,* (Washington D.C., May 27, 1998).

__________________, *China: Leadership Dynamics after Deng*

Xiaoping, (Washington DC, February 26, 1997).

________________________, *China: Possible Missile Technology Transfers from U.S.*

Satellite Export Policy- Background and Chronology, (Washington DC, March 16, 1999).

________________________, *China: Suspected Acquisition of U.S. Nuclear Weapon Data*, (Washington D.C., September 14, 2000).

________________________, *China-US Relations: Chronology of Developments during the Clinton Administration*, (Washington DC, August 28, 1998).

________________________, *China-US Summit*, October 1997, (Washington DC, October 16, 1997).

________________________, *Chinese Nuclear Weapons and Arms Control Policies: Implications and Options for the United States*, (Washington DC, March 25, 1994).

________________________, *Nuclear, Biological, Chemical, and Missile Proliferation Sanctions: Selected Current Law*, (Washington DC, May 27, 1998).

________________________, *Nuclear, Biological, and Chemical Weapons and Missiles: The Current Situation and Trends*, (Washington DC, October 2, 2000).

________________________, *The 1985 U.S.-China Agreement for Nuclear Cooperation: Moving Towards Implementation?* (Washington DC, April 10, 1997).

________________________, *The Nuclear Posture Review: Overview and Emerging Issues* (Washington DC, January 31, 2002).

"Current and Projected National Security Threats to the United States," Statement by Lowell E. Jacoby, US Navy Director, Senate Armed Services Committee, March 17, 2005.

Davis, Lynn, Under Secretary of State, US Congress, House International Relations Committee Hearing, *Review of the Clinton Administration Nonproliferation Policy*, 104th Congress, 2nd Session, June 19, 1995.

Einhorn, Robert, Deputy Assistant Secretary of State for Nonproliferation, Testimony before the Senate Governmental Affairs Committee, Subcommittee on International Security, April 10, 1997.

Holdridge, John H., *Crossing the Divide: An Insider's Account of the Normalization of US - China Relations* (Lanham, Maryland: Rowman & Littlefield Publishers, Inc., 1997).

"*Implementation of the US-China Nuclear Cooperation Agreement: Whose Interests are Served?*", Hearing before the Committee on International Relations; House of Representatives, 105th Congress, 1st Session, Washington DC, October 7, 1997.

Kissinger, Henry A., *The White House Years,* (Boston: Little, Brown and Company, 1979).

"*Missile Proliferation in the Information Age*", Hearing before the Subcommittee on International Security, Proliferation, and Federal Services of the Committee on Governmental Affairs, United States Senate, 105th Congress, 1st Session, Washington D.C., September 22, 1997.

National Intelligence Council, "Foreign Missile Developments and the Ballistic Missile Threat through 2015," December 2001.

Nixon, Richard M., *The Memoirs of Richard Nixon* (New York: Grosset and Dunlap, 1978).

"*North Korean Missile Proliferation*", Hearing before the Subcommittee on International Security, Proliferation, and Federal Services of the Committee On Governmental Affairs, United States Senate, 105th Congress, 1st Session, October 21, 1997.

Peking Review Supplement, "Communist Chinese Announcement," October 16, 1964.

Pentagon Report, *Nuclear Posture Review,* US Department of Defense, Submitted to U.S. Congress, Washington D.C., December 31, 2001.

Pentagon Report, *United States Security Strategy for the East Asia-Pacific Region,* US Department of Defence, Office of International Security Affairs, Washington D.C., February 1995.

"*Proliferation: Chinese Case Studies*", Hearing before the Subcommittee on International Security, Proliferation, and Federal Services of the Committee On Governmental Affairs, United States Senate, 105th Congress, 1st Session, Washington D.C., April 10, 1997.

"*Proliferation and U.S. Export Controls*", Hearing before the Subcommittee on International Security, Proliferation, and Federal Services of the Committee on Governmental Affairs, United States Senate, 105th Congress, 1st Session, Washington D.C., July 11, 1997.

"*Proliferation Threats Through the Year 2000*", Hearing before the Committee on Foreign Relations, United States Senate, 105th Congress, 1st Session, October 8, 1997.

"*Review of the Clinton Administration Nonproliferation Policy*", Hearing before the Committee on International Relations; House of Representatives, 105th

Congress, 2nd Session, Washington D.C., June 19, 1996.

Richard L. Armitage, *A Comprehensive Approach to North Korea,* U.S. Congressional Records, Washington D.C., March 4, 1999.

Donald H. Rumsfeld Commission Report, Findings and Recommendations, July 31, 1998.

Secretary of Defence, William Cohen, *Annual Report to the Congress for FY 2001,* Department of Defense (Washington D.C., January 2001).

Taiwan Relations Act (Public Law 96-8), U.S. Statutes At Large, April 10, 1979.

Talbott, Strobe, *U.S. Diplomacy in South Asia: A Progress Report,* (Washington D.C.: Remarks at the Brookings Institution, November 12, 1998).

Testimony of Charles E. McQueary, before the US Senate Armed Services Subcommittee on Strategic Forces, Office of the Secretary of Defense, April 11, 2007.

Testimony of CIA Director James Woolsey before the US Senate Governmental Affairs Committee, *"Proliferation Threats of the 1990s,"* February 24, 1993.

Testimony of Henry A. Obering, Director, Missile Defense Agency, Fiscal Year 2009 Budget, before the Senate Armed Services Committee, Subcommittee on Strategic Forces, April 1, 2008.

Testimony of Stanley O. Roth, Assistant Secretary of State for East Asian and Pacific Affairs, House International Relations Committee Asia and the Pacific Subcommittee, February 10, 1999.

Testimony of Lowell E. Jacoby, US Navy Director "Current and Projected National Security Threats to the United States," Senate Armed Services Committee, March 17, 2005.

Unclassified Statement of Director, Missile Defense Agency, Henry A. Obering, on *Missile Defense Program and Fiscal Year 2008 Budget*, Senate Armed Services Committee, Strategic Forces Subcommittee, April 11, 2007.

Unclassified Summary of the National Intelligence Estimate, *Pakistan*, Foreign Missile Developments and the Ballistic Missile Threat through 2015 (Washington, D.C.: US Central Intelligence Agency, December 2001).

Unclassified Report to Congress on, *Acquisition of Technology Relating to Weapons of Mass Destruction and Advanced Conventional Munitions,* (Washington D.C.: U.S. Central Intelligence Agency, November13, 2003).

U.S.-China Economic and Security Review Commission, *China's Proliferation Practices and the North Korean Nuclear Crisis*, 108th Congress, 1st Session, July 24, 2003.

U.S. Department of Defense Report, "Missile Defense Test Results", Backgrounder, May 31, 2002.

U.S. Department of State, *"Proliferation of Missiles and Essential Components of Nuclear, Biological and Chemical Weapons,"* Annual Report, September 1996.

U.S. Department of State Report, *"Nonproliferation Efforts in South Asia,"* January 21, 1997.

White House Transcript, Speech by President George W. Bush at the National Defense University, (Washington D.C., May 1, 2001).

William J. Perry, *Review of US Policy toward North Korea: Findings and Recommendations,* Unclassified Report, US Department of State (Washington D.C., October 12, 1999).

Secondary Sources

Reports

Abramowitz, Morton I., and James T. Laney, *"Managing Change on the Korean Peninsula",* Report of an Independent Task Force, Council on Foreign Relations, (New York, 1998).

Agmon, Marcy, James L. Bonomo, Michael Kennedy, Maren Leed, Kenneth Watman, Katherine Webb and Charles Wolf, Jr., *"Arms Proliferation Policy: Support to the Presidential Advisory Board",* A Report by the RAND National Defense Research Institute (CA: Santa Monica, 1996).

Arnett, Eric, *"Military Technology: The Case of China,"* Stockholm International Peace Research Institute, SIPRI Yearbook 1995: Armaments, Disarmament, and International Security (Oxford University Press, 1995).

Byman, Daniel and Roger Cliff, "China's Arms Sales: Motivations and Implications," RAND's Project AIR FORCE (Santa Monica, CA: RAND Corporation, 2003).

Eikenberry, Karl W., *Explaining and Influencing Chinese Arms Transfers,* McNair Paper 36, Institute for National Strategic Studies, National Defense University, (Washington DC, 1995).

Gill, Bates, *Silkworms and Summitry: Chinese Arms Exports to Iran and US-China Relations,* The Asia and Pacific Rim Institute of the American Jewish Committee, 1998.

Hathaway, Robert M., and Wilson Lee, eds., *"George W. Bush and East Asia: A First Term Assessment",* Study by the Asia Program, Woodrow Wilson International Center for Scholars (Washington, DC, 2005).

Hickey, Dennis V. and Michael R. Chambers, *"China's 'Good Neighbor' Diplomacy: A Wolf in Sheep's Clothing?"* Asia Program Special Report, Woodrow Wilson International Center for Scholars, no. 126, January 2005.

Johnson, Stuart E. and William H. Lewis, eds., *"Weapons of Mass Destruction: New Perspectives on Counterproliferation,"* Report by the Center for Counterproliferation Researc (Washington DC: National Defense University Press, 1995).

Kyung-won, Kim, Tommy Koh and Farooq Sobhan, *"America's Role in Asia: Asian Views,"* A Study by The Asia Foundation (CA: San Francisco, 2004).

Papayoanou, Paul A., and Scott L. Kastner, *"Assessing the Policy of Engagement with China,"* Institute on Global Conflict and Cooperation, Policy Paper, no. 40, (University of California), 1998.

Perkovich, George, Jessica T. Mathews, Joseph Cirincione, Rose Gottemoeller and Jon B. Wolfsthal, *"Universal Compliance: A Strategy for Nuclear Security"*, A Report by the Carnegie Endowment for International Peace (Washington, D.C., March 2005).

Perry, William J., and Ashton B. Carter, *"The Content of US Engagement with China,"* Special Report of the Preventive Defense Project (A Research Collaboration of Stanford University and Harvard University), vol. 1, no. 2, July 1998.

"U.S. Strategy in the Asia-Pacific Region," A Conference Report, Co-sponsored by the U.S. Army's Dwight D. Eisenhower National Security Series and The Sorrento Group in partnership with The Asia Program, Woodrow Wilson International Center for Scholars, (Washington, D.C., May 5, 2003).

Wan, Ming and Ezra F. Vogel, *"The U.S.-Japan-China Triangle: Who's the Odd Man Out?"* Asia Program Special Report, Woodrow Wilson International Center for Scholars, no. 113, July 2003.

Books

Abbas, Hassan, *Pakistan's Drift into Extremism* (New York: M.E. Sharpe, 2004).

Armacost, Michael H., *Friends or Rivals? The Insider's Account of U.S.-Japan Relations,* (New York: Columbia University Press, 1996).

Barnett, A. Doak, *Communist China and Asia: Challenge to American Policy* (New York: Harper and Brothers for the Council on Foreign Relations, Inc., 1960).

Bennett-Jones, Owen, *Pakistan: Eye of the Storm* (London: Yale University Press, 2005).

Blackwill, Robert D., and Paul Dibb, eds., *America's Asian Alliances* (Massachusetts: The MIT Press, 2000).

Bowman, Robert M., *Star Wars: A Defense Insider's Case Against the Strategic Defense Initiative* (New York: St. Martin's Press, 1986).

Brown, Harold, *The Strategic Defense Initiative: Shield or Snare?* (Colorado:

Westview Press, Inc., 1987).

_____________, *Thinking About National Security: Defense and Foreign Policy in a Dangerous World,* (Colorado: Westview Press, Inc., 1983).

Brzezinski, Zbigniew, *Promise or Peril: The Strategic Defense Initiative* (Washington, D.C.: Ethics and Public Policy Center, 1986).

Bundy, Mc George, *Danger and Survival: Choices about the Bomb in the first Fifty Years* (New Delhi: East West Press Pvt. Ltd., 1988).

Carter, Ashton B. and David N. Schwartz, eds., *Ballistic Missile Defense,* (Washington, D.C.: The Brookings Institution, 1984).

Carus, W. Seth, *Cruise Missile Proliferation in the 1990s* (Washington D.C.: Center for Strategic and International Studies, 1992).

Chang, Gordon H., *Friends and Enemies: The United States, China and the Soviet Union, 1948-1972,* (Stanford: Stanford University Press, 1990).

Clarfield, Gerard H., and William M. Wiecek, *Nuclear America: Military and Civilian Nuclear Power in the United States, 1940-1980,* (New York: Harper & Row Publishers, 1984).

Cohen, Warren I., *America's Response to China: A History of Sino-American Relations* (New York: Columbia University Press, 1990, 2000).

_____________, ed., *New Frontiers in American- East Asian Relations,* (New York: Columbia University Press, 1983).

Cordesman, Anthony H., *Strategic Threats and National Missile Defenses: Defending the U.S. Homeland* (Westport, CT: Praeger Publishers, 2002).

Corera, Gordon, *Shopping for Bombs: Nuclear Proliferation, Global Insecurity and the Rise and Fall of the AQ Khan Network* (London: C. Hurst Publishers Ltd, 2006).

Davis, Zachary, and Benjamin Frankel, eds., *The Proliferation Puzzle: Why Nuclear Weapons Spread and What Results* (Essex: Frank Cass, 1993).

Diehl, Sarah J. and James Clay Moltz, *Nuclear Weapons and Nonproliferation* (California: ABC-CLIO Inc., 2002).

Dutta, Sujit, China's Emerging Power and Military Role: Implications for South Asia, in Jonathan D. Pollack and R. Yang, eds., *Under the China Shadow* (Santa Monica: RAND, 1998).

Eisendrath, Craig and Melvin A. Goodman and Gerald E. Marsh, *The Phantom Defense—America's Pursuit of the Star Wars Illusion* (Westport, CT: Praeger Publishers, 2001).

Funabashi, Yoichi, *Alliance Adrift* (New York: Council on Foreign Relations Press, 1999).

Garver, John W., *Foreign Relations of the People's Republic of China* (New Jersey:

Prentice-Hall, Inc., 1993).

Gill, Bates, *Chinese Arms Transfers: Purposes, Patterns, and Prospects in the New World Order* (Westport, CT: Praeger Publishers, 1992).

Graham, Bradley, *Hit to Kill: The New Battle Over Shielding America from Missile Attack* (New York: Public Affairs TM, 2001).

Handberg, Roger, *Ballistic Missile Defense and the Future of American Security: Agendas, Perceptions, Technology and Policy* (Westport, CT: Praeger Publishers, 2002).

Harding, Harry, *A Fragile Relationship: The United States and China Since 1972* (Washington D.C.: The Brookings Institution, 1992).

______________, ed., *China's Foreign Relations in the 1980s* (New Haven: Yale University Press, 1984).

Holdridge, John H., *War and Peace with China* (Lanham, MD: Dacor-Bacon House, 1994).

Hsiao, Gene T. and Michael Witunsky, eds., *Sino-American Normalization and its Policy Implications* (New York: Praeger, 1983).

Hsueh, Chun-tu, ed., *China's Foreign Relations: New Perspectives* (New York: Praeger Publishers, 1982).

Huntington, Samuel P., *Political Order in Changing Societies* (New Haven and London: Yale University Press, 1968).

Hwang, Byong-Moo, and Mel Gurtov, *China's Security: The New Roles of the Military* (London: Lynne Rienner Publishers, Inc., 1998).

Jencks, Harlan, *From Muskets to Missiles* (Colorado: Westview Press, 1983).

Kanter, Arnold and Linton F. Brooks, eds., *U.S. Intervention Policy for the Post-Cold War World: New Challenges and New Responses* (New York: The American Assembly, 1994).

Kanwal, Gurmeet, *Nuclear Defence: Shaping the Arsenal* (New Delhi, Knowledge World, 2001).

Kaufman, Daniel J., and Jeffrey S. McKitrick and Thomas J. Leney, eds., *U.S. National Security: A Framework for Analysis* (Lexington: D.C. Heath and Company, 1985.)

Khalilzad, Zalmay, *The United States and Asia: Toward a new U.S. Strategy and Force Posture* (Santa Monica: RAND, 2001).

________________ and Ian O. Lesser, eds., *Sources of Conflict in the 21st Century: Regional Futures and U.S. Strategy* (Santa Monica, CA: RAND Publication, 1998).

Kim, Samuel S., ed., *China and the World: Chinese Foreign Policy in the Post-Mao Era* (Boulder, CO: Westview Press, 1984).

Lampton, David M., *Same Bed Different Dreams: Managing U.S.-China Relations, 1989-2000* (California: University of California Press, 2001).

___________________, ed., *The Making of Chinese Foreign Policy and Security Policy: In the Era of Reform* (California: Stanford University Press, 2001).

Lewis, John Wilson and Xue Litai, *China Builds the Bomb,* (Stanford, California: Stanford University Press, 1988).

Lindsay, James M. and Michael E. O'Hanlon, *Defending America: The Case for Limited National Missile Defense* (Washington, D.C.: Brookings Institution Press, 2001).

Lindsay, James M., *Congress and the Nuclear Weapons* (Baltimore: The Johns Hopkins University Press, 1991).

Mahapatra, Chintamani, *Indo-U.S. Relations: Into the 21st Century* (New Delhi: Knowledge World, 1998).

Mahmood, Safdar, *Pakistan: Political Roots and Development 1947-1999* (Oxford: Oxford University Press, 2000).

Mann, James, *About Face: A History of America's Curious Relationship with China, from Nixon to Clinton* (New York: Alfred A. Knopf, Inc., 1998).

Manning, Robert and Ronald Montaperto and Brad Roberts, *China, Nuclear Weapons and Arms Control* (New York: Council on Foreign Relations Press, 2000).

Meisner, Maurice, *Mao's China and After: A History of the People's Republic* (New York: Free Press, Inc., 1986).

Moltz, James Clay, *The Politics of Space Security: Strategic Restraint and the Pursuit of National Interests* (Palo Alto, CA: Stanford University Press, 2008).

Nye, Jr., Joseph S., and James A. Schear, eds., *Seeking Stability in Space: Anti-Satellite Weapons and the Evolving Space Regime* (Lanham, MD: University Press of America, Inc., 1987).

Oksenberg, Michel and Elizabeth Economy, *Shaping U.S.-China Relations: A Long- Term Strategy* (New York: Council on Foreign Relations, Inc., 1997).

Overholt, William H., *China: The Next Economic Super Power* (London: Orion Publishing House, 1993).

Perkovich, George, *India's Nuclear Bomb* (Berkeley: University of California Press, 1999).

Pollack, Jonathan D. and Richard H. Yang, eds., *In China's Shadow: Regional Perspectives on Chinese Foreign Policy and Military Development*, RAND Corporation, 1998.

Rajain, Arpit, *Nuclear Deterrence in Southern Asia* (New Delhi: Sage Publications

India Pvt. Ltd., 2005).

Richelson, Jeffrey T, *Spying on the Bomb* (New York: WW Norton & Company, 2006).

Rodman, Peter W., *Shield Embattled: Missile Defense as a Foreign Policy Problem* (Washington, D.C.: The Nixon Center, 2001).

Ross, Robert S., *Negotiating Cooperation: The United States and China, 1969-1989* (Stanford: Stanford University Press, 1975).

Roy, Denny, *China's Foreign Relations* (London: Macmillan Press Ltd., 1998).

Russell, Richard L., *Weapons Proliferation in the Greater Middle East* (Oxford: Routeledge Press, 2005).

Schlesinger, Jr., Arthur M., *The Dynamics of World Power: A Documentary History of United States' Foreign Policy, 1945-1973* (New York: Chelsea House Publishers, 1973).

Shinn, James, ed., *Weaving the Net: Conditional Engagement with China* (New York: Council on Foreign Relations Press, 1996).

Singh, Jasjit, ed., *Asia's New Dawn: The Challenges to Peace and Security* (New Delhi: Knowledge World, 2000).

__________, ed., *Asian Security in the 21st Century* (New Delhi: Knowledge World, 1999).

__________, ed., *Reshaping Asian Security* (New Delhi: Knowledge World, 2001).

Smoke, Richard, *National Security and the Nuclear Dilemma* (New York: Random House, 1984).

Snyder, Craig, ed., *The Strategic Defense Debate: Can "Star Wars" Make Us Safe?* (Pennsylvania: University of Pennsylvania Press, 1986).

Sokolski, Henry and James M. Ludes, eds., *Twenty- First Century Weapons Proliferation,* (Oregon: Frank Cass Publishers, 2001).

Spector, Leonard S., with Jacqueline R. Smith, *Nuclear Ambitions: The Spread of Nuclear Weapons, 1989-1990* (Colorado: Westview Press, Inc., 1990).

Stebbins, Richard P., *The United States in World Affairs 1966* (New York: Council on Foreign Relations and Harper and Row Publishers, 1967).

Timmerman, Kenneth, *Countdown to Crisis: The Coming Nuclear Showdown with Iran* (New York: Crown Forum, 2005).

Vogel, Ezra F., ed., *Living with China: U.S./China Relations in the Twenty-First Century* (New York: W.W. Norton & Company, Inc., 1997).

Wilcox, Francis O., ed., *China and the Great Powers: Relations with the United States, the Soviet Union and Japan* (New York: Praeger Publishers, 1974).

Wirtz, James J. and Jeffrey A. Larsen, eds., *Rockets Red Glare: Missile Defenses and the Future of World Politics* (Colorado: Westview Press, 2001).

Worden, Simon P., *SDI and the Alternatives* (Washington, D.C.: National Defense University Press, 1991).

Yager, Joseph A., ed., *Nonproliferation and U.S. Foreign Policy* (Washington, D.C.: Brookings Institution, 1980).

Yuzawa, Takeshi, *Japan's Security Policy and the ASEAN Regional Forum: The Search for Multilateral Security in the Asia-Pacific* (New York: Routledge, 2007).

Zhao, Suisheng and Carol Lee Hamrin, eds., *Decision-Making in Deng's China: Perspectives from Insiders* (Armonk, NY: M.E. Sharpe, Inc., 1995).

Articles

Ahn, Byung-joon, "The Man Who Would Be Kim," *Foreign Affairs*, vol. 73, no. 6, November/December 1994.

Ahn, Yinhay, "North Korea in 2001: At a Crossroads," *Asian Survey*, vol. 42, no. 1, January/February 2002.

Ahrari, M. Ehsan, "China, Pakistan, and the 'Taliban Syndrome'," *Asian Survey*, vol. 40, no. 4, July/August, 2000.

Becker, Elizabeth, "Missile Deployment Uncertain – Setback for scaled – down 'Star Wars' Plan," *The New York Times*, January 19, 2000.

Berkowitz, Bruce D., "Portending the Future of Proliferation," *Review Essay in Orbis*, vol. 39, no. 2, Spring 1995.

Bermudez Jr., Joseph S., "Exposing North Korea's Secret Nuclear Infrastructure – Part One", *Jane's Intelligence Review*, vol. 7, no.1, July 1999.

Bernier, Justin, "Asia's Shifting Strategic Landscape: China's Strategic Proxies," *Orbis*, vol. 47, no. 4, Fall 2003.

Bitzinger, Richard A., "Arms to Go: Chinese Arms Sales to the Third World," *International Security*, vol. 17, no. 2, Fall 1992.

Bhaskar, C. Uday, "Bush Outlines New US Nuclear Policy," *Strategic Analysis*, vol. 25, no. 3, June 2001.

Bijian, Zheng, "China's 'Peaceful Rise' to Great-Power Status," *Foreign Affairs*, vol. 84, no. 5, September/October 2005.

Binnendijk, Hans and George Stewart, "Toward Missile Defenses from the Sea," *The Washington Quarterly*, vol. 25, no. 3, Summer 2002.

Broad, William J., "A Missile Defense with Limits: the ABC's of the Clinton Plan," *The New York Times*, June 30, 2000.

Broad, William J., David E. Sanger and Raymond Bonner, "A Tale of Nuclear Proliferation: How Pakistani Built His Network," *The New York Times*,

February 12, 2004.

Bromley, Mark, "European Missile Defense: New Emphasis, New Roles," *BASIC Paper* no. 36, May 2001.

Brown, David G., "North Korea in 1998: A Year of Foreboding Developments," *Asian Survey,* vol. 39, no.1, January/February 1999.

Calder, Kent E., "The New Face of Northeast Asia," *Foreign Affairs,* vol. 80, no.1, January/February 2001.

Carpenter, Ted Galen, "Life after Proliferation: Closing the Nuclear Umbrella," *Foreign Affairs,* vol. 73, no. 2, March/April 1994.

Cha, Victor D., "Korea's Place in the Axis," *Foreign Affairs,* vol. 81, no. 3, May/June 2002.

Chanda, Nayan, "Technology Cocooned," *Far Eastern Economic Review,* November 5, 1987.

Changsu, Kim, "South Korea-U.S. Security Issues Amid Improving Inter- Korean Relations," *Korea Focus,* vol. 9, no. 3, May-June 2001.

Chansoria, Monika, "Nuclear North Korea: Shifting Strategic Calculations?" *Asian Defence Review*, Annual Issue, (New Delhi: Knowledge World Pvt Ltd, 2007).

Chellaney, Brahma, "India's Nuclear Planning, Force, Structure, Doctrine and Arms-Control Posture," *Australian Journal of International Affairs,* vol. 53, no. 1, 1999.

__________________, "New Delhi's Dilemma," *Washington Quarterly*, Summer 2000.

Cheung, Tai Ming, "Proliferation is Good, and There's Money in it Too," *Far Eastern Economic Review*, June 2, 1988.

Chin Lee, Wei, "Thunder in the Air: Taiwan and TMD," *The Nonproliferation Review,* vol. 8, no. 3, Fall-Winter 2001.

Chittaranjan, Kalpana, "North Korea: Nuclear Issues" *Strategic Analysis,* vol. 23, no. 8, November 1999.

__________________, "U.S. NMD: An Issue that Just Won't Go," *Strategic Analysis,* vol. 24, no.10, January 2001.

Christensen, Thomas J., "Chinese Realpolitik," *Foreign Affairs,* vol. 75, no. 5, 1996.

Christoffersen, Gaye, "The New American Strategy of Containment," *Asian Survey,* vol. 42, no. 3, May/June 2002.

Cirincione, Joseph, "The Asian Nuclear Chain Reaction," *Foreign Policy,* no.118, Spring 2000.

__________________, "Why the Right lost the Missile Defense Debate," *Foreign*

Policy, no.106, Spring1997.

Croddy, Eric, "China's Role in the Chemical and Biological Disarmament Regimes," *The Nonproliferation Review,* vol. 9, no.1, Spring 2002.

Coyle, Philip, "Rhetoric or Reality? Missile Defense under Bush," *Arms Control Today,* vol. 32, no. 4, May 2002.

Cumings, Bruce, "Toward a Comprehensive Settlement of the Korea Problem," *Current History,* vol. 98, no. 632, December 1999.

Daalder, Ivo H., James M. Goldgeire and James Lindsay, "Deploying NMD: Not Whether, But How," *Survival,* vol. 42, no.1, Spring 2000.

Daalder, Ivo H., and James M. Lindsay, "A New Agenda for Nuclear Weapons," *Brookings Policy Brief,* no. 94, February 2002.

Davis, Zachary S., "China's Nonproliferation and Export Control Policies," *Asian Survey,* vol. 35, no. 6, June 1995.

Delpech, Therese, "Nuclear Weapons and the 'New World Order': Early Warning from Asia?" *Survival,* vol. 40, no. 4, Winter 1998-99.

Dreyer, June Teufel, "The Military's Uncertain Politics," *Current History,* vol. 95, no. 602, September 1996.

Eberstadt, Nicholas, "North Korea's Interlocked Economic Crises: Some Indications from 'Mirror Statistics'," *Asian Survey,* vol. 38, no. 3, March 1998.

Gabel, Josiane, "The Role of U.S. Nuclear Weapons after September 11," *The Washington Quarterly,* vol. 28, no.1, Winter 2004-05.

Gaffney, Frank J., "China Arms the Rogues," *Middle East Quarterly,* September 1997.

Gelb, Leslie H., "Pakistan Links Peril U.S.-China Nuclear Pact," *The New York Times,* June 22, 1984.

Gill, Bates, "Chinese Arms Exports to Iran," *China Report,* vol. 34, no. 3&4, 1998.

__________, "Curbing Beijing's Arms Sales," *Orbis,* Summer 1992.

Gill, Bates, and Andrew Thompson, "A Test for Beijing: China and the North Korean Nuclear Quandary," *Arms Control Today,* vol.33, no.4, May 2003.

Glanz, James, "Other Systems Might Provide a U.S. Missile Shield," *The New York Times,* September 4, 2000.

Glaser, Charles L., and Steve Fetter in "Correspondence," by James M. Lindsay and Michael E. O'Hanlon, *International Security,* vol. 26, no. 4, Spring 2002.

__________, "National Missile Defense Policy and the Future of U.S. Nuclear Weapons Policy," *International Security,* vol. 26, no.1, Summer 2001.

Glenn, John, "On Proliferation Law, a Disgraceful Failure," *International Herald Tribune,* June 26, 1992.

Godwin, Paul, and John J. Schulz, "Arming the Dragon for the 21st Century: China's Defense Modernization Program," *Arms Control Today,* vol. 23, no. 10, December 1993.

Godwin, Paul H.B., "China's Nuclear Forces: An Assessment," *Current History,* vol. 98, no. 629, September 1999.

Goldstein, Avery, "Great Expectations: Interpreting China's Arrival," *International Security* vol. 22, no. 3, Winter 1997/98.

Goldstone, Jack, "China's Coming Collapse," *Foreign Policy,* no. 99, Summer 1995.

Gordan, Michal, "Beijing Avoids New Missile Sales Assurances," *The New York Times,* March 30, 1990.

Gourdon, Come Carpentier De, "The War Machine and New Security Hazards," *World Affairs,* vol. 5, no. 2, April-June 2001.

Gupta, Amit, "Third World Militaries: New Suppliers, Deadlier Weapons," *Orbis,* vol. 37, no.1, Winter 1993.

Harland, Bryce, "For a Strong China," *Foreign Policy,* Spring 1994.

Harnisch, Sebastian, "U.S.-North Korean Relations Under The Bush Administration: From 'Slow Go' to 'No Go'," *Asian Survey,* vol. 42, no. 6, November/December 2002.

Hibbs, Mark, "China Accord Would Turn Up U.S. Heat on Pakistani Reactor," *Nucleonics Week,* August 14, 1997.

Hibbs, Mark, "Sensitive Iran Reactor Deal may Hinge on MFN for China", *Nucleonics Week,* October 1, 1992.

Hsiung, James C., "China's Omni-Directional Diplomacy: Realignment to Cope with Monopolar U.S. Power," *Asian Survey,* vol.35, no.6, June 1995.

Huntley, Wade L., and Robert Brown, "Missile Defense & China," *Foreign Policy in Focus,* Nautilus Institute, vol. 6, no. 3, January 2001.

Jianying, Li and Zhang Yijun, "Ups and Downs in Sino-U.S. Relations," *Foreign Affairs Journal,* no. 63, March 2002.

Jisi, Wang, "China's Search for Stability With America," *Foreign Affairs,* vol. 84, no. 5, September/October 2005.

Jun, Bong-Geun, "North Korean Nuclear Crises: An End in Sight?" *Arms Control Today,* vol. 36, no. 1, January/February 2006.

Kak, Kapil, "Missile Proliferation and International Security," *Strategic Analysis,* vol. 23, no. 3, June 1999.

Kampani, Gaurav, "Second Tier Proliferation: The Case of Pakistan and North Korea," *The Nonproliferation Review,* Fall-Winter 2002.

Kang, David C., "Rethinking North Korea," *Asian Survey,* vol. 35, no. 3, March

1995.

___________, "The Avoidable Crisis in North Korea," *Orbis,* vol. 47, no. 3, Summer 2003.

Kartha, Tara, "Ballistic Missile Defenses: The Debate in the U.S.," *Strategic Analysis,* vol. 24, no.1, April 2000.

Khan, Shahid-ur-Rehman, "China Agrees to Supply 300-MW PWR to Pakistan," *Nucloenics Week,* March 1, 1990.

Kim, Pan Suk, "Will North Korea Blink? Matters of Grave Danger?" *Asian Survey,* vol. 34, no. 3, March 1994.

Kim, Samuel S., "North Korea in 1994: Brinkmanship, Breakdown and Breakthrough," *Asian Survey,* vol. 35, no.1, January 1995.

___________, "North Korea in 1999: Bringing The Grand Chollima March Back In," *Asian Survey,* vol. 40, no.1, January/February 2000.

___________, "North Korea in 2000: Surviving through High Hopes of Summit Diplomacy," *Asian Survey,* vol. 41, no.1, January/February 2001.

Kimball, Daryl G., "Nonproliferation through Disarmament," *Arms Control Today,* vol. 35, no.1, January/February 2005.

Knowlton, Brian, "North Korea Arms Pact is Now Dead, Powell Says," *International Herald Tribune,* October 21, 2002.

Kondapalli, Srikanth, "Towards a Lean and Mean Army: Aspects of China's Ground Forces Modernization," *Strategic Analysis* vol. 26, no. 4, October- December 2002.

Krauthammer, Charles, "Why We Must Contain China," *Time,* July 31, 1995.

Kurian, Nimmi, "Defence Modernization in China: An Overview," *International Studies,* vol. 37, no. 3, July-September 2000.

Lacey, Marc, "Missile Defense Issue Lands in the Middle of the Gore-Bush Campaign," *The New York Times,* September 2, 2000.

Lampton, David M., "China and Clinton's America: Have They Learned Anything?" *Asian Survey,* vol. 37, no. 12, December 1997.

Lee, Manwoo, "North Korea: The Cold War Continues," *Current History,* vol. 95, no. 605, December 1996.

Lewis, John W., Hua Di and Xue Litai, "Beijing's Defense Establishment: Solving the Arms-Export Enigma," *International Security,* vol. 15, no. 4, Spring 1991.

Lewis, John, and Hua Di, "Chinese Ballistic Missile Programs," *International Security,* Fall 1992.

Lieberthal, Kenneth, "A New China Strategy," *Foreign Affairs,* vol. 74, no. 6, November/December 1995.

_________________, "The United States and Asia in 2001: Changing Agendas,"

Asian Survey, vol. 42, no.1, January/February 2002.

Lindsay, James M. and Michael E. O'Hanlon, "Missile Defense after the ABM Treaty," *The Washington Quarterly,* vol. 25, no. 3, Summer 2002.

Mahapatra, Chintamani, "The Eagle and the Dragon: After the Cold War," *Strategic Analysis,* vol.19, no. 2, May 1996.

__________, "The US, China and the Ghauri Missile," *Strategic Analysis,* vol. 22, no. 3, June 1998.

__________, "American Approach to Sino-Pakistan Nuclear and Missile Cooperation," *Strategic Analysis,* vol. 21, no. 10, January 1998.

__________, "Withstanding the Patron's Pressure," *Strategic Analysis,* vol. 16, no. 8, November 1993.

Mahbubani, Kishore, "Understanding China," *Foreign Affairs,* vol. 84, no. 5, September/October 2005.

Marquis, Christopher, "US Declares 'Rouge Nations' are now 'States of Concern'," *The New York Times,* June 20, 2000.

McLaughlin, Kevin, "Would Space-Based Defenses Improve Security?" *The Washington Quarterly,* vol. 25, no. 3, Summer 2002.

Merrill, John, "North Korea in 1993: In the Eye of the Storm," *Asian Survey,* vol. 34, no. 1, January 1994.

Miller, Judith, "U.S Is Holding Up Peking Atom Talks," *The New York Times,* September 19, 1982.

Mitchell, Alison, "Bush says U.S. Should Reduce Nuclear Arms," *The New York Times,* May 24, 2000.

Moltz, James Clay, "Missile Proliferation in East Asia: Arms Control Vs TMD Responses," *The Nonproliferation Review,* no. 4, Spring-Summer 1997.

__________, "The Impact of NMD on Nonproliferation Regimes," *The Nonproliferation Review*, vol. 7, no. 3, Fall-Winter 2000.

Mullins, Robert E., "The Dynamics of Chinese Missile Proliferation," *The Pacific Review*, vol. 8, no. 1, 1995.

Muralidharan, Sukumar, "Missiles and Concerns," *Frontline,* July 16, 1999.

Myers, Steven Lee, "U.S. Missile Plan Could Reportedly Provoke China," *The New York Times,* August 10, 2000.

Myers, Steven Lee, and James Glanz, "Taking a Look at the Workings of a Missile Shield," *The New York Times,* May 3, 2001.

Nayan, Rajiv, "North Korea and Missile Trade," *Strategic Analysis,* vol. 22, no. 12, March 1999.

__________, "Trends in the Missile Technology Control Regime," *Strategic Analysis,* vol. 22, no. 6, September 1998.

Newhouse, John, "The Missile Defense Debate," *Foreign Affairs,* vol. 80, no. 4, July/August 2001.

Nishihara, Masashi, "Japan has Cause to Worry about Chinese Ambition," *International Herald Tribune,* July 12, 1994.

Noland, Marcus, "Why North Korea Will Muddle Through," *Foreign Affairs,* vol. 76, no. 4, July/August 1997.

Norris, Robert S. and Hans M. Kristensen, "US Nuclear Forces, 2008," *Bulletin of the Atomic Scientists,* vol. 64, no. 1, March/April 2008.

Nye, Jr., Joseph S., "East Asian Security: The Case for Deep Engagement," *Foreign Affairs,* vol. 74, no. 4, July/August 1995.

Oh, Kongdan, and Ralph Hassig, "North Korea Between Collapse and Reform," *Asian Survey,* vol. 39, no. 2, March/April 1999.

O'Hanlon, Michael E., "Pyongyang: Reform or Abyss," *Financial Times,* October 11, 2006.

Pande, Savita, "Chinese Nuclear Doctrine," *Strategic Analysis,* vol. 23, no. 12, March 2000.

__________, "Missile Technology Control Regime: Impact Assessment," *Strategic Analysis,* vol. 23, no. 6, September 1999.

Park, Kyung-Ae, "Explaining North Korea's Negotiated Cooperation with the U.S.," *Asian Survey,* vol. 37, no. 7, July 1997.

Payne, Keith B., "The Case for National Missile Defense," *Orbis,* Spring 2000.

Pincus, Walter, "Hints of North Korean Plutonium Output," *Washington Post,* January 31, 2003.

Pollack, Jonathan D., "Asia's Shifting Strategic Landscape: China and the United States Post-9/11," *Orbis,* vol. 47, no. 4, Fall 2003.

Pratt, Erik K., "Missile Defense Sponsors: Shifting Political Support for Strategic Defense after Reagan," *Asian Perspective,* vol. 25, no. 1, 2001.

Rappai, M.V., "China's Nuclear Arsenal and Missile Defense," *Strategic Analysis,* vol. 26, no. 1, January-March 2002.

Richardson, Michael, "A Resurgent China Sets Off Alarms Over 'Containment'," *International Herald Tribune,* July 7, 1995.

Robbins, Carla A., "Nuclear Nonproliferation Effort Snags," *The Wall Street Journal,* January 27, 2005.

Roberts, Brad, Robert A. Manning and Ronald N. Montaperto, "China: The Forgotten Nuclear Power," *Foreign Affairs,* vol. 79, no. 4, July/August 2000.

Roy, Denny, "Rising China and US Interests: Inevitable vs. Contingent Hazards," *Orbis,* vol. 47, no. 1, Winter 2003.

__________, "The 'China Threat' Issue: Major Arguments," *Asian Survey,* vol.

36, no. 8, August 1996.

Roy-Chaudhury, Rahul and Swaran Singh, "Post- Cold War Trends in Arms Transfers," *Strategic Analysis,* vol. 17, no. 12, March 1995.

Russell, Richard L., "Swords and Shields: Ballistic Missiles and Defenses in the Middle East and South Asia," *Orbis,* vol. 46, no. 3, Summer 2002.

Sachdev, A.K., "Chinese Missiles: Winning the Limited War," *Strategic Analysis,* vol. 24, no. 3, June 2000.

______________, "North Korea's Missile Programme: A Matter of Concern," *Strategic Analysis,* vol. 24, no. 9, December 2000.

Samore, Gary, "US-DPRK Missile Negotiations," *The Nonproliferation Review,* vol. 9, no. 2, 2002.

Sanger, David, "U.S. is Punishing 8 Chinese Firms for Aiding Iran," *The New York Times,* January 18, 2005.

Satterwhite, David H., "North Korea in 1996: Belligerence Subsiding, Hunger Worsens," *Asian Survey,* vol. 37, no. 1, January 1997.

Saunders, Phillip C., "Confronting Ambiguity: How to Handle North Korea's Nuclear Program," *Arms Control Today,* vol. 33, no. 2, March 2003.

______________, "New Approaches to Nonproliferation: Supplementing or Supplanting the Regime?" *The Nonproliferation Review,* vol. 8, no. 3, Fall-Winter 2001.

Scheinman, Lawrence, "Disarmament: Have the Five Nuclear Powers Done Enough?" *Arms Control Today,* January/February 2005.

Schmitt, Eric, "President Decides to Put off Work on Missile Shield," *The New York Times,* September 2, 2000.

Scobell, Andrew, "China and North Korea: The Close but Uncomfortable Relationship," *Current History,* vol. 101, no. 656, September 2002.

Segal, Gerald, "East Asia and the 'Constrainment' of China," *International Security,* vol. 20, no. 4, Spring 1996.

Seigle, George, "Russia and China Worried over U.S. Plans for NMD System," *Jane's Defense Weekly,* March 24, 1999.

Sethi, Manpreet, "US Pursuit of Nuclear Non-Proliferation: Check and Checkmate," *Strategic Analysis,* vol. 23, no. 6, September 1999.

Shambaugh, David, "Containment or Engagement of China? Calculating Beijing's Responses," *International Security,* vol. 21, no. 2, Fall 1996.

______________, "Facing Reality in China Policy," *Foreign Affairs,* vol. 80, no.1, January/February 2001.

Shen, Dingli, "Ballistic Missile Defense and China's National Security," *Jane's*

Special Report, April 17, 2000.

__________, "Iran's Nuclear Ambitions Test China's Wisdom," *The Washington Quarterly,* vol. 29, no. 2, Spring 2006.

Singh, Swaran, "China's Arms Trade: Taking off Again," *Strategic Analysis,* vol. 17, no. 7, October 1994.

Sokolski, Henry, "Fighting Proliferation with Intelligence," *Orbis,* vol. 38, no. 2, Spring 1994.

______________, "U.S. Satellites to China," *International Defense Review,* April 1994.

Solomon, Jay and Gordon Fairclough, "Troubled Power Project Plays Role in North Korea Showdown," *Wall Street Journal,* January 30, 2002.

Soon-young, Hong, "Thawing Korea's Cold War: The Path to Peace on the Korean Peninsula," *Foreign Affairs,* vol. 78, no. 3, May/June 1999.

Southerland, Daniel, "U.S., China Sign Accords," *Washington Post,* August 28, 1985.

Squassoni, Sharon, "Closing Pandora's Box: Pakistan's Role in Nuclear Proliferation," *Arms Control Today,* vol. 34, no. 3, April 2004.

rivastava, Anupam, "China's Export Controls: Can Beijing's Actions Match its Words?" *Arms Control Today,* vol. 35, no. 9, November 2005.

Steinberg, Gerald, "Chinese Policies on Arms Control and Proliferation in the Middle East," *China Report,* vol. 34, no. 3&4, 1998.

Sutter, Robert, "Why does China Matter?" *The Washington Quarterly,* vol. 27, no.1, Winter 2003-04.

Talbott, Strobe, "Unfinished Business: Russia and Missile Defense under Clinton," *Arms Control Today,* vol. 32, no. 5, June 2002.

Timmerman, Kenneth, "Tehran's A-Bomb Program Shows Startling Progress," *Washington Times,* May 8, 1995.

Tompkins, Joanne, "How U.S. Strategic Policy Is Changing China's Nuclear Plans," *Arms Control Today,* vol. 33, no. 1, January/February 2003.

Twomey, Christopher P., "Chinese-US Strategic Affairs: Dangerous Dynamism," *Arms Control Today,* vol. 39, January/February 2009.

Urayama, Kori J., "Chinese Perspectives on Theater Missile Defense," *Asian Survey,*

ol. 40, no. 4, July/August 2000.

Weeks, Jennifer, "Sino-U.S Cooperation at a Crossroads," *Arms Control Today,* vol. 27, no. 4, June/July 1997.

Weiss, Leonard, "Turning a Blind Eye Again? The Khan Network's History and Lessons for U.S. Policy," *Arms Control Today,* vol. 35, no. 2, March 2005.

Wolfsthal, Jon Brook, "U.S. and Chinese Views on Proliferation: Trying to Bridge the Gap," *The Nonproliferation Review*, Fall 1994.

Wonacott, Peter, "Korea Tensions Put Beijing in a Tight Spot," *The Wall Street Journal,* January 3, 2003.

Woon, Eden Y., "Chinese Arms Sales and U.S.-China Military Relations," *Asian Survey*, vol. 29, no. 6, June 1989.

Wortzel, Larry M., "China Pursues Traditional Great-Power Status," *Orbis,* vol. 38, no. 2, Spring 1994.

Wu, Anne, "What China Whispers to North Korea," *The Washington Quarterly,* vol. 28, no. 2, Spring 2005.

Xuetong, Yan, "China's Post-Cold War Security Strategy," *Contemporary International Relations,* vol. 5, no. 5, May 1995.

Zaborsky, Victor, "Does China Belong in the Missile Technology Regime?" *Arms Control Today,* vol. 34, no. 8, October 2004.

Zeking, Jin, "--------------------," *China Daily,* June 5, 1999.

Zimmerman, Peter D., "Proliferation: Bronze Medal Technology is enough," *Orbis,* vol. 38, no. 1, Winter 1994.

Zongwei, Shao, "US Nuke Action Concerns China," *China Daily,* April 14, 2000.

Zukang, Sha, "The Global Strategic Balance and Stability Brook no Disruption," *Beijing Review,* August 2000.

__________, "U.S. Missile Defense Plan: China's View," *Disarmament Diplomacy,* January/February 2000.

Websites Accessed

http://in.today.reuters.comm
http://northkorea.ssrc.org
http://online.wsj.com
http://www.acronym.org.uk
http://www.armscontrol.org
http://www.atomicarchive.com
http://www.brookings.edn
http://www.carlisle.army.mil
http://www.carnegieendowment.org
http://www.cdiss.org
http://www.cecc.gov
http://www.ceip.org
http://www.cfr.org
http://www.china.org.cn

http://www.chinadaily.com.cn
http://www.china-embassy.org
http://www.china-un.ch
http://www.chinaview.cn
http://www.cia.gov
http://www.cnduk.org
http://www.cns.miis.edu
http://www.csis.org
http://www.cwc.gov
http://www.defenselink.mil
http://www.dia.mil/publicaffairs
http://www.dod.gov
http://edition.cnn.com
http://www.facts.com
http://www.fas.org
http://www.firstgov.com
http://www.fmprc.gov.cn
http://www.fr-aktuell.de
http://www.globalsecurity.org
http://www.house.gov
http://www.iht.com
http://www.iiss.org
http://www.iranian.ws
http://www.kimsoft.com
http://www.missiledefenseadvocacy.org
http://www.mofa.go.jp
http://www.nautilus.org
http://www.news.sina.com.cn
http://www.nci.org
http://www.nti.org
http://www.nytimes.com
http://www.rand.org
http://www.senate.gov
http://www.sipri.org
http://www.state.gov
http://www.unidir.org
http://www.usembassy-china.org.cn
http://www.usinfo.state.gov

http://www.usip.org
http://www.uspolicy.be
http://www.washingtonpost.com
http://www.whitehouse.gov
http://www.wmdinsights.com

INDEX